Understanding International Social Work: A Critical Analysis

Richard Hugman

palgrave
macmillan

First published 2010 by
PALGRAVE MACMILLAN

Palgrave Macmillan in the UK is an imprint of Macmillan Publishers Limited, registered in England, company number 785998, of Houndmills, Basingstoke, Hampshire RG21 6XS.

Palgrave Macmillan in the US is a division of St Martin's Press LLC, 175 Fifth Avenue, New York, NY 10010.

Palgrave Macmillan is the global academic imprint of the above companies and has companies and representatives throughout the world.

Palgrave® and Macmillan® are registered trademarks in the United States, the United Kingdom, Europe and other countries.

ISBN-13: 978-0-230-21959-5

This book is printed on paper suitable for recycling and made from fully managed and sustained forest sources. Logging, pulping and manufacturing processes are expected to conform to the environmental regulations of the country of origin.

A catalogue record for this book is available from the British Library.

A catalog record for this book is available from the Library of Congress.

10   9   8   7   6   5   4   3   2   1
19 18 17 16 15 14 13 12 11 10

Printed in China

Understanding International Social Work

Also by Richard Hugman

*Power in Caring Professions**
*Ageing and the Care of Older People in Europe**
Ethical Issues in Social Work (edited with David Smith)
Concepts of Care (edited with Moira Peelo & Keith Soothill)
*Social Welfare & Social Value**
*New Approaches in Ethics for the Caring Professions**

* *also published by Palgrave Macmillan*

Cho tất cả bạn dồng nghiệp ơ Việt Nam để công việc lịch sư tạo ra Công tác Xã hội Việt – chúc mừng hạnh phúc và thành công

Contents

Preface

As the impact of globalization becomes more and more apparent in our daily lives, social workers increasingly are recognizing that our profession is international. That it has always been so may not always be noticed in the day-to-day demands of professional life. Yet, the shape of social work in all the different countries around the world where it is now practised would not be the same without exchanges of ideas and the movement of people, both social workers and services users, between countries. Even those issues and problems that are regarded as 'local' are now very likely to be impacted by global trends and forces. Not only can social workers pursue careers by moving between countries to an extent not previously seen, but at the same time there are increasing demands for social work services for people who also have crossed borders, either as migrants or as refugees. In such a world social workers, including those who are in training and those who teach or do research, cannot afford to ignore the field of international social work.

A study of international social work must be seen as more than 'knowing about other countries'. Although knowledge of the profession, our colleagues and service users in other places is valuable, it is vital that questions are asked about the way in which social work has developed in different places. How has it developed? What is the influence of different parts of the world on each other? What sort of problems and issues can be seen as crossing national borders? Is social work a unified profession around the world, or should it be seen as different in different places? How should social workers be educated and trained – should there be one model or many? Are social work values and ethics the same everywhere or are they different in different places?

This book seeks to answer these questions through a critical analysis of international social work in relation to areas of practice, relationships within the profession between different global regions, and key issues for the work of the international professional organizations. Ultimately, it considers the way in which such an analysis informs an understanding of social work as a whole.

As in any part of our work, our own identity is reflected in the views that we hold and the questions that we ask. The origins of this book lie in my own experience of being (or becoming) an 'international social worker': as a migrant moving to live and work in 'another' country; as someone actively involved in the international professional organizations and working with colleagues from different parts of the world; and as a practitioner working with an international agency in the role of a consultant. Each of these experiences provides the challenge to discover more of the richness in the diversity of the profession around the world, to learn more about my own identity, including the experience of myself as a global Northerner and through that as 'other', and to encounter in a very tangible way the questions identified above. (See the glossary for an explanation of why the terms global 'North' and 'South' have been favoured over other ways of dividing the world in this analysis.) In noting this I am not claiming a privileged viewpoint to fend off debate (although I am aware that as someone from a European background and as male I can be privileged in all sorts of ways) but rather positioning myself as a means of reflecting on the types of questions that I have identified and giving the reader the opportunity to grasp some of what I bring personally to this analysis.

Inevitably, a study of this kind had benefitted from the support of many others. My colleagues at the University of New South Wales provide a dynamic context in which to teach and write. They covered my absence on a sabbatical in which much of the ground work for this book was undertaken, during which I was welcomed by other colleagues at Massey University, the University of California at Berkeley and the University of Durham. For conversations and debates in these and other places that have contributed to my development of this particular analysis I would like to thank Eileen Baldry, Sarah Banks, Linda Bartolomei, Vivienne Bozalek, Helen Charnley, Elaine Congress, Bob Chazin, Lena Dominelli, Doug Durst, Gracy Fernandes, Mel Gray, Sue Green, Arne Groenningsaeter, Lynne Healy, Siobhan King, Tracie Mafile'o, Duncan McDui-Ra, James Midgley, Mehmoona Moosa-Mitha, Otrude Moyo, Robyn Munford, Mary Nash, Kieran O'Donoghue, Joan Orme, Leila Patel, Eileen Pittaway, Vishanthie Sewpaul, Wheturangi Walsh-Tapiata and Angie Yuen-Tsang. Research assistance and many challenging questions were provided by Ivana Codarini and Mim Fox. Anonymous reviewers also contributed greatly by forcing me to focus on my arguments. Most especially, I would like to acknowledge the inspiration of friends and colleagues in Vietnam in their dedication to the creation of an authentic social work for their country and to thank them for all that I have learned from their insights and questions – Nguyễn Thủy Hồng, Nguyễn Thị Thai Lan, Le Hồng Loan, Bui Xuân Mai, Nguyễn Thị Lan, Nguyễn Văn Hồi, Nguyễn Thị Oanh, Pham Kieu Oanh, Vu Thị Le Thánh, Le Văn Phú, Mai Kim Thánh, and for assistance and support (as well as lots of ideas) Vu Thánh Vân, Nguyễn Lan Phường and Văn Thị Minh Hiên.

Parts of Chapter 5 have previously appeared in my article 'But is it social work? A case of mistaken identities', in *British Journal of Social Work*, vol. 39, no. 6, pp. 1138–53 and I am grateful to Oxford University Press and the editors, Eric Blyth and Helen Masson, for permission to reproduce these sections here.

Finally, as ever it has been a great pleasure to work with Catherine Gray and her colleagues at Palgrave Macmillan, who throughout showed their usual patience and critical support.

Richard Hugman
Sydney 2009

1

Introduction – The Global Growth of Social Work

The Early Days of Professional Social Work

As a formal profession, social work can be dated from the late 1800s (Payne, 2005). These early beginnings can be seen in the combination of activity to create formal education and training for the various practices that were called 'social work' at that time. The objectives of early social work were focused almost entirely on assistance for those people who were seen to be experiencing problems of daily life that were grounded in poverty. Whether we consider the work of the Charity Organization Societies, hospital almoners and 'police court missionaries' (focused on assistance to individuals and families) or the work of the Settlement Movement (focused on communities) the common factor was the impact of industrialization, urbanization and modernization on those people who were regarded as lacking resources to deal effectively with the problems that they encountered.

These main types of early professional social work can be seen to have developed at around the same time in many countries of Northern Europe, Scandinavia and North America. A significant aspect of professionalization was the move to establish education and training programmes at a university level. This has been identified as having been particularly significant given the numbers of women from middle-class backgrounds who entered social work at this time, but whose opportunities for a professional identity were limited (Walton, 1975). Different claims are made about which of the various national developments of professional social work education can be considered the 'first' instances of formal tertiary level programmes. For example, Riga (2008, p. 73) refers to the Amsterdam School of Social Work as 'the world's oldest school' (it was founded in 1899 and is now the School of Social Work and Law in the Hogeschool van Amsterdam). In the United Kingdom, training programmes

1

conducted by members of the Charity Organization Society and of the Settlement House movement from the 1870s coalesced in the London School of Sociology in 1903 (Parry & Parry, 1979). In the United States, the School at Columbia University traces its origins to the New York Charity Organization Society summer course of 1898 (which led to the founding of the School in 1904) (Healy, 2008a, p. 138).

In whatever way we date the beginnings of professional social work, however, the underlying importance of such a debate is often lost in the detail. In other words, the important point to note about these various claims to the origins of professional social work is that they span many countries. For example, Healy (2008b, p. 1) notes that when the First International Conference of Social Work convened in Paris in 1928 there were delegates from 42 different countries. The Second and Third Conferences were held in the 1930s and by 1939, 75 schools of social work from 18 countries were in membership of the International Committee of Schools of Social Work (ICSSW) (Healy, 2008b, p. 4). Also emerging from the First International Conference on Social Work was the International Permanent Secretariat of Social Workers, which initially represented social workers from eight countries (Healy, 2008a, p. 177). As will be discussed in more detail in Chapter 6, these organizations grew respectively into the International Association of Schools of Social Work (IASSW), the International Council on Social Welfare (ICSW) and the International Federation of Social Workers (IFSW). At this point, however, what is equally as important, if not more so, than considering in which country different aspects of social work first emerged is that from its earliest days social work as a profession can be seen as international.

By the 1930s social work had also spread from the advanced industrial countries of the global North to some countries of the South, through colonial relationships (Midgley, 1981). In particular, we can note that schools of social work were founded in various countries of the South through the 1920s and 1930s, including programmes at Yanjing University (now Beijing, China) (1922), the University of Buenos Aries (Argentina) (1924), the Tata Institute of Social Sciences in Mumbai (India) (which was, until 1944, the Sir Dorabji Tata Graduate School of Social Work) (1936) and the University of Cairo (Egypt) (1936) (Badran, 1975, p. 38; Viera, 1976, p. 261; Queiro-Tajalli, 1995, p. 87; Department of Urban and Rural Community Development, 2004, p. 31). Professional education was often the driving force in the growth of social work in these countries, with appropriate services being initiated to make use of the graduate workforce, such as the Ministry of Social Affairs and Labour in Egypt which was founded in 1939 (Walton & El Nasr, 1988, p. 153). That these educational programmes and services were modelled on the work of, and in many instances actually founded by, social workers from the global North is not in question and this point will be discussed in depth in the subsequent chapters.

What is important to note here is that from the early decades of the twentieth century professional social work was spreading rapidly throughout the world.

Social Work Internationally Post-1945

The worldwide conflict of 1939–45 had a major impact on the development of social work. Not only were individual social workers caught up in the conflict in many different ways, but the course of development of the profession as a whole was affected. Among the many individual stories of that time are examples such as that of the founder of the School of Social Work at the University of Warsaw, Helena Radlinska, whose own house as well as the School buildings were destroyed; two-thirds of her colleagues also were killed (Healy, 2008b, p. 6). These events of destruction and loss were repeated in different ways in many places. At the same time social workers also played positive roles embodying values that have come to be seen as core to the profession, such as Irena Sendler who, amongst many others, worked at personal risk to protect the lives of Jewish children in the middle of the Holocaust (Wieler, 2006).

Social work was also part of the post-war reconstruction. At a national level, in different countries, social workers participated in the rebuilding of social infrastructure. Internationally, too, social work played an important post-war role. For example, the ICSSW (as it still was until 1955) was involved from the earliest days in the fledgeling United Nations (UN). It was granted consultative status with the Economic and Social Council (ECOSOC) in 1947 and the various organizations that grew from the ICSSW and the Permanent Secretariat (IASSW, ICSW and IFSW) have maintained this link to the present time. The then president of the ICSSW, René Sand (who was both a physician and a social worker), played a prominent role in the establishment of the World Health Organization (WHO) (Eilers, 2008, p. 65), and one of his successors as president of the IASSW, Herman Stein, was very influential in the early days of the United Nations Children's Fund (UNICEF) (Kendall, 2008, pp. 111–13). As we will see in subsequent chapters, the UN and its various constituent organizations (especially UNICEF) in different ways have been part of the development of social work internationally, both in the form of having key international social workers in influential roles within them and in providing institutional support for the development of the profession. (We will also see, paradoxically, that there are strong arguments in favour of the view that other entities of the UN act in such a way as to create the conditions that necessitate social work and related forms of intervention.) Significant international non-government organizations (INGOs), such as the International Committee of the Red Cross (ICRC), have also had a close relationship with social work since the immediate post-war era, with the same mixture of social work action in their formation and in their contribution to the development of international social work (Healy, 2008a, p. 123).

One of the significant global trends of the 1950s through to the 1970s was the achievement of independence from colonial rule by many countries in Africa and Asia. It is in this period that an increasing concern with social development became part of the debates about international social work (Hall & Midgley, 2004). In some countries social work either emerged in this period as part of the social development movement or became associated with social development as a practice. In other countries, however, this connection was not made or else the development of social work followed a Western model of what Midgley (1981, 1997) has described as 'remedial welfare'. Thus, social work in this period has to be understood in the context of what has come to be known as 'post-colonialism' or 'neo-colonialism'.

Social work in 'post-colonial' settings has, in many instances, been part of a struggle between processes of modernization and a critical rejection of the dominance of Western influences. It is in this period that the ideas of 'indigenization' and 'authentization' came to identify a central debate in the field of international social work (Walton & El Nasr, 1988; Osei-Hwedie, 1993; Nimagadda & Cowger, 1999). The question is whether forms of social work from countries of the global North can be adapted appropriately for the national and cultural contexts into which they are introduced (indigenization) or whether it is necessary to construct a genuinely local professional model (authentization) (Walton & El Nasr, 1988, pp. 148–9; see discussion in Chapter 5). Critics of the processes by which social work spread from the countries in which it originated, especially those who consider that 'international social work' has effectively been the importation of (often individualized American models) theory and practice from the global North into other countries, have even at times questioned whether the very concept of social work itself is relevant in the global South (Midgley, 1981; also see Gray & Fook, 2004; Payne & Askeland, 2008). At the same time, the professionalization of social work has been a part of the wider processes of modernization in countries of the global South that has been embraced by practitioners and academics in the social welfare field in much the same way that it was also sought enthusiastically in earlier decades by those in the global North.

From the 1980s through to the present day we can continue to see the growth of professional social work in various parts of the world, including Africa, Asia, Eastern and Southern Europe, the Pacific Island states and South America (see, e.g.: Yuen-Tsang & Sung, 2002; Ku et al., 2005; Mafile'o, 2006; Osei-Hwedie et al., 2006; Hugman et al., 2007). The debates about indigenization and authentization continue to be central in all of these regions (Osei-Hwedie, 1993; Yan & Cheung, 2006), as do those between micro-level 'remedial' practices that focus on individuals and families and macro-level 'development' approaches that focuses on organizations, policies and systems (Mendes, 2007; Olson, 2007). Thus, although social work is now established as a profession in 90 countries (as understood in terms of membership of the IFSW [2008b]), and social workers from around the world regularly engage in dialogue through meetings and conferences, it could be said that the understanding of social work internationally is now more diverse than ever.

But, assuming that such a description is plausible, is this necessarily a negative situation? Recent critical scholarship has questioned the pursuit of a unitary view of social work that embraces all countries and situations (Gray & Fook, 2004). This argument is based on the idea that any sense of the commonalities of social work around the world must, necessarily, be both broad and limited. In so far as social work theory and practice is required to take account of cultural differences then comparisons will have to focus on the ways in which social work can be authentically contextualized. From this point of view, an emphasis on difference is desirable, even if it leads to a sense that there is no one single entity called 'social work'. Against this view, as has already been implied above, is the idea that there is a sufficient degree of commonality in goals and values that unite social workers in all parts of the world for a common purpose. From this point of view, it can be said, international social work is more than simply a series of connections between particular countries but in recent years has come to represent a more thoroughly 'global' phase in the development of the profession. As is made clear in the subsequent chapters of this book, this question of similarity and difference is now one of the most critical issues in understanding international social work.

Social Work and Globalization

The similarities and differences between countries and cultures is one of the central elements in discussions of the phenomenon that has come to be known as 'globalization'. This concept refers to an analysis of the contemporary world that sees all national economic, political, social and cultural systems as having become increasingly integrated (Bauman, 1998; George & Wilding, 2002). As Sklair (1999) notes, there is not only one theory of globalization but rather this concept is a collection of ideas that variously emphasize the economic, the political, the social or the cultural dimensions of the integration between nation states. Although Sklair himself tends to favour the notion of a 'global capitalist model', because of what he sees as the importance of transnational practices (i.e., where individuals and organizations act across national borders without being tied to any one location), at the same time he also notes that political, social and cultural aspects are also important. Indeed, he argues that although there are many negative aspects to this process, to the extent that it is now inevitable it also represents a positive opportunity if used for the pursuit of humanitarian, democratic and just ends.

As many discussions of international social work such as Lyons (1999), Lyons et al. (2006) and Cox and Pawar (2006) have noted, it is not possible to begin to analyse all the different issues that constitute international social work without grasping the significance of globalization and its impact on both social work practices and the social systems within which it is located. For example, the actions of social work are contextualized by the impact of economic, political and cultural globalization. Lyons (1999, pp. 31–5) traces the way in which various major international events of the last 50 years have established the background for international social work. These include the post-war reconstruction policies; the 'Cold War'; the formation of the World Bank and the International Monetary Fund (IMF); the oil crisis of the mid-1970s; the evolution of the General Agreement on Tariffs and Trade (GATT) into the World Trade Organization (WTO); the breakdown of the political bloc dominated by the Soviet Union; the growth of other blocs such as the European Union (EU) and the Association of South-East Asian Nations (ASEAN); the influence of neo-liberal economics and the 'structural adjustment' policies of the IMF and the World Bank. ('Structural adjustment' refers to shifts within national economic policies from state to private ownership of key industries, the deregulation of markets and reduced trade barriers such as tariffs – all of which are intended to increase trade and hence national wealth.) All of these events have contributed to major shifts in the possibilities for the projects that characterize international social work.

Two particular world events serve to illustrate the way in which such events impact on social work. The first of these is the breakdown of the Soviet bloc in Eastern Europe. The shift over the last two decades from managed economies and political systems to Western-style democracy and market economies has brought significant changes both in daily life for the populations of these countries and the opening up of possibilities for greater communication with other parts of the world. Of particular concern to social workers has been the disclosure and rise of the incidents of social needs in these countries. In the post-Soviet era, for example, there have been opportunities for INGOs of various kinds to develop projects in the countries of Eastern Europe. Some of these have involved professional social workers, while others have not. Some also can be described as having used progressive approaches, while again others have implemented projects and used practices that from the value position of professional social work can be said to be questionable (Payne & Askeland, 2008, p. 125).

The impact of the 'structural adjustment' policies and programmes of the IMF and World Bank also have had a marked impact on the terrain of social work. This is most frequently recognized in discussions of social development (Midgley, 1997; Dominelli, 2007). In some parts of the world economically driven development has led to industrial manufacturing and commercial agriculture replacing more traditional local economic activity. As markets have shifted geographically in order to provide high rates of return for international business, local populations, usually in developing countries, have then found themselves simultaneously without employment and no longer having the infrastructure to provide alternative sources of income from their own labour. At the same time, structural adjustment policies had required national governments either to cease development of, or to drastically reduce, social security systems (Deacon, 2007, p. 47). So the net effect was that, at least in some countries, large sections of the population ended up in situations of as much or greater poverty than previously, sometimes because of growing disparities in wealth despite increasing average per capita levels of income (UNDP, 1999; George & Wilding, 2002). Women and children were particularly negatively affected by the impact of these policies (UNICEF, 1999). Moreover, it should be recognized that the impact of such policies is to create conditions in which the more individual and family focused concerns of social workers are exacerbated, including problems of children's well-being and safety, domestic violence, substance misuse and other social issues that can be associated with social stress.

Over the last half-century, the longer-term trajectory of the impact on social welfare of global economic, political and cultural developments can be described as that of an increasing emphasis on state-based institutions and systems of the post-1945 period which faltered in the 1970s and then was subsequently replaced by various forms of privatization, with the drivers in both directions being economic and political in combination. For writers such as Midgley (1997) and Stiglitz (2003) this rise and fall of social approaches to human well-being must be seen as part of the impact of neo-colonialism. The demise of the 'welfare consensus' in the member countries of the Organization for Economic Co-operation and Development (OECD) was imposed more widely through institutions such as the IMF, World Bank and WTO in ways that echo the manner in which earlier social structures and political systems had been imposed around the world through colonial administrations. For example, the policy goal of 'rolling back the welfare state' was a priority of domestic policy not only in these Western countries, but such changes were buttressed by the restructure of global aid and development as well as a concern with trade and international economic relations. Social welfare was retrenched in the domestic sphere and at the same time in relations between nation states. Indeed, the latter strategy was intricately bound up with the former. In this sense it may even be plausible to see the process as that of applying the same principle to both domestic and foreign policies: those who had come to depend on the provision of direct welfare were to be required to learn to 'fend more for themselves' (i.e., cease to rely on the support of these governments, whether of their own nation or as part of the international community).

The Nation State and Globalization

In so far as each of these definitions of international social work is based on the idea of movement between countries they assume the existence of the nation state and the political, cultural and moral authority exercised by the state. Thus they raise the question of whether it is possible to envisage a social welfare system or social work practice that is not shaped in some way by the nation state within which the system or practice is to be found. The conventional answer to this question would be to say that the history of social work as a modern profession is often articulated around the growth, or otherwise, of welfare states (compare Esping-Andersen, 1990, and George & Wilding, 2002, with Payne, 2005). Consequently, the various forms of the profession can be seen in terms of the differences between such states, such as in the extent to which social work is provided directly by state institutions, by NGOs or through a private market (Barnes & Hugman, 2002). For this reason, the form of social work that is possible in any particular location is structured by the type of welfare regime in that country. Thus it can be argued that the possibilities for social work are circumscribed by national borders and that this is the case even if we are talking about 'international' social work.

Both in scholarly analysis and popular discussions, the notion of 'globalization' has come to be part of standard terminology in the last two decades. Underlying this concept is the idea that through the rapidly increasing complexity and potential of technology, economic, political, legal, social, cultural and environmental systems have become integrated across the world (Mishra, 1999; Seitz, 2008). Some analysis argues that there is now, effectively, a single global market and a single global political system at the supra-national level (Stiglitz, 2003). Others have suggested that a single 'global' culture is developing, in the phenomenon that Ritzer (2000) has called 'McDonaldization' (in which the sameness of this fast food chain in every country serves as a metaphor for worldwide uniformity). From this point of view, even though national governments continue to exercise authority within their own countries, such authority is effectively limited by the impact of global systems and relationships, so that in economic and political matters national governments now operate as a local level to global society. This view argues that under conditions of globalization we must begin to contend with the possibility that national borders are weakening and that social, political and economic systems are becoming both more fluid and more interconnected, leading to a global homogenization of the human condition.

At the same time, many of the analysts of globalization have also questioned the limits of this process. Bauman (1998), for example, challenges the extent to which globalization is to be seen as having succeeded in weakening national borders, as opposed to having reconfigured the relations between states. Some states may have been brought closer together, such as in the EU or ASEAN, but these remain groups of states with separate national systems and identities. Indeed, as Asad (2000) notes, the causes of the international movement of capital that characterizes economic globalization come precisely from the capacity of nation states to manage their local economies differently. The movement between countries of various industries including clothing, motor vehicles or computing and other high-technology equipment occurs precisely because countries can compete with each other on the basis of labour costs that include business taxes as well as local wage rates. However, Asad (2000) also qualifies this understanding with a recognition that states are equal in terms of political sovereignty but are not equal in terms of the types of power that they can exercise. This is seen not only in classic colonial relationships, but also in contemporary neo-colonial linkages through economic and other forms of dominance by certain countries over others. Stiglitz (2003) likewise argues that the argument for a single global system is overstated, pointing to the dominance of economics in such an argument and noting that not only in areas of society and culture does greater technological and communicative integration highlight *difference* as much if not more than commonality, but also that dissent (including terrorism) has increased along with trade and economic integration. George and Wilding note that such differences are almost always in the favour of the global North as against the global South (2002, pp. 110–12), which may serve as an explanation, at least partially, of the globalization of violent dissent and terrorism.

This is not to suggest, however, that there is not a widespread agreement among theorists that the contemporary world is marked by highly integrated economic, political and cultural systems. What happens in one part of the world impacts on many other parts and the extent and speed of such effects has been increased greatly by the 'new' technologies (Sklair, 1999; Seitz, 2008). These have not only enabled previously existing forms of information to be transmitted more quickly, but have also provided the basis for the development of new forms of economic or political structures. The spread of international financial institutions (which in themselves combine previously separate sectors such as banking and insurance) and the formation of new supra-national political entities such as the EU and ASEAN are examples of this. In the political realm the management of populations, for example in the control of population migrations, has been expanded through the use of technology in tracking the movement of individuals across national borders.

The effects of these more recent developments of globalization can be seen not only in relation to economics and politics, but also in the realm of social welfare. Examples of issues that are particularly relevant for international social work that can be seen in these terms include health and human services, education, social security and poverty, work and (un)employment, housing, migration, crime and so on (George & Wilding, 2002; Deacon, 2007). As we will see in subsequent discussion, dialogue and action between nations now concerns not only trade, security and other issues that previously had been part of global relationships, but also matters of social policy such as access to social services and social security by people moving between countries. As part of this, the increasing connections being made by some governments between trade and aid and development policies have seen a shift from the dominant neo-liberal policies of the previous 20 years. This is illustrated, for example, by the commitments made regarding the alleviation of worldwide poverty by the G8 Summit of 2005 at Gleneagles in Scotland. Notwithstanding the limited impact of action by some countries following from the summit (Deacon, 2007, p. 115), it was notable because of the way in which globalized communication was used to mobilize widespread popular debate and pressure on national governments towards conclusions that were favourable to social democratic rather than neo-liberal policies. The positive actions of many countries following this particular meeting should also be recognized, although it is as yet somewhat early to reach conclusions about their impact.

Deacon (2007) identifies five ways in which the processes of globalization have implications for social policy in general and which for the purposes of this discussion raise questions about the impact on international social work. The first of these implications is that the globalized economy potentially creates a competition between countries producing what Deacon refers to as a 'race to the welfare bottom' (2007, p. 9). By this, Deacon is referring to the argument that in order to secure inward investment from international business, countries are under pressure to reduce the costs of the provision of social welfare (including health, education and social security). However, as Deacon notes, this has not necessarily always been the case and he refers to recent evidence that there are differing impacts of those countries where welfare states were already relatively well-developed (mostly in the global North) and those where they are not (mostly on the global South).

The second policy implication of greater global integration is that the international quasi-governmental organizations, including those associated with the United Nations, as well as the IMF and World Bank, have entered national debates (Deacon, 2007, p. 9). This has in some cases led to the prescription of specific policies for certain countries, usually illustrated by reference to the 'structural adjustment' policies of the 1990s (UNICEF, 1999). However, this process is not monolithic, and even between entities of the United Nations there are differences of policy advice and emphasis. Examples include the defence of social expenditures to promote social cohesion and develop human capital by the International Labour Organization (ILO) or the promotion of redistributive policies by some parts of UNICEF (Deacon, 2007, p. 25).

The third can be seen in the emergence of social policy debate at the supranational level, particularly in regional groupings such as the EU and ASEAN. For example, a distinctively Asian approach to social welfare policies has been identified by some commentators (Kwon, 1998). Whether or not this is in fact the case, or whether a similar phenomenon might be ascribed to Sub-Saharan Africa is open to debate.

Fourth, globalization has created an international private market in social provision. This can be seen in health and human services, education, social insurance and even in criminal justice (such as the provision of private prisons). For example, the last decade in Australia has seen the development of the private provision of some prisons and the whole of the (largely now discredited) immigration detention centre system (Briskman et al., 2008). Similarly, services such as health care in many countries are provided by multinational firms, while university and secondary school education has also become a major transnational industry. These types of developments particularly benefit those who are already advantaged within national economic and political systems.

The fifth area of the impact of globalization and social policy identified by Deacon is that it has encouraged the global movement of people, both individually and in large numbers. Such movements present challenges to national welfare systems. This includes both of those who migrate 'legitimately' within the laws and treaties that apply between countries (in that they have prior authorization, such as obtaining visas) and those who shift as asylum seekers (George & Wilding, 2002, pp. 144–6; Cox & Pawar, 2006, pp. 267–74). The former may be welcomed, or even actively sought, by national governments whereas the latter have increasingly come to be perceived as a threat to economic prosperity and political stability. Bauman (1998) makes an ironic distinction between these two types of migrants, respectively, as 'tourists' and 'vagabonds': the former travel freely while the latter are actively excluded by processes of 'border security'.

Is Social Work 'Global'?

In relation to these debates about the reality of globalization and its implications for social policy and social welfare systems, it is necessary to consider the extent to which international social work might be considered 'global'. As we will see in more detail in subsequent chapters, organizations such as the IFSW, IASSW and ICSW could be said to be 'global' in that they seek to bring together all social work from around the world. It is even possible to see international social work as part of the process of globalization within the profession, as both cause and effect. Increased movement of social workers and transmission or exchange of practices and ideas in social work, it could be argued, lead to an increased homogeneity of the profession between regions and countries. Indeed, in so far as 'social work' is now identified as a profession in 90 countries, including on every continent (IFSW, 2008b), the view that there is a common core which unites such a body should at least be given some consideration (Hugman, 2009).

However, at the same time we may conclude that the international movement of social work (however this is understood – this point will be developed further in Chapter 2) is also reflective of the capacity of nation states to manage their welfare systems according to local needs, practices, resources, customs, values and so on. As we will see in more detail in subsequent chapters, even if we accept the idea of a common core to social work it may still be argued that the emphasis in different countries is so diverse that we should reject the idea of integration that is contained in the concept of 'global'. This argument does not discard the idea of globalization in its entirety but, as with other critical analysis, questions the extent to which the process it describes must be understood as all-embracing. At the same time, such a position can continue to regard (international) social work as part of the web of relationships between countries, even those that are made increasingly more complex through processes of globalization, and to think in terms of the variety of relationships between different national forms of social work.

This latter perspective supports Healy's assertion (2008a, p. 7), based on her wide review of the definitions of international social work, that it is most helpful to differentiate 'international' from 'global'. One of the major questions that will be addressed in this present analysis is that of the extent to which social work might be said to be the same or different in all the countries in which it has developed as a profession. An understanding of globalization as a complex phenomenon embracing economics, politics, culture and society, and as highly complex in that it has both negative and positive features, therefore provides one thread from which such an inquiry can be woven.

Healy (2008a) explains the difference between 'international' and 'global' in the following way:

> [...] *global* means pertaining to or involving the whole world, whereas *international* can mean any of the following: between or among two or more nations, of or pertaining to two or more nations or their citizens, pertaining to the relations between nations, having members or activities in several nations, or transcending national boundaries or viewpoints (Healy, 2008a, p. 7 – emphasis original).

So to put it simply, for Healy what distinguishes international social work is that it involves any aspect of social work in which there is some relationship between two or more countries or nations. This is a very useful approach, because it allows a lot of flexibility in considering a variety of practices and structures. It enables the discussion to include, for example, a situation in which a social worker goes from one country to another country in order to practice, or in which there are exchanges between social work academics at universities in two countries, as well as circumstances that affect many or all countries in which social work is practised. (The implications of this definition will be considered in much more detail in Chapter 2.) For the purposes of this discussion, therefore, we can begin with a recognition that 'global' (as in the issue of 'globalization', for example) is a particular aspect of 'international' in relation to social work, implying some degree of integration across the world as a whole.

The Framework of this Book

From the discussion so far, it will be seen that the question of the extent to which social work can be regarded as a globalized profession remains open. This book is partly directed towards providing an answer to this question, along with addressing various other matters concerning the dynamic nature of the profession internationally. So we will return to this point in the final chapter.

The question about the global nature of social work depends, as the starting point, on the way in which we understand international social work. Mention has already been made of the different ways in which international social work can be defined, and so we turn to this particular crucial point in Chapter 2. This chapter articulates the various ways in which international social work can be characterized and the implications that follow from each particular part of the definitions that have been developed by key writers on the subject. The chapter examines what it means to say that social work is 'international' and considers who are 'international social workers'.

In Chapter 3 the analysis focuses on the international issues with which social work is concerned. Existing literature has identified the most crucial of these areas: refugees and forced migration; famine and drought; other natural disasters; poverty; human trafficking; the impact of rapid industrialization, including economic migration within and between countries (with implications about the way in which economic globalization has impacted on local social structures) (Lyons, 1999; George & Wilding, 2002; Hall & Midgley, 2004; Cox & Pawar, 2006; Lyons et al., 2006; Dominelli, 2007). The discussion here examines the opportunities and challenges presented for social work in terms of both programmes and practices. In particular, this chapter is centrally concerned with the role played by social work in responding to these various issues and the way in which social workers act in doing so.

One particular issue that affects many parts of the social welfare field internationally is that of the co-ordinated attempt to deal with poverty in many countries, particularly developing nations. This can be seen not only in specific events such as the G8 summit of 2005, discussed above, but also (perhaps even more so) in the preceding formulation of the United Nations Millennium Development Goals (MDGs) (UN, 2000a; Hall & Midgley, 2004; Deacon, 2007). Very little has been written about the relationship between the MDGs and international social work. Therefore Chapter 4 examines the nature of the MDGs and looks at their implications for international social work. It also then examines the contribution that social work can make in responses to the MDGs and the challenges that they pose for international social welfare.

One of the most long-running debates about the nature of social work, stemming from the earliest date of professionalization, has been the question of whether social work should focus on social issues and human needs at the micro- or the macro-level. As has already been noted, this debate not only continues in those countries where social work first developed, but it is also highly relevant in considering the growth of professional social work in other parts of the world. For example, is a different focus for social work necessary in developing countries compared to those that have advanced industrial structures and well-developed social welfare systems? Or, is the nature of social work such that practices which emphasize working with individuals and families are applicable in any situation? In order to provide answers to these questions, Chapter 5 looks at the variety of forms of social work practice and their relationship to international social work. It also considers ways in which social work in different national contexts can be informed by an international comparative view of the nature and identity of professional social work.

As noted above, attempts to create international organizations in social work date back to the early part of the twentieth century. There are now three major organizations that bring social workers together from around the world and which have a major influence on knowledge, skills and values. These are the International Federation of Social Workers (IFSW), the International Association of Schools of Social Work (IASSW) and the International Council on Social Welfare (ICSW). In addition, there are linked organizations, such as the International Consortium on Social Development (ICSD) and the Commonwealth Organization of Social Workers (COSW). Semi-autonomous regional groupings also exist within some of these organizations. Chapter 6 examines the work of these organizations and the contribution that they make to international social work. In particular, the chapter looks at the way in which the function of these organizations can create a tension between a universal view of the nature of social work and the national and local particularities that shape social work in each setting. It also considers the place of other organizations, such as INGOs and the UN sector in international social work.

Two particular issues are of importance in considering the relationship between the international professional organizations and social work in different parts of the world. These are education and training and professional ethics. In many respects, it might be argued that the growth of social work is being driven increasingly, at least in those countries where it is relatively new, by a concern for appropriately high levels of education and training for practitioners in the social welfare field (compare, e.g., Namdaldagva, 2004; Osei-Hwedie et al., 2006; Hugman et al., 2007; Tsang et al., 2008). Alongside this, social work is sometimes defined as much by its value base as by particular sets of skills and knowledge (Payne, 2005). The international professional organizations have for a long time played an active role in the development of both these aspects of social work professionalization. In 2004 the IFSW and IASSW approved documents to establish international guidelines for education and training and to revise extensively their previously existing statements on ethics (IASSW/IFSW, 2004; IFSW/IASSW, 2004). Both of these documents have accelerated an already existing debate about the way in which thinking about social worker should be sensitive to cultural and national differences as against notions of commonality (Gray, 2005). Chapters 7 and 8 respectively examine in detail the international statement on standards for education and training and on professional ethics, looking particularly at the critical questions that arise from them in relation to notions of difference and similarity.

Following on from a consideration of education and training, and values and ethics, Chapter 9 revisits Midgley's (1981) now classic critique of 'professional imperialism'. This work firmly established the debate about the extent to which the internationalization of social work hands essentially being the transmission of skills and practices derived from 'Western contexts' into other parts of the world. This discussion extends themes that have already been introduced concerning the importance of diversity, with the implication that social work internationally would better be understood as a set of different practices, compared to the possibility that there is a common core to social work. The chapter raises the idea that those parts of the world in which social work is or may be a product of colonial or neo-colonial relations, namely the global South, have much to contribute to thinking about the profession in the global North.

In conclusion, Chapter 10 draws together the themes of the book with a particular focus on key debates: between micro- and macro-theories and practices, between universal and particular understandings of social work and concerning the dynamics of professionalization internationally. This chapter looks not only at the ways in which international social work might develop in the future, and overcome problems of 'professional imperialism', but also the contribution that a critical understanding of international social work can make to a wider understanding of social work as a whole.

Throughout this discussion there is one particular underlying debate that appears in several forms, namely that between a universal perspective on social work practices, theories and values and that based on the differences between cultures and societies. This debate can been seen especially in Chapter 5 in relation to different forms of social work and the questions of 'indigenization' and 'authentization', in Chapters 7 and 8 concerning social work education and professional ethics and in Chapter 9 in the analysis of 'professional imperialism'. However, it lies behind all the issues that are explored here. In the concluding discussion this debate is highlighted as a central contemporary question that must be grasped in order to understand international social work: it is, in many ways, the central theme of this analysis. But first we must set out the scope of our field of inquiry and, therefore, in the next chapter we start to examine the question of how international social work can be defined and the various elements that have been suggested as important aspects of this phenomenon.

2

Different Visions of 'International' in Social Work

The Elements of 'International Social Work'

When we think about international social work we are effectively combining a number of different elements into one concept. In the previous chapter we briefly considered an important difference between 'global' and 'international' in relation to social work. In this chapter we bring to the discussion of various approaches to the meaning of 'international' and how these relate to our understanding of social work as a professional activity. So, to understand the concept fully we need to disentangle the separate strands.

A range of approaches to the question of how we should regard the 'international' in social work have been stated, in various ways and for a range of purposes, by many commentators including Midgley (1981), Healy (1995, 2008a), Lyons (1999), Hokenstad and Midgley (2004), Cox and Pawar (2006), Lyons et al. (2006) and Payne and Askeland (2008). One key example can be found in Midgley's analysis of 'professional imperialism' (1981), which emphasizes the way in which social work practices and models of professional education have been taken from the global North to the global South. In what has become a classic work, this critique argued that the reality of international social work was far from being a process that could be described using words such as 'transmission' or 'exchange', which imply some sort of equality or openness of relationship. Rather, for Midgley, it reflected the colonial and post-colonial political and economic structures within which it was practised. In other words, just as the relationships between countries through the early to mid-twentieth century can only be grasped using the concept of colonialism, so too the spread of social work from countries of the global North to other countries ought to be understood in the same terms. (We will return to this critique in more detail in Chapter 9.)

Without denying (or even, at times, explicitly addressing) the argument presented by Midgley, other commentators on international social work have emphasized various aspects of this type of relationship between countries. For example, Lyons and her colleagues (1999, 2006) discuss contemporary practices with an emphasis on the activities of social workers from the global North, especially in their work either in countries of the global South or with problems whose origins can be identified with those countries (such as refugees and forced migrants). Cox and Pawar (2006), in their opening chapter, emphasize the debate about indigenization and the need to recognize a diversity of approaches to social work practices. Similarly, Payne and Askeland begin 'from experiences in Western countries, where social work originated' (2008, p. 4) and their analysis goes on to examine the implication that this origin is the foundation of a 'Western' bias in a lot of social work theory and practice.

By combining these different analyses we can identify five elements in the concept of international social work. Of these, the way in which the first four are set out here is influenced particularly by the insights of Healy, who seeks to build a comparative framework (and intentionally builds on ideas that go back at least to the First International Conference of Social Work which took place in Paris in 1928) (Healy 2008a, pp. 8–9).

1. Probably the most common usage of the term more widely in the profession, international social work can be seen as *the practice of social work in a country other than the home country of the social worker*. In this sense, social work is international when a social worker goes from her or his own country to work as a social worker in another country. In the early years of professionalization in the global North, social workers travelled between European countries, or between Europe and North America, to practise and to establish services. Others travelled in order to be trained (both in formal university programmes and in practice) before returning to their countries of origin to establish professional social work there. For example, Norma Parker, a leading figure in the development of social work in Australia, studied in the United States and the United Kingdom in the 1930s (Lawrence, 1965). However, by the end of the twentieth century this definition of international social work, at least in many instances, had come to mean the transmission of social work from the countries where it was well institutionalized (the global North) to those where it was developing (the global South). Many social workers continue to travel in order to practise or to receive education and training, to pursue their careers or to undertake specific projects in 'another' country.

2. Through the twentieth century the idea of international social work increasingly also came to mean *working with individuals, families or communities*

whose origins are in a country other than that where the social worker is practising. In other words, in contrast to the first definition, it is social work undertaken with service users who are not in their home country. So, in this sense, social work services provided for various types of migrant populations may be seen as 'international', because the nature of the needs experienced by these groups, and the causes of those needs, cross national borders (war, famine, natural disasters and so on). The most obvious example of this would be social work undertaken with refugees and forced migrants (Cox & Pawar, 2006). Other migrant communities also form part of this dimension of international practice in that they too may have particular needs that arise from their experience of migration and settlement, ethnic differences from the majority population in their new country and so on.

3. *Working with international organizations,* such as INGOs like the ICRC, International Social Service (ISS) or Save the Children Fund (SCF), or quasi-governmental organizations such as the United Nations agencies (UNICEF, UNDP, UNHCR and so on) is the third meaning of international social work. This understanding does not depend on whether the social worker actually moves between their country of origin and another country. For example, a social worker employed in the headquarters of an INGO in their own country of origin could be regarded as engaged in international social work in this definition as much as would someone who 'goes overseas' to work 'in the field'. The focus of these types of agencies can combine other definitions in that they can be concerned with both practice and issues that require intervention shifting in many ways across and between national borders.

4. The fourth definition can be found in *collaborations between countries in which social workers exchange ideas or work together on projects that cross national borders.* Examples of this include visits between practitioners to learn about services in each others' countries, or university teachers and researchers working together on projects that combine knowledge from two or more countries. For example, as has been noted in Chapter 1, this has a long history. In the early twenty-first century such exchanges still take place, between practitioners, policy makers and academics. This definition also includes international conferences and similar events. Student exchanges, either for short visits or for practice learning at qualifying or post-qualifying levels (variously known as practicum, field education or internships), might also come within this notion, especially if such interactions are constructed in such a way that they can promote mutual learning. The key difference between this definition and that described previously of social workers 'working in another country' (see 1 above) is the bi-lateral or multi-lateral relationships between social workers in the various locations that are mutual in terms of both the contribution made and the benefit

derived by each partner in the process. Also, over time it may involve people going from each country to the other.

5. More recently, discussions of international social work have started to recognize the interplay of 'global' and 'local', in *practices that address locally issues that originate in globalized social systems* (Dominelli, 2003, 2007; Lyons et al., 2006). Examples include the impact of the global economy on local (un)employment and the social problems that follow as a result, the impact of pan-national structures on the employment of social workers and on social welfare policies and so on. This notion differs from the other definitions presented in this chapter in that both the service users and the social workers may be in their country of origin, while it is the structural issues affecting their lives which have their foundations elsewhere.

So, in summary, we may say that 'international social work' refers to practice and policy concerning situations in which professionals, those who benefit from their services or the causes of the problems that bring these two actors together, have travelled in some way across the borders between nations. That is, social work is international when the social worker, the service user or the social issue moves between or connects two or more countries. As we will see below, such movement/connection can be interpreted variously as international according to (1) who or what has moved and (2) what is the impact of this movement on other people and institutions, or on wider social issues, in the location(s) of the social work practices being considered. International social work thus has several identities and in thinking about it critically we must bear both of these factors in mind. In order to examine this more closely we will turn to each of the above five definitions in turn, through a brief examination of critical and/or reflective writing about these issues.

Social Work(ers) in 'Other' Countries

The first of the five definitions is that in which the social worker moves to a country other than that from which they originate in order to practise in some way. In the light of recent critical discussions of international social work these sorts of movements raise several important questions. These can be summarized as:

a. To what extent are models of social work developed in one national and cultural context useful or appropriate in other situations?

b. What is the relationship between a social worker whose origins are in one situation and the local colleagues and clients with whom they may work in another context?

c.   In particular, who makes decisions concerning the appropriateness of fit of theories and practices that a social worker from another country might bring to the situation in which they are working as an international social worker, or on what basis is this determined?

d.   How do social workers whose identity and training are derived from one context, whether this is the global North or South, learn about other contexts and adapt their practice appropriately to them?

e.   At what point might an international social worker, defined in these terms, cease to be 'international' and become part of the profession 'locally'?

To examine these questions, two cases will be used as illustrative examples.

Example 2.1: American Social Work Teachers in Ukraine and Vietnam

The work of a group of social work educators from New York provides one picture of 'going overseas' (Forgery et al., 2000; Chazin et al., 2002; Forgery et al., 2003). In these projects, American social work academics and practitioners (associated with Fordham University School of Social Service) undertook to provide short programmes for colleagues in Vietnam and in Ukraine as both these countries sought to develop social work. In Vietnam the group provided a programme to help university teachers developing social work education, while in Ukraine they provided advanced training for practitioners.

In Vietnam, the project was invited by the Open University of Ho Chi Minh City to 'provide curriculum development training in two areas identified as priorities by Vietnamese faculty members' (Forgery et al., 2003, p. 148). These areas were 'generalist practice with individuals, families and groups' and 'human behaviour and the social environment' (p. 149). Forgery and her colleagues (2000, 2003) describe how these ways of constructing social work theory and practice are culturally grounded in America and that a central part of the process was in working collaboratively with Vietnamese participants as colleagues to develop a shared understanding of how they could be adapted to a new situation and how more genuinely local ideas and actions could be developed (see discussions of 'indigenization' and 'authentization' elsewhere in this book).

In Ukraine the project was to present a short advanced training course for school-based practitioners (social workers, teachers and others) who provide counselling and other similar interventions for students and their families in areas affected by the Chornobyl nuclear disaster of 1986 (Chazin et al., 2002, p. 90). (See Chapter 3 for further discussion of social work and responses to disasters.) The focus of the programme was to assist the Ukraine practitioners in developing greater skills in working with their service users in addressing the psycho-social problems that they face. The goal was to construct a participatory educational process that emphasized the local knowledge and experience of participants, as against the 'expertise' of the international programme providers (pp. 95–6). For instance, this involved the Ukrainian participants providing appropriate practice material as the basis for exploring ideas and thinking about new ways of working.

In both contexts, a central issue that was identified was that there were expectations on the part of colleagues in countries where social work is less professionalized regarding the expertise of those from a country such as the United States. This was also something that the team themselves had to deal with, in addition to their anticipated need to learn about the history and culture of the countries in which they were to work (Forgery et al., 2000). Consequently, the discussions of these projects raise questions of cultural appropriateness in theories and practices for social work, as well as an explicit recognition of questions of social power in relations between local and international participants, as central to engaging in 'social work in another country'. They also show that when social workers travel as experts they can also be recipients or learners as much as givers or teachers if they are open and reflexive.

Example 2.2: A Hong Kong Worker in Canada

Yan (2005, p. 4) proposes that the international social worker who settles in a new country should be considered as having 'crossed over' a boundary between territories. Yan's description of his own origins is that he was part of the 'native elite' (here he draws on the work of Said (1994) and positions himself within his own country/culture). Yan describes his social work education in terms of an acculturation to a Western professional model: for example, he learned notions of confidentiality or self-determination that made little sense in relation to his own culture (compare with Yip, 2004). His professional journey then took Yan to London (a 'secular pilgrimage' to the 'imperial capital' – 2005, p. 6) to undertake higher-level education. On returning to Hong Kong, Yan then became involved in the processes of using aspects of the social work curriculum as part of the preparation for the reintegration of Hong Kong into China – in that process he describes how the profession prioritized internationalization both as a survival mechanism and also to contribute to the development of social work in China (2005, p. 8). Yan, too, can be seen as having 'internationalized': the next phase of this is seen in his move to Canada as a practitioner. In this role he experienced rejection both by clients, including other migrants, and by mainstream professional structures. Undertaking his doctorate involved a further form of internationalism, in that from his Canadian university he then spent some time in China as part of a 'collaboration' between institutions (Yan, 2005, p. 10 – also see Tsang et al., 2000). From there, an academic position at an American university was a further international step (following which Yan has returned more recently to Canada).

Discussion

These two cases demonstrate different paths to becoming international social workers in the sense of the social worker moving between countries. The first embodies a movement of theory and practice from the global North to the South, in which the social workers who moved did not become part of the local context. The second portrays a movement from the global South to the North, in which the social worker then eventually settled in a new situation. In both cases the social workers in question demonstrate a reflexive awareness of the differences between these contexts and their own role in 'carrying' or 'transmitting' ideas and practices. Yet the dynamic of this movement, in many senses, is the same: the underlying pattern is that the prevailing sources of ideas about what it is to practice and theorize social work are grounded in the North and are brought to the South. So, the issue for international social work is to challenge this dynamic. In this regard, social workers from the South often appear to be better placed to identify and respond to this process, in that they are more likely already to be aware of the way in which the 'truth' about social work is 'received' by some countries from others. The work of Yan and his colleagues exemplifies this, being concerned as so much of it is with questions of appropriate 'contextualization' and 'recontextualization' across cultural boundaries (Tsang et al., 2000; Yan, 2005; Yan & Tsang, 2005; Yan & Cheung, 2006). Nonetheless, as the first example demonstrates (Forgery et al., 2000, 2003; Chazin et al., 2002), when grasped by those from the North this also can form the basis for a more equal exchange.

However, at the same time, it is important not to construct colleagues of the global South as if they were simply passive recipients of ideas and lacked agency (Sewpaul, 2006). The group from Fordham University were invited to the Ukraine and Vietnam and it is the case that a great amount of this type of international social work is now conducted on such as basis. This is not to deny the post-colonial nature of the globalized world in which such movements occur, but it does point to a shared nature of the responsibility for making such dynamics explicit and seeking to overcome the imbalance of power that results when a relationship is based on one party having resources (including knowledge and practical expertise) that another lacks. The responsibility for colleagues in the countries of the South, it has been argued, is to recognize this and to seek to find ways of achieving 'indigenization', 'authentization' and 'recontextualization' (Walton & El Nasr, 1988; Osei-Hwedie, 1993; Nimagadda & Cowger, 1999; Yan & Tsang, 2005); for those from the global North it is essential also to become aware of the potential risks in this dynamic and to seek to work as a partner.

Akimoto (1997, pp. 26–7) has posed a somewhat different question: if a social worker from Australia or Kenya travels to Japan and does exactly what a

Japanese social worker would do there, how can this be understood as 'international social work'? The practitioner, he argues, is simply 'doing' social work. In response we can note that in the examples used above it is clear that, in both cases, the social workers concerned did act in ways that local social workers did not, as well as perceiving their situation very differently. For instance, Yan's (2005) reflective discussion demonstrates that the social worker who has travelled may continue to approach the context that has now become 'local' with an awareness of differences, of other possibilities or problems and of their own strengths and limitations enhanced by the journey they have taken. We may reasonably expect that the Australian or Kenyan social worker in Japan may learn to do Japanese social work without ever fully letting go of what they brought to the situation. Where the local social worker must learn to be an effective practitioner, international social workers are always, to some extent, required to take explicit responsibility for how they use the knowledge and skills they bring from 'other' contexts. If social workers making such moves, in either direction, do not practice with this degree of reflexivity then they may well be regarded by others as acting inappropriately. Where Akimoto's question may prove fruitful is in that he draws attention to examples where social workers travel from the global South to countries of the North: he cites an instance of an Indian nun working in the United States and asks if this is also 'international' practice (Akimoto, 1997, p. 27). The answer suggested by this discussion is 'yes, it is' and any lack of attention to this is a reflection of the neo-colonial dimensions of globalization and, it may be argued, the social work literature.

'International' Clients

People may move between countries for a variety of reasons. Consequently social workers may find themselves involved in different types of intervention to support migrants. As we have noted above, a group of people who are likely to require assistance from social workers and that has become most clearly identified as 'international', in the sense that they have moved to a country other than their homeland, is that of refugees and asylum seekers (Cox & Pawar, 2006; Nash et al., 2006; Payne & Askeland, 2008). This group has rapidly become a major focus for social work, in both the global North and South. The core questions for this vision of international social work include the following:

a.   Can the local social work profession grasp and respond appropriately to the needs of migrant communities or individuals and how might it seek to do so?

b. In what ways are the needs of migrant communities or individuals different from those of other service users and should social work for such communities be approached as a different form of practice?
c. What are the challenges for practice for locally trained social workers in working with clients whose culture and language are different to the local 'mainstream'?

For the purposes of discussion we will look at examples from New Zealand and the United States.

Example 2.3: Refugee Support in New Zealand

Nash and Trlin (2004) and Nash et al. (2006) describe social work with refugees and forced migrants in New Zealand, much of which is provided by non-government organizations (NGOs). These agencies have experienced a substantial rise in the number of refugees seeking help in recent years (Nash et al., 2006, p. 350). This was largely due to New Zealand developing a positive approach to receiving a planned annual quota of refugees selected by the United Nations High Commission for Refugees (UNHCR). Following a six-week orientation programme, these refugees are then expected to 'begin making their own way in society, with [...] community sponsors' and with assistance provided by community-based services (Nash et al., 2006, p. 347).

An important aspect of social work with refugee communities presented in these studies is that it brings together macro-, mezzo- and micro-practices. There is an interweaving of community development, social education, counselling and practical assistance. Social workers in refugee support services also regularly find that they act as a bridge between service users and other professions, as well as services such as housing, education, employment and health. Of crucial importance, it is necessary for local social workers to become appropriately acquainted with the unique cultural values of the people with whom they are working. These studies point to the importance of recognizing that although cultural differences may present social workers who have been trained in mono-cultural contexts with challenges for adapting techniques to the needs of a diverse service users, this must not be understood as problematizing people from ethnic or linguistic minority backgrounds. Furthermore, not only is it important to recognize that people from similar cultural backgrounds may interpret their culture differently, but that in the context of working with refugee communities some factors that can be understood as cultural may also need to be understood in relation to the refugee experience which is always, to some degree, traumatic (compare with Pittaway et al., 2003). From their discussion of practice in New Zealand and their identification of literature from other countries on this topic, Nash et al. (2006, p. 356) suggest that social work with refugees can be identified as a new 'field of practice'.

Example 2.4: Preparing for Practice with Caribbean Immigrants to New York City

Carten and Goodman (2005) report a collaborative project to train Master of Social Work (MSW) graduates to work more appropriately with West Indian families in New York. This project was a partnership between New York University School of Social Work, the University of the West Indies and the Children's Services Administration of New York City. It was undertaken because it was recognized that the distinctive needs of the Anglophone Caribbean migrants to New York were not appropriately being met (Carten & Goodman, 2005, p. 774). The curriculum was jointly prepared between these three partners and students undertook focused field education placements as well as completing specialized classes. In this way, the students who were selected for the project were able to study relevant background material on Caribbean culture and families, as well as issues such as the movement between the United States and the West Indies that are marked for migrants by 'extended periods of separation or multiple re-unifications and anticipated loss' (Carten & Goodman, 2005, p. 774). Students were encouraged to integrate individual, family and community approaches and to draw on various relevant theories, in order to recognize the range of roles that constitute social work with this client group, including 'case manager, planner, advocate, facilitator, researcher, collaborator, program developer, broker, and mediator' (Carten & Goodman, 2005, p. 781).

Discussion

These examples together summarize many of the key issues in social work with 'international service users'. First, they highlight the way in which, taken as a whole, it is usually inappropriate to consider social work in 'either/or' terms regarding techniques and approaches. In such situations social work is normally a practical combination of the macro, mezzo and micro. Second, working with people from different cultural backgrounds is not simply a matter of knowing about such factors as foods, music or religious festivals (although these things can be important at the right time) but of understanding deeper issues of culture and of recognizing that language may form a distinct issue that has to be resolved (e.g., in working appropriately with interpreters where clients are not from the majority language culture). Understanding what it is to live as a member of a minority community is an important aspect of this, as culture is closely interwoven with social structures. Third, whether the client is a refugee or a migrant, issues of loss and continuing attachment to one's country of origin have to be considered. While this varies between individuals and may find different cultural expression, such factors are frequently present. In addition, although none of the studies addresses this explicitly, social work with refugees and other migrants also often involves dealing with questions of racism and other forms of discrimination (Choi & Choi, 2005; Dominelli, 2008). Working with international service users also challenges social workers, especially those from the majority local culture, to examine their own ethnic identity and to work across cultural differences (Nash & Trlin, 2004; Carten & Goodman, 2005). As with the previous definition, there is a responsibility for social workers to develop and apply a conscious capacity to reflect on their own background and its relationship to social structures.

Working with International Organizations

There is a diverse range of international organizations in which social workers may practice, from the quasi-governmental agencies of the United Nations, through the large INGOs, to a plethora of smaller NGOs that are based in one country and provide services in others. Miller (2007, p. 353) suggests that in 2000 there were over 37,000 NGOs, covering both social and economic development, as well as the environment, media and culture and political activities. In these organizations social workers undertake a wide variety of tasks, including organization of relief and humanitarian aid, need assessment, research, or training and support of local social welfare personnel in recipient countries, as well as ongoing direct provision of services that include counselling, casework and community development (Cox & Pawar, 2006). It is also necessary to acknowledge that international organizations are not 'neutral', ethically or politically, in that they exist to promote particular policies and practices, with goals that may or may not have their origins in the national or cultural contexts in which they are implemented (Fisher, 1997; Koggel, 2007). In understanding this dimension of international social work, therefore, it is important to ask three questions.

a.   What are the processes for problem definition and implementation of responses in the work of INGOs?
b.   What is the relationship between an INGO, local NGOs and other stakeholders, including local communities? (This includes the question of accountability.)
c.   What role does social work play in these institutions?

Example 2.5: International Social Service

The agency International Social Service (ISS) is one of the oldest INGOs in the social welfare field. Its primary role is to provide child and family social work between countries. Since being founded in 1945 it has become particularly focused on the matters of children's placement with their families and with alternative care providers and is based in several countries, with a headquarters in Geneva (Switzerland). Forrest and Rushton (1999) describe the focus of social workers of ISS as that of providing expert assessment and advice regarding the placement of children, particularly when care is being sought by alternative members of families or with regard to applications for adoption between countries. In research conducted in the late 1990s in the United Kingdom, they identified that approximately one-third of the children in the sample who had been considered for international placement actually were placed outside the United Kingdom, whereas the other two-thirds remained in the country (Forrest and Rushton, 1999, p. 157).

A particular example of practice on ISS is provided by the case history of 'Telisha', an eight-year-old girl who had come to the United Kingdom from Jamaica, following her mother who had migrated in order to study (ISS, n.d.). The mother had then died unexpectedly, leaving this small girl without a carer. A social worker from ISS then contacted a comparable social work agency in Jamaica, which was able to locate the girl's grandmother. Subsequently the girl returned to Jamaica to the care of her grandmother. In all the cases used by ISS to illustrate its work, social workers operate by liaising with their immediate colleagues in other countries, or where ISS does not have a branch with those local social workers who have responsibilities for undertaking such tasks, rather than by travelling internationally themselves. In this sense international practice involves collaboration and communication, knowledge of agencies and resources in other countries and the capacity to work in partnership across national boundaries.

Example 2.6: Community Development in Zambia

Quinn (2003) describes a particular approach to social work as part of an international relationship between NGOs. As part of the support for a Zambian organization, Reformed Open Community Schools (ROCS), provided by Tear Australia and Australian Volunteers International, Quinn worked for two years as a community and education advisor. Tasks included consultation with communities to identify needs and solutions, followed by project design and applications to external agencies for resources (Quinn, 2003, p. 41). This led, among other things, to the establishment of successful schools and also to projects delivering clean water and improved sewerage. For Quinn, the central feature of these projects was the involvement of community members in all aspects of the process, from identifying specific needs, through project design to implementation.

One of the crucial elements of this example is that the sponsoring inter-national organizations, Tear Australia and Australian Volunteers International (who effectively employed Quinn), work only through partnership with local NGOs. That is, they neither have 'in-country' staff nor direct the specifics of the projects undertaken by their partners. Rather, Tear Australia provides resources, which may be in the form of finance (including direct funding) and support to local NGO workers, while both may facilitate some provision of expertise in the form of volunteers or time-limited paid workers to assist local NGOs under the direction of those organizations. So, in this sense, the principles articulated by Quinn (2003, p. 41), that

> communities set their own goals and priorities and are actively involved all the way through the process[, that] resources are drawn from within communities them-selves wherever possible [and that] where external resources are necessary they are used in ways that foster and complement community endeavour[,]

are replicated in the relationships between NGOs internationally.

Discussion

These two examples have been chosen deliberately to illustrate particular aspects of social work in or for international organizations. The example of the ISS is one in which social workers may be based in any of many countries. Further-more, their practice is focused on situations in their own country in relation to connections with other countries. So in this way they engage in international social work without 'leaving home'. In contrast, the example of Quinn's work in Zambia did involve the social worker travelling. (Indeed, this project could also be understood as an instance of 'social work in "other" countries' as discussed above and to that extent demonstrates that these distinctions are not mono-lithic.) The ISS provides family casework, whereas Tear Australia and Australian Volunteers International are concerned with social development. But, impor-tantly, both illustrate ways in which social work across national borders can be undertaken on the basis of partnership rather than simply in a giver–receiver relationship. Both these examples show organizations that are independent, non-government and not-for-profit. Social work in other types of international organizations, such as agencies of the United Nations, may be somewhat dif-ferent because of the specific relationships that they might have with national governments (see, e.g., the instances referred to by Cox & Pawar, 2006). Simi-larly, both the examples discussed here are of direct forms of practice as opposed to policy, research or other more indirect practices. However, the issue of the relationship between countries, especially in terms of North and South, remains crucial.

Social Work 'Exchanges'

To some extent, thinking about exchanges in international social work has been relatively widely considered, possibly because such projects are undertaken by academics as well as practitioners and it is academics who tend to produce much of the available literature. As indicated above, this is a separate category concerning situations in which the movement of social workers and social work ideas between two or more countries occurs through a mutual partnership in which the degree of mutuality of relationship can be observed. That is, it differs from situations in which a social worker from one country might go to another country in order to undertake training or some other developmental activity (see Example 2.1) because of the *mutuality* that exists in the relationship. There are several collections of reports from partnership arrangements in social work education and research that provide a range of concrete examples (see, e.g., Dominelli & Bernard, 2003; Healy et al., 2003; Hokenstad & Midgley, 2004). Just one instance will be used here to illustrate some central themes in this dimension of international social work.

Example 2.7: A partnership between Universities in Texas and Mexico

Elliott et al. (2003) report an evaluation of a joint doctoral programme in social work between the University of Texas at Arlington and the Universidad Autónoma de Nuevo León. This programme is taught partly at UANL and partly at UTA, with both Mexican and American students participating. A working capacity in both English and Spanish is required (p. 71) and the students may select the language in which they are assessed (p. 77). The programme commenced in 1997 and at the time of the reported evaluation, 2002, it was continuing despite some problems in the complexities of universities working together, with 17 students enrolled (and it is still continuing in 2009 – personal communication).

The objectives of the two universities differed. In Mexico the government had determined that all university teachers should have doctorate qualifications; in Texas there was a growing recognition of the multi-cultural nature of the State (having the second largest Hispanic population in the USA) and also the need for a greater international awareness in social work practice and policy (pp. 72–3). To meet both these aims, the programme has a 'speciality in international comparative social policy'.

Particular difficulties facing this programme included the financial challenges for students undertaking part of their studies in another country (which included the American as well as the Mexican students), co-ordination and management of the programme between two quite different university systems and the lack of faculty members fluent in both languages. Of particular note, although not discussed at length, is the implication for recruitment of American students given 'the program's policy focus in the face of U.S. students' predominant interest in clinical practice' (p. 77). The programme had at that time succeeded in recruiting approximately equal numbers of Mexican and US students, although more than half of the latter are noted as being ethnically Hispanic (p. 74).

Discussion

This particular project is summarized here because it demonstrates an important difference from many descriptions of 'international exchanges'. Most particularly, the way in which mutuality is realized in practice makes it quite different from the majority of projects, in which there is an explicit 'North to South' transfer of ideas and expertise (as well as movement of people) (compare, e.g., with Shera, 2003, and Wilson, 2003). Of course, mutuality may be achieved in many ways and does not have to be an exact exchange of identical actions and benefits; nor must equity mean sameness of all parties (Maxwell & Healy, 2003). However, the UANL/UTA programme embodies the goal of a *two-way* transaction between colleagues working from a basis of professional equity.

This example also highlights the way in which many discussions of 'international exchange' are based on social work education and research, almost entirely in universities. There may be very good reasons for this, including the mandate of universities to undertake such activities. At the same time, this reality in itself continues to present a significant challenge in how such work might be undertaken as an 'exchange' as opposed, say, to constructing it carefully as 'working in another country' (see above) in which social work academics (often from the North) effectively provide a service (to countries of the South). Again, we are brought back to the implications of the critique of the dynamic in international relationships in social work, especially in that they may reproduce other ways in which the global North can dominate the South. We need to continue to ask whether such arrangements are 'exchanges' or a 'uni-directional flow' of ideas and expertise (Midgley, 1992, p. 23). Where such relationships are not based on a two-way flow of ideas and expertise, issues of control and decision-making become vital. If the relationship is one in which colleagues in the South are provided with Northern ideas and models of practice, while the 'exchange' is that those from the North can undertake research, then the measure of mutuality might more appropriately be seen as whether those of the South are in control of the process. Otherwise a 'service providing' model appears to be a more accurate way of constructing such arrangements, with implications for responsibility and accountability that parallel other such relationships in social work practice (compare with Hugman, 1991).

Global/Local Social Issues

Defining an 'international' social issue is actually somewhat difficult if we begin from the assumption that globalization has affected all aspects of contemporary society. From that perspective, many social issues or problems have an international dimension. For example, the impact of neo-liberal economic policy can be seen worldwide, in terms of increased poverty, insecure employment and the reduction of public sector provision (where this had previously been the norm) (Ferguson & Lavalette, 2005; Lyons, 2006; Sewpaul, 2006; Lyngstad, 2008). As a consequence, issues or problems that are faced by service users may have immediate and overwhelming international dimensions. These include, among other things, issues as varied as the impact on local communities of economic decisions made in other countries or by multi-national corporations that have no one single national base, the effect of the trafficking of children and young women on their families and communities of origin and the consequences of the spread of HIV/AIDS in countries where health and other services have been scaled back in response to economic 'structural adjustment' programmes (Hall & Midgley, 2004). In some respects, the implications for social work differ according to both the type of issue faced and its relationship to international forces. These can be seen in terms of the following questions.

a. What is the nature of the issue or problem and what are the international dimensions of it?
b. What are the implications for social work of the issue or problem?
c. How may social workers locally be better prepared to work with international issues and problems?

Unlike the other four areas of international social work that have been considered, however, in this area it is effectively impossible to point to particular programmes or projects that embody the notion of 'working with the impact of international issues' that do not simply describe aspects of everyday social work. We are returned to the question posed by Akimoto (1997) concerning whether we may speak of 'international social work' if the social worker is engaged in practice that is the same as all other practice in the surrounding context. In response, recognizing that the impact of globalization is endemic, it might be more appropriate to ask if there is any aspect of social work that might be considered to be entirely 'local'. So we may conclude that by recognizing that our colleagues elsewhere are dealing with comparable situations, that there is much that can be learnt by considering interventions that are practised in other countries: in other words, this is an argument for an 'international' vision for social work generally.

Forms of 'International Practice' – Some Broader Issues

In a reflective discussion of the way in which international social work has developed, Drucker argues that in many situations international social work ought to be concerned with the provision of relief and humanitarian aid or other forms of material or practical assistance, combined with a foundational focus on promoting social change and challenging social injustice (Drucker, 2003, p. 53). Yet, he asserts, many discussions of international social work tend to have what might be described as an 'individualistic focus'. For example, Drucker is critical of what he describes as an emphasis on therapeutic models of practice, even in discussions of indigenization of social work theory in practice. (Similarly, Mohan [2008] berates international social work for losing sight of its concern with the structural causes of social issues and, hence, with questions of social justice.) Indeed, as we will see in Chapter 5, this has been an ongoing theme in debates about the nature of social work (Lundy, 2006; Olson, 2007). The question not only concerns whether or not models are inappropriately exported and imposed through colonial processes (as confronted in Midgley's critique [1981]) but also whether social work in any one country ought to favour macro-, mezzo- or micro-theories and practices.

So, to begin to explore this issue, at this point we will look at three particular questions. These concern the development of apparently 'western' forms of welfare-oriented social work in the global South, the definitions of international social work in social welfare agencies in the United States and wider considerations of the role of 'relief and humanitarian work' in different parts of the world.

First, to explore why welfare-oriented professional social work might develop, we will look at three Asian countries where it has been developing very rapidly, where previously it either did not exist or where it had been abandoned under Communist governments. Since the 1980s social work has been growing as a profession in China, in Mongolia and in Vietnam (Yuen-Tsang & Sung, 2002; Namdaldagva, 2004; UNICEF Vietnam/MOLISA, 2005). The extent of professionalization and the speed of this development differ between these three countries, but for the purposes of this particular discussion there are some important common features. One of the major issues in all three countries is that as they have shifted rapidly from centrally planned to market economies (both within continuing socialist regimes as in China and Vietnam or as part of a move to a multi-party system as in Mongolia), there have been major social upheavals, with growing disparities of wealth between the different socio-economic strata and between urban and rural areas. This has exposed social problems that can be seen, in many ways, as similar to those experienced in countries of the global North, exemplified by very rapid changes in patterns of family life, the types of risks to which children and other vulnerable people are exposed and so on.

Each of these countries, therefore, has turned to existing examples of social work from those parts of the world where it is more highly developed as a basis for constructing their own models (Namdaldagva, 2004; Yan & Cheung, 2006; Hugman et al., 2007). The aim is to create professional social work that is congruent with the local national and cultural milieu.

Yan and Cheung suggest that the context in which the professionalization of social work occurs should be understood as a 'regulative discourse' (2006, p. 70). This notion describes the way in which culture and the prevailing political ideologies combine to produce distinct possibilities for the 'shape' of professional social work. In China this can be described in terms of 'Chinese socialist characteristics' (loc. cit.). (Similarly, in Vietnam 'social work with a Vietnamese face' is being created within the realities of 'Vietnamese socialist characteristics' – see Hugman et al., 2007.) In this type of situation there is often a sense that the pressing needs for a social work profession are questions of child well-being and safety, the care of vulnerable adults who are no longer as protected by family or local community structures as they might once have been, the social dimensions of HIV/AIDS or drug misuse and so on (Namdaldagva, 2004; UNICEF Vietnam/MOLISA, 2005). Tackling structural poverty or challenging 'distorted development' (Midgley, 1997) in these contexts may be defined as 'political work' and not the province of a profession such as social work, in much the same way as it can be regarded in parts of the global North (compare with Hugman, 1998; Ferguson & Lavalette, 2005). It may also be argued that addressing the needs of vulnerable children, such as in situations of exploitation in dangerous work, in being subject to human trafficking, as well as domestic abuses arising from the pressures of industrialization and urbanization, are all part of the social justice focus in social work.

Second, in some detailed research undertaken in the Bay area of northern California, Xu (2006) shows that in practice there are varying ideas about international social work in social welfare agencies. Xu compared 96 social service agencies with regard to the way in which they claimed that they 'served international clients[,] had an office in another country[,] had working relationships with international organizations or foreign social service agencies [or] had been working on international issues such as human rights concerns abroad' (which encompasses three of the definitions summarized above) (2006, p. 685). While 62.5 per cent of agencies claimed to have been involved in some sort of international social work practice using these criteria, the reality was that *on average* just 28 per cent of clients were described as immigrants or refugees and only one organization had an office overseas. Xu concludes that, even when working with immigrants and refugees, these agencies tended to focus on local issues and not to place their practices in a more international context. Xu (2006, p. 689) adds a qualifying statement that this should not be taken as a criticism of 'often severely underfunded' agencies which necessarily have to target their interventions because, when faced with pressing demands from the individuals and communities with who they were in direct contact, these agencies focused on meeting the tangible needs that were directly in front of them. Arguments from other countries of the global North suggest that this conclusion is likely to be generalizable in many places (e.g., see Lyons, 2006; Lyngstad, 2008).

Third, however, having identified some of the pressures that are faced by everyday social work in many parts of the world, we also should ask whether 'relief and humanitarian work' is a sufficient way of understanding the macro in international social work, or whether concern with 'social change, social injustice and the conditions of the poor' (Drucker, 2003, p. 53) is a complete description of social work (also see Lundy, 2006; Mendes, 2007; Olson, 2007; Mohan, 2008). It is not that a concern with the provision of relief for people facing immediate needs is inappropriate, as faced with people who are starving a direct, immediate and practical response is entirely necessary. However, most social work is not of this kind. The important question being posed here is whether or not social work should look *only* to the personal dynamics of any given problem, focusing on individuals and their immediate relationships, or whether it is necessary for the profession to build its practices on an understanding of social structures and systems. However, in asking this question, it is also necessary that we continue to ask *which* practices and theories are appropriate and relevant for any given national and cultural context.

Concluding Remarks

This chapter has examined different ways in which social work may be considered as international. It has identified the importance of understanding the ways in which relationships between countries affect contemporary theory and practice. In doing so, it has established that there are various dimensions each of which can be explained in terms of who and what crosses national borders. Importantly, it has emphasized that it is not necessary for a social worker to travel in order for their practice to require an understanding of the international dimensions of issues and problems. It is not only social workers themselves, but service users and, more abstractly, social issues that can move between countries.

There are several key themes that have emerged in this discussion. These include culture, political structures, the legacy of history, economics and the ways in which the role and tasks of social work itself perceived. In the chapters follow each of these themes will contribute to the underlying framework for the discussion. In various ways, some of these themes will emerge as having a particular importance in relation to different aspects of international social work; all have some relevance. In this chapter it has been possible only to give very brief summaries of the particular social issues and problems with which international social work intervenes. Therefore, the next chapter examines some important substantive 'international' areas in which social work is practised.

3

Social Work with International Issues

Focusing on International Issues

In the previous chapter we saw how international social work has five major dimensions, which can be understood in terms of whether it is a social worker, a service user or a social problem that can be seen to have crossed national borders. Yet we have also noted that although this distinction has some explanatory value, at the same time it may tend to oversimplify what is happening in the practice of international social work. So this chapter will look in greater detail at particular examples of substantive international issues and the way in which our understanding of these helps to construct an analysis of social work 'between countries'. There is an extensive range of topics that could be addressed, so to some extent any discussion necessarily has to be selective. In this chapter we will focus particularly on those areas of social work that are concerned with some sort of movement between countries and across national borders. As far as possible, this discussion will avoid simply looking at a comparative analysis of the situation in specific countries, although such a focus can inform the study of international social work so, where appropriate, some international comparisons will be considered.

By the very nature of the sort of issues with which social workers are concerned some of the topics are highly contested. Existing literature identifies the most crucial of these as: refugees, asylum seekers and forced migrants; human trafficking; natural disasters; poverty, including the impact of rapid industrialization and economic migration within and between countries; the impact of globalization on social structures (i.e., the localized impacts of international processes); and within all of these there are specific challenges for children, women, disabled people, older people, Indigenous people and those from ethnic minority communities (Healy, 1995, 2008a; Lyons, 1999; Hokenstad & Midgley, 2004; Cox & Pawar, 2006; Lyons et al., 2006; Dominelli, 2007; Payne & Askeland, 2008). Many of the areas in which social work is engaged internationally relate to the core values of social work as these are widely understood (IFSW/IASSW, 2004). They raise questions of human rights, with associated challenges to human agency, dignity and other related values, questions of social justice and the way in which people's well-being is challenged by inequality and inequity, and also questions of the ways in which social work can most appropriately assist people in the improvement of their lives. Our central question is not only that of what are the issues faced by particular groups of people but also, crucially, that of what social work can do in response to the situations and needs that are identified.

Refugees, Asylum Seekers and Forced Migrants

The United Nations Convention on Refugees Article 1 (UN, 1951) defines a refugee as a person who:

> owing to well founded fear of being persecuted for reasons of race, religion, nationality, membership of a particular social group or political opinion, is outside the country of his nationality and is unable or, owing to such fear, is unwilling to avail himself of the protection of that country; or who, not having a nationality and being outside the country of his former habitual residence as a result of such events, is unable or, owing to such fear, is unwilling to return to it (from UNHCR, 2007a, p. 16; *gender specific terms as in original*).

While the original Convention also attached the constraint that the events causing such fear had to have occurred before 1951 (because the prime concern at that time was the impact of the 1939–45 War), this was subsequently modified in 1966 to include ongoing situations (in the 'New York Protocol', ratified in General Assembly Resolution 2198 (XXI) – UNHCR, 2007a, pp. 48, 53). The most recent figure at the time of writing is that 9.877 million people worldwide are recognized by the UNHCR as refugees (UNHCR, 2007b, p. 11).

A survey of social work literature published since 2000 (using the Ovid database 'Social Work Abstracts') indicates that the apparent predominant concern of the profession with regard to refugees and asylum seekers has been with its role in assisting in the process of settlement in countries of the global North (compare with Xu, 2006). Within this body of analysis it is also possible to identify a particular concern with children and families and with women in their role as mothers. Thus, it is clear that social workers of the global North tend to identify the issues faced by refugees and asylum seekers as those of settlement and adaptation to a new country of residence. In this sense refugees and asylum seekers represent international social work in the form of service users moving between countries, with an emphasis on particular directions in such movement.

In working with refugees and asylum seekers in a country of settlement there are many factors that must be considered. The first of these is that refugees and asylum seekers arrive in a new country with their own unique histories, which almost inevitably include experiences of trauma and loss (Nash & Trlin, 2004; Pine & Drachman, 2005; Briskman et al., 2008). Second, the institutional framework within which assistance may be offered to refugees and asylum seekers creates a new reality for them and at the same time forms the basis on which social work can play a role. Related to this, third, there are wider issues relating to the economic circumstances, social structures and the political climate of the country of settlement (Cemlyn & Briskman, 2003; Humpage & Marston, 2005). It is not only a question of how these different factors are addressed but also the way in which they are addressed together that forms a basis for effective social work intervention (Snyder et al., 2005).

From the later 1990s onwards the policies and practices of countries in the global North rapidly have become more restrictive with regard to the interpretation of the UN Convention and Protocol as 'border security' was increasingly a heightened political issue (Okitikpi & Aymer, 2003; Weber, 2006). The worldwide number of refugees identified by the UNHCR peaked in 1993 at 17.8 million people (UNHCR, 2007b, p. 11) and this appears to have triggered a political response that was similar across many countries (Christie, 2003; Engebrigsten, 2003; Okitikpi & Aymer, 2003; Briskman et al., 2008). As a consequence of their involvement in programmes to assist refugees, asylum seekers and forced migrants, social workers often find themselves drawn into practices that seek to challenge the atmosphere of mistrust in such countries and also to engage in political advocacy for more humane responses to refugees and asylum seekers. This is especially the case where children and families are concerned. Briskman et al. (2008) describe how children were incarcerated in Australia, sometimes for years, in camps that were mostly located in desert areas. Social workers, along with others, both advocated for a change in these policies and practices and worked both to provide practical assistance to refugee families and to support them in dealing with the trauma of their journey and arrival in a new country. Christie (2003) argues that the legal and policy responses in Ireland were similarly engaged in constructing such families as threat to the security and stability of society. Consequently, social workers frequently found that although they had a clear role in arranging accommodation, providing support for children and families in the process of making an asylum application and linking asylum seekers with other services (compare with Nash & Trlin, 2004; Nash et al., 2006), at the same time this was frustrated by a lack of resources and the limitations of policies designed to make seeking asylum more difficult. In the United Kingdom social workers can experience reluctance on the part of asylum seekers to receive assistance because of a high level of mis-trust based on assumptions that all professionals and officials are concerned with defining all claimants as 'bogus' (Okitikpi & Aymer, 2003). Likewise, in Nor-way immigration policies and practices have come to express only the interests of the state, even in situations of child welfare when notions of the child's best interests are supposed to prevail (Engebrigsten, 2003). Thus, critical social work is inextricably engaged in practice at the most macro-levels of policy and politics.

This macro-response does not diminish the individual and community needs experienced by refugees, asylum seekers and forced migrants. Social work prac-tice with refugees and asylum seekers also needs to be focused on several different levels at the same time. For example, attention to the psychosocial impact on individuals and families of the trauma and loss involved in flee-ing one's homeland is important part of the social work response (Nash & Trlin, 2004; Pine & Drachman, 2005). Such a role is unambiguously a cen-tral part of social work as it is widely conceived in the global North, in that it attends to the psychosocial functioning of individuals and families. However, in work with refugee families and communities it is now widely regarded that there is often either a reluctance or practical inability to acknowledge and to work with cultural expressions of trauma and loss (Kreitzer, 2002, p. 49). In recent years social work more generally has come to recognize that focusing on the strengths and capabilities of service users is an essential aspect of 'starting where the person is' which is at the heart of the notion of the 'person-in-their-social-environment' (Pine & Drachman, 2005, p. 550). At the same time social workers need to be sensitive to the needs of refugees and asylum seekers to find appropriate ways of coping with the implications of trauma and loss in a way that enables them to engage with life in a new situation.

Social workers also have to attend to the material needs of refugees and asy-lum seekers (Humpage & Marston, 2005, pp. 142–3; Jaiswal, 2005). Although some refugees might arrive to join friends and relatives in a country of set-tlement, many will require assistance in securing income, education, access to health, housing and other essential services, as well as help in obtaining clothing, food and other practical aspects of daily life. Social workers and other colleagues in human services therefore have a crucial role to play in the practical ways in which refugees and asylum seekers might begin process of settlement from the point of arrival and often for a considerable time following. Nash and Trlin (2004, 2006) describe services in New Zealand in which social workers com-bine these practical activities with trauma counselling and other psychosocial support. Funding for such services was predominantly a combination of gov-ernment, charitable and local fundraising; approximately 75 per cent of these services were secular with the remaining proportion provided by religious orga-nizations (Nash et al., 2006, p. 8). The religious organizations all provided services without focusing on the religion or other cultural origins of the refugees and asylum seekers in question (i.e., their practice was 'non-sectarian'). While many of the agencies included in their study provided services for refugees and asylum seekers and also other parts of the community, they predominantly either specialized in working with refugees or else provided such assistance only as a minor part of their work (Nash & Trlin, 2006, p. 14).

Yet, of the 9.877 million people currently identified as refugees, most do not become asylum seekers in countries of the global North. The very large majority move to adjoining countries and a significantly large proportion of these people then become resident in camps that are established solely for the purpose of providing shelter to refugees (Kreitzer, 2002; Pittaway et al., 2003). The reality of life in such camps is one of considerable hardship, often with limited access to water, food, adequate shelter and in many situations personal safety. Women and children are particularly at risk, with large numbers facing the prospect of rape and interpersonal violence (Kreitzer, 2002; Pittaway & Pittaway, 2004; Pittaway & Bartolomei, 2005). This is not to suggest that women refugees should be considered only as victims, as it is often women who provide the focal point that holds families and kin groups together in both the refugee situation and repatriation (Ross Sherrif, 2006). However, in many situations little is done to recognize and respond to the risks faced by women and children in refugee camps. Some critics also argue that social work and social development interventions in refugee camps have often effectively been the extension of political or religious interests, whether or not this was intended, with limited attention to either the psychosocial or the longer-term community needs and interests of the refugees themselves (Drumm et al., 2003). A detailed study undertaken by Kreitzer (2002) in Liberia demonstrates that the improvement of the lives of refugees in camps requires participation in planning and implementing development programmes, especially of women. This study also points to the frequent lack of qualified and skilled personnel in programme administration.

One example of practice with refugees and asylum seekers in such camps is that undertaken by the Centre for Refugee Research at the University of New South Wales in Australia. Over a number of years social workers and others associated with this Centre have undertaken extensive 'action research' in refugee camps in Asia and Africa (Pittaway et al., 2003; Pittaway & Bartolomei, 2005). This series of projects combines practical education for residents of the camps, most especially women, to make use of international human rights instruments in order to seek better conditions and to advocate for change in their circumstances, with support for women to further develop ways in which they might deal with and challenge the risks faced by themselves and other women in these situations (Pittaway & Pittaway, 2004; Pittaway & Bartolomei, 2005). Working in conjunction with the UNHCR, these projects have enabled women refugees from particular camps to make representations about the risks faced by women in such situations on the international stage, culminating in the approval by UNHCR of a Conclusion, which constitutes 'soft law', in relation to the use of rape as a tactic in war and an endemic problem in the camps as well as more generally to promote the defence of women's rights (UNHCR, 2006). Within this work there is also some provision of support to individual women who have faced the trauma of rape, torture, the loss of partners and children and of their homes and ongoing work to develop capacities within refugee and forced migrant communities themselves to respond to such needs. From this example, it can be seen that macro-, mezzo- and micro-levels of practice are combined in every aspect.

Human Trafficking

Human trafficking can also be considered as a form of forced migration. Here again, a UN Protocol has been produced to define the nature of a problem and to spell out the commitment of member states to deal with it (UN, 2000b). This emphasizes that the core issues concern the use of force, abduction or some other form of coercion, fraud or deception, or the abuse of power or a position of vulnerability (which, it could be argued, is another way of understanding coercion or duress); these uses of social power may be direct or they may be indirect, for example being exerted over a carer or legal guardian of another person, but in all cases they are intended to lead to the exploitation of the person who is 'trafficked' (Lowe, 2007, p. 50). As Lowe emphasizes, human trafficking must not be confused with people smuggling in that it is not simply about the illegal movement of people but concerns movement that is undertaken contrary to a person's autonomy and with the purpose of abusing the person in some way. It is on this basis that 'slavery' is considered an appropriate term to describe human trafficking by some commentators (Batstone, 2007).

There is also a strong debate about the extent to which we should understand human trafficking in terms of sexual exploitation. This debate can be situated in relation to feminist debates about prostitution and sex work (Desyllas, 2007, p. 59). On one side is an argument that all sex work is exploitative of women (and boy as well as girl children) and that therefore all commercial sex work ought to be suppressed, while on the other side it is asserted that the issue is that of autonomy and human rights such that the issue is whether women engage in sex work by their own choice or are coerced. For Desyllas (2007) the dominant discourse in American policy and practice is one that tends to bring together more conservative stances (with negative views of both sexuality and of migration) with that of radical feminist arguments for the abolition of pros- titution. This, she states, has provided an impetus to American-based NGOs to pursue an abolitionist goal. This appears to be in opposition to the UN Protocol (2000b) definition that emphasizes the element of coercion and focuses on working conditions and crime in relation to all types of labour rather than on morality and (women's) sexuality (Desyllas, 2007, p. 63; also see Jones et al., 2007, p. 115–16).

It is clear that the majority of people who are trafficked are being traded for purposes related to sex work (Hodge & Lietz, 2007; New Internationalist, 2007). There are indeed also many people who are trafficked for the purpose of enforced labour of other kinds, whether domestic or industrial, and in parts of Africa to serve in military forces and even in sports teams (Jones et al., 2007, p. 109; New Internationalist, 2007, pp. 12–13). Commercially arranged transnational marriages (so-called 'mail order brides') can also often be little more than a form of trafficking (UNICEF Vietnam, personal communication). Nevertheless, current estimates are that as many as 80 per cent of trafficked persons are female, among whom approximately 70 per cent are trafficked for the purposes of sexual exploitation (Hodge, 2008, p. 143). The majority of people who are trafficked are women and girls, while around 98 per cent of those trafficked to the sex industry are female (New Internationalist, 2007, p. 12). So, while the general issue of human trafficking is clearly of concern to international social work because it is a matter of human rights abuses, the centrality of a market for coerced sex work cannot be ignored. The question is what might be an appropriate response from social workers within the context of a concern with human rights and the particular injustices and harms that are perpetrated on vulnerable people of whom those coerced into the sex industry are the major part.

Along with the debate about the emphasis on sex and morality in discussions of human trafficking there is a related contention between those who argue that responses should focus on the demand or the supply sides of the problem. In other words, should law, policy and practice concentrate on 'rescuing' those who are trafficked and 'catching criminals' or should there be an emphasis on dealing with issues of poverty and racial and gender inequalities that lead people to become easier targets for traffickers (Roby, 2005, p. 142; Lowe, 2007, pp. 51–2)? As Lowe notes, many people who are trafficked are not abducted by force but, at least at the beginning of the process, are drawn in by the promise of work, opportunities to pay off debts and so on, or may be sold by families who are convinced that a young person will have a better life (also see Roby, 2005, p. 139; Hodge, 2008, p. 146). Responses to poverty and discrimination therefore may provide more long-term solutions, including the relevance of working conditions for all migrant workers (Desyllas, 2007, p. 75; Jones et al., 2007, p. 118). In countries such as Australia there is specific legislation concerning sex tourism where this concerns minors, targeting men who travel for the purpose of having sex with children, although this can be complex to enforce. Nevertheless, there appears to be clear agreement between all analysts of this issue, whatever their stance on other aspects, that the trafficking of children should always be regarded as coercive and abusive in every respect (Jones et al., 2007).

There is also the question about what can actually be done to assist those who are at risk of being trafficked or who are released from forced labour after they have been trafficked. Lowe (2007, p. 54–5) suggests several approaches to direct work with people who are trafficked or at risk of being drawn into being trafficked. The first of these is in education and publicity, generally raising awareness of risk. Second is in being prepared in a variety of practice settings to respond to those who are able to leave such a situation, in both practical terms and in providing psychosocial support. Hodge and Lietz (2007) draw strong parallels between the impact of trafficking and domestic violence or child abuse on those who have been trafficked. They argue, therefore, that social workers encountering women who have been trafficked should think in similar terms in relation to appropriate interventions and we might add that the same principle ought to be applied to work with trafficked children.

But there are many complex issues in recognizing the needs of people who have been trafficked. Most particularly, in many countries when those who have been trafficked are identified they become subject to immigration laws, are defined as 'illegal migrants' and deported to situations where there is a high risk they may be trafficked again (Van Hook et al., 2006). Moreover, especially where young women have been trafficked into the sex industry, returning home may not be possible (e.g., see Datta, 2007, p. 15). Families and communities can find it impossible to accept the person back, even in situations where the person was actually abducted. Indeed, European research suggests that those who are tricked into being trafficked (as opposed, say, to very young children being sold by parents or other relatives) often have backgrounds of being subject to violence (Bullens & Van Horn, 2002, pp. 44–5). Once trafficked, the dynamics of their relationships with those who had bought them might at times be equivalent to imprisonment, but more often control is exerted through abusive relationships quite similar to those observable in situations of domestic violence.

In respect to all these issues advocacy for people who have been trafficked is currently lacking. Provision of alternative sources of livelihood is also an important question. For example, Roby (2005, p. 142) refers to a project in northern Thailand in which a combination of school sponsorship, income generation assistance for families and informal education about the realities of trafficking are being used to provide alternatives for communities where girls are at risk. Integrating services with policy development is therefore a priority in this field. Without such practices and policies in place direct intervention in situations where people are thought to be working under these conditions is likely to be counter-productive, as it exposes those who have been trafficked to other serious risks and in the sex industry also may make life worse for those who are willingly working in that industry (Datta, 2007; Desyllas, 2007). In these latter situations there may be scope for social workers and other professionals to collaborate with sex workers to develop strategies to assist those who are trafficked and working against their will. In all of this, international co-operation is vital, but this is extremely difficult to achieve because of the political and cultural sensitivities to issues of human trafficking, in countries of the global North as well as the South, especially when this concerns the sex industry.

'Natural' Disasters

Natural disasters take many forms. In general terms they concern the impact on human life of the interplay between climate, land and sea. They include drought, flood and the extreme ocean events such as the Asian tsunami of 2004. In all cases these types of situations have a devastating effect on communities, often involving the loss of homes, livelihoods and in many circumstances the death of community members. Social workers are often involved in responses to natural disasters through their normal roles in a variety of social service and other community agencies.

While in many ways the immediate physical effects of natural disasters can be understood as objective, whether in terms of the destruction of property or of the failure of crops and so on, the way in which such natural disasters strike different communities and different individuals within communities is highly socially structured (Alston, 2007; Rivera & Miller, 2007; Hawkins & Rao, 2008; Moyo & Moldovan, 2008). Park and Miller (2006) assert that, on this basis, there could be said to be no such thing as a 'natural' disaster. For example, the impacts of Hurricane Katrina in the United States, of the recent serious drought in Australia and of the Asian tsunami affected different people in different ways. First, those people who lack access to resources or who lived in poorer circumstances tend to be worst affected in the immediate impact. Second, the pre-existing distribution of access to resources, whether material or social, greatly assists individuals in dealing with the aftermath of major events. For these reasons, the impact of disasters is unequally distributed along socially structured lines, including socio-economic class, sex, 'race' and ethnicity and age (Alston, 2007; Spence et al., 2007).

Social work responses also can be understood in terms of the immediate and longer time scales (Kreuger & Stretch, 2003). In the time immediately after an event, whether or not there are strategies in place will determine the effectiveness of responses. So, several studies have emphasized the importance of planning before any particular event occurs (Kreuger & Stretch, 2003; Park &

Miller, 2006; Mathbor, 2007; Spence et al., 2007; Moyo & Moldovan, 2008). At this point social workers can be involved in assisting in the formulation of practical plans. Social workers will often also be involved in undertaking a basic needs analysis, identifying families and individuals who have been affected and in beginning to put into place immediate debts to make practical needs for shelter, food and drink and other basic daily requirements.

In the medium term, responses begin to shift towards the repair to damaged homes and other essential property and the identification of the need for counselling and other post-traumatic interventions at an individual level (Galambos, 2005; Park & Miller, 2006). Studies also emphasize that as the time since a major event elapses responses tended to shift more towards psychosocial interventions, especially post-traumatic stress counselling (Kreuger & Stretch, 2003; Puig & Glynn, 2003). While this is regarded as relevant and appropriate, at the same time there is a growing argument that at this period it is also timely to begin to involve communities in future planning. Although the lack of preparedness has been linked to the low socio-economic status that tends to be seen in such ethnic minority communities, this is through lack of attention and not because such planning cannot be undertaken.

Hawkins and Rao (2008) show from an example of continuing post-tsunami intervention in Tamil Nadu, India, how social development goals including the promotion of human capital, social capital and employment opportunities are a necessary part of the post-disaster recovery. Supported by the Madras School of Social Work (Chennai, India), this project (known as CEDER) began with the provision of relief (immediate direct giving of supplies) and continued in the establishment of a longer-term plan for the recovery of the community, including 'reviving livelihoods [. . .] forming self-help groups and introducing income generation programs [. . .] creating groups for career counselling and establishing leadership programs [. . . supporting] full school enrolment [. . .] conducting general health camps [and] facilitating home repairs and reconstruction [of] the primary school (for the whole village)' (Hawkins & Rao, 2008, p. 41). A similar range of responses was also observed in social work responses after an earthquake in Bam, Iran (Javadian, 2007).

As already noted, there is also an indication that certain groups within at risk communities are themselves especially vulnerable. Children and young people require particular attention, because they may find it more difficult to adjust when the world they have previously trusted to be reasonably stable has proved not to be so (Kreuger & Stretch, 2003). As with refugee situations, it is also the case that in natural disasters women and girls may be particularly at risk of rape and other forms of gender-based violence (Pittaway et al., 2007).

Puig and Glynn (2003) detail an example of international practice in which a group of social work students from the United States travelled to Honduras in order to assist in the relief and reconstruction work after Hurricane Mitch in 1998, in conjunction with an NGO. The objective was the students to participate in assessment of families' needs, the provision of counselling and the development of community management. This also involved negotiation with local authorities over disputes about land, the organization and distribution of material relief and other practical tasks such as repairs to homes as well as helping teachers to get the local school re-opened (Puig & Glynn, 2003, p. 58–9). The students resided with local families whose homes had not been damaged. This meant that they were able to learn more quickly about the local culture and about the way in which families had been affected by the hurricane. By being involved in the daily life of the community in this way preparatory cross-cultural learning was grounded in reality as seen by local residents. Puig and Glynn (2003, p. 62) also note that the students learned about important social and political differences, such as the role of the military in Honduran society as well as gaining a more realistic understanding of how their own nation and culture is perceived in other parts of the world.

In summary, therefore, we can see that social work in response to natural disasters requires a wide range of skills, from individual counselling through organization and administration, to social development and advocacy. In both the domestic and the international context it also requires attention to cross-cultural knowledge and skills to underpin and inform good practice and greater attention to the impact of social inequalities on the way in which the 'natural' world relates to human society.

Poverty

In many parts of the world social work is closely allied with struggles against poverty (Burke & Ngonyani, 2004; Mendoza Rangel, 2005). Cox and Pawar (2006, p. 161) refer to this as 'the most significant problem facing the modern world', with one-third of the global population affected significantly. They also note that it appears in many ways to be so extensive and complex that it is formidable, perhaps even impossible to resolve. Consequently, the meaning of poverty and its causes attract a great deal of debate. It is vital that poverty is understood as having both social and economic dimensions, which are interwoven (Odulana & Olomajeye, 1999; Cox & Pawar, 2006: 194–6; Deacon, 2007; Morazes & Pintek, 2007). In the following chapter we will see how this particular issue is the focal point of the UN Millennium Development Goals (UN, 2000a). Here we will focus specifically on poverty alleviation as an important aspect of international social work practice, one that relates to many other issues, as we have already noted.

The strategies and practices used by social workers tend to be oriented towards the community level, although those social workers who are involved in policy and advocacy may also be concerned with economic issues at national and international levels. At the local level, approaches can be divided broadly into two groups: promoting social services and income generation. The first of these can be described in general terms as focusing on the development of human capital. That is, the objective is to equip individuals and communities to engage in productive activity. This goal concerns the human attributes and capacities that are necessary for people to participate in all aspects of their communities and seeks to develop programmes that will actually provide such capacities. So, such activities might be directed towards building community infrastructure, including schools and health facilities (Odulana & Olomajeye, 1999). They might also involve informal education, skill development and other related ways in which people can participate in gaining access to personal and social resources with which they can deal with poverty.

An example of social work in this context is provided by Ku et al. (2005) in their discussion of capacity-building as a goal within a poverty reduction programme in Yunnan Province in China. The project was based on a team of social work students and educators from Hong Kong working with the residents of one township in what is referred to as a 'community services experiment model' (Ku et al., 2005, p. 220). Although the regional government had attempted to provide education, road building and tourism projects, as well as the development of cash crops, community members were largely uninvolved. The capacity-building programme therefore sought a way of engaging the local residents as active partners in thinking about and planning development projects, such as 'the generation of methane gas, adult education and income-generating projects' (Ku et al., 2005, p. 228). The method used was that of 'oral history', in which the local residents were encouraged to reflect on their own problem-solving capacities, prior experience and strengths, and which involved people who might otherwise have been marginalized, including older people, women and children. 'In short, oral history was only a start for us in terms of implementing participatory development in Au Village' (Ku et al., 2005, p. 224).

Second, income generation programmes seek to create tangible ways in which individuals and groups can improve their access to financial resources through their own labour. Probably the best-known framework for this approach is that of 'micro-credit' (Brook et al., 2008). In this model a small loan is made to an individual in order to provide resources for that person to undertake an activity that will generate income. The loan is repaid, with interest, and the remaining income can be used for both further investment and consumption. The difference between this model and 'normal' banking is that it is specifically directed to the very poor who would otherwise not be able to obtain loans. The most widely known programme is the Grameen Bank in Bangladesh, founded by Mohammed Yunus, who gained a Nobel Prize for this work (Bernasek, 2003;

Selinger, 2008). The Grameen Bank built its programmes, and its reputation, providing loans to rural women in order to give them an opportunity to create their own economic activity and so help lift their own families and communities out of poverty. This model has been adapted in many countries of the global South; in the North similar schemes have also developed, either in the Credit Unions or in the form of Individual Development Accounts sponsored by community banks (e.g., see Stoesz & Saunders, 1999).

Various analyses indicate that this type of approach can be very successful but there are some limitations that have to be recognized. Two meta-analyses of the Grameen Bank's impact produce apparently contradictory findings. Bernasek (2003), including primary research undertaken herself, considers that the evidence broadly is that women have been enabled to make choices and have been able to contribute economically to their families, reducing poverty and achieving better health, housing and educational outcomes for their children. In contrast, in a secondary analysis specifically focused on one aspect of the Grameen Bank, the Village Phone programme, Selinger (2008) examines arguments that the popularity of micro-credit has depended on an overarching idea that micro-credit has 'empowered' rural women, which a small number of critical studies has suggested is not the case. Moreover, critics argue that the terms of the Grameen Bank loans mean that women have their independence curtailed as they are effectively drawn into compliance with many lifestyle requirements (including hygiene, food and other household matters, cultural requirements such as not using the loans for dowry payments and so on). In their conclusions, however, Bernasek and Selinger come close to agreement that the main impact of these schemes has been to raise levels of income of poorer parts of the population and to support some gains in health and so on. However, they also agree that claims to have empowered women are less easy to substantiate. Together they raise the question of whether it is possible in the time scale, and using one approach, to have radically altered the social structures of Bangladesh, challenged patriarchy and eradicated poverty. This is especially the case given that one of the underlying ideas was to use traditional social norms as a basis for ensuring that people taking loans would seek to make use of them and to be able to make repayments. So, if the ambitions of such schemes are pitched more modestly, then it can be seen to have a positive impact (Bernasek, 2003). As Selinger puts it (2008, p. 41), these schemes create new 'relations of dependence and independence' which could be said to pertain in any context.

Other forms of micro-credit are, indeed, operating in other parts of the world, such as China (Gao & Hu, 2005). In China, support for micro-credit has come from a combination of government agencies, international agencies (including UNDP and direct donor countries), private foundations and NGOs and commercial banks (operating through rural credit unions). Gao and Hu suggest that although many of these projects have been successful in respect of assisting the reduction in overall poverty levels, there have also been problems of repayments and sustainability. Therefore they argue that in the Chinese context micro-credit should follow the successful models of other countries and be non-profit and oriented towards supporting not-for-profit or social enterprises (Gao & Hu, 2005, pp. 42–4).

In Malawi, Hazarika and Sarangi (2008) show, through detailed research, that micro-credit schemes have an impact on child labour. That is, in families that have access to micro-credit and who have landholdings there is an *increase* in the amount of work that children are expected to undertake to assist their family enterprises. Hazarika and Sarangi note that this does not seem to be at the expense of participation in education in terms of school attendance, but they express concern that in the longer term there may possibly be negative effects on children's health and formal educational attainments due to fatigue.

Many aspects of direct social work practice therefore can be said to address issues of poverty. The two approaches that have been highlighted here share concern with giving people opportunities to exercise their own agency and to act, either for themselves or, more frequently, as part of their local communities. Attention to poverty alleviation as a goal in international social work therefore tends to emphasize social development and community development practices (compare with Ife & Tesoriero, 2006). At times it will also involve social workers engaging with advocacy in relation to the structural and political dimensions of responses to poverty.

Indigenous Peoples

An aspect of international social work that has been discussed only rarely in the literature is that of Indigenous peoples. As a consequence of centuries of colonialism, there are many countries in the world where the dominant sections of society are descended from settlers. This can be seen in both North and South America, in Australia and New Zealand, and although in recent decades there has been significant change in Africa the history of colonialism continues to leave its mark (e.g., see Odulana & Olomajeye, 1999). Two meanings of 'indigenous' can therefore be identified within the social work literature. One is that it refers specifically to peoples who can be regarded as First Nations or Aboriginal in countries such as Australia, Canada, New Zealand and the United States (for example, see Weaver, 1997; Yellow Bird, 1999; Baldry & Green, 2002). There are also parts of Asia in which people now regarded as 'ethnic minorities' identify themselves as the Indigenous inhabitants of their regions. The other meaning, more widely used, refers to all non-Western countries in which social work has been adapted from Western sources (see summaries in Coates et al., 2006; Gray et al., 2007). The second meaning is discussed in detail elsewhere in this book. For the purposes of this discussion we will focus specifically on the First Nations or Aboriginal peoples.

One of the common features of settler societies is the overrepresentation of Indigenous people among the users of social welfare systems, in indices of poor physical and mental health, and within criminal justice systems (Baldry & Green, 2002; Weaver, 2002; Briskman, 2007; Green & Baldry, 2008). Social work with Indigenous peoples can be considered under the heading of international social work because in these situations it might be said that entire social and cultural systems have been transplanted across borders. Indeed, as Weaver (1997) comments, Indigenous social workers may have to face tensions between their own cultures and that of the profession.

One of the common features shared between these Indigenous societies is a very close relationship between people and land. In addition, there are particular attachments to kinship relationships and the social obligations of group membership which creates social dynamics that are rarely understood by mainstream society and which can present difficulties because they can lead to clashes between the expectations of Indigenous people and officialdom (Green & Baldry 2008). For example, Heske (2008) provides an illustrative example of a young woman living in an Aboriginal community who has been asked to provide evidence concerning the domestic violence perpetrated against her by her husband. Although this young woman has the same rights as any other member of the wider society (to freedom from violence and the threat of violence), she not only faces her own feelings about her relationship with her husband (as might any married woman, see Wise, 1995) but also has to take into account community expectations about her role within the family and the stance taken in relation to the community's relationship with the White 'mainstream'. As Heske (2008, p. 5) notes, this presents 'mainstream' professionals with many difficulties in reconciling expectations that it is appropriate to encourage the woman to protect herself and to ensure her own safety with a recognition that the woman's Indigenous culture should be respected. The situation is exacerbated by the young woman's feeling that the White 'mainstream' has come onto her people's land without respecting cultural requirements. (We will return in subsequent chapters to the question of whether it is possible to think cross-culturally about questions of human rights, social justice and other values.)

Another crucial issue facing social work with First Nations or Aboriginal people is that of the way in which the welfare system was used in the twentieth century as part of the process of assimilation and the obliteration of cultural difference (Palmer & Cooke, 1996; Baldry & Green, 2002; Briskman, 2003; Coates et al., 2006, p. 385). Although these policies had many dimensions, one of those that currently presents a major challenge is the systematic removal of children from Indigenous mothers and their placement in institutional care or, sometimes, with foster families. There are two aspects to the legacies of these practices that continue to face social workers today. The first of these is a significant number of children who were ill-treated while in institutional care. The lasting psychological, emotional and spiritual damage can be seen in high rates of alcohol and drug-related problems, problems in family and community relationships, high levels of physical ill-health and high incidence of early death (Weaver, 2002; Briskman, 2007). For these reasons, Indigenous people are overrepresented as service users in proportion to their numbers in populations (Baldry & Green, 2002).

The second aspect of the legacy of the removal of Indigenous children is a lasting impact on communities and on the relationship between Indigenous peoples and the 'mainstream' (Briskman, 2003). Indigenous communities have been fragmented and many people have been denied the opportunity to know their own biological family and to be brought up with the knowledge of their own culture. These events, and their lasting effects, have also made it particularly difficult for Indigenous people to see the social welfare services as having the potential to provide assistance. For contemporary social workers in the child protection field such a legacy makes a highly complex part of social work practice particularly fraught. The same applies in Canada, New Zealand and other countries with Indigenous populations. In a country such as Australia this has been compounded by years of denial especially among political leaders. The reconciliation process, as it is known, that seeks to find a new way in which Indigenous people and 'mainstream' society can live together more harmoniously is, therefore, an important issue for social work. This not only requires that social workers are able to grasp knowledge and skills relevant to cross cultural practice, but also that they recognize the implications of the history and politics of this situation for thinking about practice (Green & Baldry, 2008).

One particular example of practice in this area is that of the development of child welfare practices and policies that are focused on the needs and rights of Indigenous children. Ban (2005) describes the Aboriginal Child Placement Principle (ACPP) that operates across Australia. This principle is that an Aboriginal child who is removed from the care of her or his parents should be placed with other kin, if they are not available with other members of the child's own community, if this is not possible with another Aboriginal family and only with non-Aboriginal people as a last resort. If the 'last resort' is reached, then there should be ongoing contact through Aboriginal family welfare services to ensure that all possible contact with family, community and culture is maintained. This policy and practice is modelled on very similar policies and practices in New Zealand, which were developed because of the same issues for Maori families in the child welfare system (Worrall, 2006), and comparable practices and policies exist also in Canada for the same reasons (Blackstock et al., 2004; Trocmé et al., 2004). However, Ban argues (2005, pp. 388–9), in Australia this policy is often breached in practice because it fails to take account of the relatively low socio-economic circumstances of many Aboriginal families and the resulting lack of resources. His solution is to make greater use of family conferencing to make decisions about children in such situations, a practice that also comes from Maori traditions. This is a process where family members come together to share ideas and to support one another in finding solutions to identified problems, and in the statutory field this is done with support from social workers and others. This idea is also used in other situations, such as elder abuse in Indigenous American communities (Holkup et al., 2007). The challenge for social workers, especially given the highly contested area of child protection, is to support families in making decisions and then supporting them in following through, rather than family conferencing being just a token way of appearing to recognize Indigenous community strengths (Ban, 2005; Worrall, 2006).

International Social Work Issues

In this chapter we have considered several issues facing international social work, including refugees, asylum seekers and forced migrants, human trafficking, natural disaster, poverty alleviation and Indigenous peoples. This is not intended to be an exhaustive coverage of issues but rather to focus on particular examples that can be used in order to identify particular questions that face social work and also to tease out some broad questions. So to conclude this discussion we will look briefly at some of the common points that are identified by this selective consideration of international issues.

The first common feature is that in all cases relevant knowledge and skills combine macro-, mezzo- and micro-levels. In no instance could it be said that social work should only be focusing on one or another of these ways at analysing and responding to particular issues. This is important, because the history of social work has many times been characterized by strenuous debate between those who wish to define the profession exclusively in terms of one or another. International social work, it would appear, requires social workers to have a breadth of vision and the flexibility to work in a number of different ways in order to address all the relevant aspects of the issues with which they are working.

Second, in each situation there are important questions about the way in which social workers respond to people who are marginalized by social structures and relationships. In particular, in each of these issues it can be seen that gender and age are often crucial factors. Women, children and older people are all identified across the range of issues as having particular interests and needs that have to be recognized and addressed.

Third, international social work inescapably requires that we address questions of culture. This begins with a recognition of the importance of cross-cultural knowledge and sensitivity in practice. However, it goes further because in each of these situations it is clear that particular regions and their dominant cultures continue to also be dominant globally. So, it is not simply a matter that those from the global North learn to recognize the perspectives and values of people from the global South, but also that our analysis of social work issues pays attention to the way in which the issues themselves are grounded in forms of neo-colonialism and racism (Dominelli, 2008). We will return to this point in Chapter 9.

4

Social Work and the UN Millennium Development Goals

The UN Millennium Development Goals in Context

Underlying the issues that have been discussed in the previous chapter is the sense that the development of human society, in all of its aspects, can be described as 'distorted' (Midgley, 1997). At the same time as human ingenuity has produced ever more complex technology, for example extending dramatically the way in which food can be produced, the development of human society continues to see disparities between different parts of the world and between people on grounds of socio-economic class, sex, age, ethnicity and 'race', sexuality and (dis)ability. Debates about the causes of and solutions to poverty and other factors limiting social development have, of course, proceeded over many decades. In the 1990s, at an international level, and increasingly in many individual countries, these debates were dominated by economic concerns couched in the terms of the theoretical and ideological position which is usually referred to as 'neo-liberalism' (Deacon, 2007; Correll, 2008). That is, social development (including human advances in health, education, cultural activity, community and family life and so on) was seen among the most powerful institutions and decision makers to be entirely dependent on, and in some cases simply a derivative of, economic growth.

In 1995 the World Summit for Social Development (WSSD) took place in Copenhagen (UN, 1995). A total of 117 nations participated and the summit ended with a Declaration containing ten overarching commitments, together with an Agreement and an accompanying Programme of Action (UN, 1995). The core of this Declaration can be summarized as a commitment to:

1. creating an economic, political, social, cultural and legal environment that will enable people to achieve social development;

2. eradicating poverty;
3. promoting full employment as a basic priority of economic and social policy;
4. promoting social integration by fostering societies that are stable, safe and just (based on human rights and social justice);
5. promoting human dignity, including the achievement of equality and equity between women and men and enhancing the position of women in all aspects of society;
6. attaining universal and equitable access to quality education, the highest standard of physical and mental health and primary health care;
7. accelerating the development, in all respects, of Africa and the least developed countries;
8. ensuring that when structural adjustment programmes are agreed to that they include social development goals (with a particular focus on the eradication of poverty, promoting full and productive employment and enhancing social integration);
9. increasing significantly and/or utilizing more efficiently resources allocated to social development;
10. an improved and strengthened framework for international, regional and sub-regional co-operation for social development.

(The full text of the Declaration and its supporting documents is available through the WSSD web pages which can be accessed at http://www.un.org/esa/socdev/wssd/).

At the heart of the Agreement, the Declaration and the Programme of Action is the statement that governments undertook to 'place people at the centre of development and direct our economies to meet human needs more effectively' (section 26(a)). The background principles were wide ranging, and variously addressed the centrality of the family as the key human institution, the particular issues arising from the history of colonialism and the treatment of Indigenous peoples, the specific needs of disadvantaged groups within societies, and a particular emphasis on the needs of children and of older people. From the previous chapter, and as we will consider again later in this chapter, it will be clear that the WSSD implicitly represents an important point in inter-governmental thinking about issues that concern social work.

In the space of only five years, however, the WSSD had effectively been superseded by the Millennium Development Goals (MDGs) (UN, 2000a). Interpretations of the reasons for this shift and the possibilities arising from it have varied. Correll (2008) is scathing about what he considers to be 'a sad and minimalist collection of random targets, disconnected from development' (p. 453), 'a remnant' (p. 455) and 'a mediocre, minimalist, disjointed selection of leftovers' (p. 460). For Correll, the explanation of a rapid movement from wide-ranging commitments that incorporated poverty reduction within a broader approach to social development to the minimum targets of the MDGs lies in the influence of neo-liberal economic and political thinking, stemming from the influence of the IMF, the World Bank and the OECD. These institutions, he argues, remain wedded to the 'Washington Consensus'. This concept was defined by Williamson (1989) to refer to broad policy agreement between the IMF, World Bank and other global financial bodies, under which aid and development support was expected to meet strict conditions, including the reduction of state expenditures and trade liberalization in return for assistance focused specifically on poverty reduction. Critics have argued that this was simply a vehicle to foster the growth of free markets for the benefit of highly developed Northern economies and unfettered business opportunities for multi-national corporations (see, e.g., George, 1988; Chomsky, 1999). Stiglitz (2003, p. 56) has argued that this position no longer holds as a consensus, but Correll disagrees, asserting that in practice it is very much alive. It is not that poverty reduction has no place in social development for Correll; indeed, as Midgley (1995) has stated, social development brings economic responses to the task of addressing the social dimensions of human development. However, in this approach economic concerns are incorporated within broader strategies as a means to the end of human development and should not become ends in and of themselves. They certainly should not be a means by which 'donor' nations gain more than they give while claiming to be engaged in aid and development (Saith, 2006). Yet, it can also be seen that the Washington Consensus, as an expression of the dominant neo-liberal perspective, has influenced national practices in which governments have subordinated social dimensions of development (such as accessible health services) to economic priorities even though this may, in fact, not be in their long-term interests economically as well as socially (Gabriele, 2006).

Deacon (2007) broadly concurs with this analysis. He describes the WSSD as 'the most significant in a line of recent summits' (2007, p. 75), as it brought together thinking from a series of conferences and summits on education, children, development, human rights and population and development. Moreover, as also noted by Correll (2008, p. 455), the language of the WSSD was one of universality, equity and equality, and achievement of highest attainable standards (Deacon 2007, p. 76). However, Deacon concurs with Correll that in place of these very strongly worded objectives the MDGs have proposed minimum targets and goals. Given the large number of countries that signed to the WSSD and that the articles of the Declaration were clearly focused on all aspects of human development, the question must be posed as to why in just a short space of time this became reduced to minimum standards. For Deacon (2007, p. 76), this movement from one approach to the other must be understood in terms of the influence of the IMF and the OECD, via the World Bank and the WHO, over the development and aid organizations of the UN (and hence over national governments and the major INGOs). Indeed, Deacon (2007, p. 77) notes somewhat ironically that the team leader of the MDGs implementation appointed by the UN was someone who had previously championed neo-liberal structural adjustment policies through those other economically focused organizations. Nevertheless, Deacon also observes that world attention regarding social development is now concentrated on the MDGs and that the United Nations Development Program (UNDP) has responsibility for coordinating their achievement. While it may be that they represent a weakening of the earlier intentions, they now define the international context of development policy, planning and practice.

The Millennium Development Goals

So, what are the MDGs? This agreement comprises eight specific goals, which as already indicated are expressed in terms of minimum attainments and which are augmented by specific targets, which it is intended will be achieved by 2015 (UN, 2000a). The goals, with their associated targets, are as follows.

1. To eradicate extreme poverty and hunger –

    • target 1 – Halve, between 1990 and 2015, the proportion of people whose income is less than $1 a day
    • target 2 – Achieve full and productive employment and decent work for all, including women and young people
    • target 3 – Halve, between 1990 and 2015, the proportion of people who suffer from hunger

2. Achieve universal primary education –

    • target 1 – Ensure that, by 2015, children everywhere, boys and girls alike, will be able to complete a full course of primary schooling

3. Promote gender equality and empower women –

    • target 1 – Eliminate gender disparity in primary and secondary education, preferably by 2005, and in all levels of education by 2015

4. Reduce child mortality –

    • target 1 – Reduce by two-thirds, between 1990 and 2015, the under-five mortality rate

5. Improve maternal health –

   - target 1 – Reduce by three-quarters the maternal mortality ratio
   - target 2 – Achieve universal access to reproductive health

6. Combat HIV/AIDS, malaria and other diseases –

   - target 1 – To have halted by 2015 and begun to reverse the spread of HIV/AIDS
   - target 2 – Achieve, by 2010, universal access to treatment for HIV/AIDS for all those who need it
   - target 3 – Have halted by 2015 and begun to reverse the incidence of malaria and other major diseases

7. Ensure environmental sustainability –

   - target 1 – Integrate the principle of sustainable development into country policies and programmes and reverse the loss of environmental resources
   - target 2 – Reduce biodiversity loss, achieving, by 2010, a significant reduction in the rate of loss
   - target 3 – Halve, by 2015, the proportion of the population without access to safe drinking water and basic sanitation
   - target 4 – By 2020, to have achieved a significant improvement in the lives of at least 100 million slum dwellers

8. Develop a global partnership for development –

   - target 1 – Address the special needs of least developed countries, landlocked countries and small island developing states
   - target 2 – Develop further an open, rule-based, predictable, non-discriminatory financial and trading system
   - target 3 – Deal comprehensively with developing countries' debt
   - target 4 – In co-operation with pharmaceutical companies, provide access to affordable essential drugs in developing countries
   - target 5 – In co-operation with the private sector, make available benefits of new technologies, especially information and communications.

(The full text of the MDGs and their associated targets is available through the MDG web pages which can be accessed at http://www.un.org/millenniumgoals/ and in languages other than English.)

The question still remains, however, whether these goals and their specific targets should be understood as a major setback for social development internationally, or whether they are to be regarded as offering a form of progress (Saith, 2006; Correll, 2008; Mathbor & Ferdinand, 2008). The promotion of education at all levels for everyone (WSSD) becomes a minimum attainment of primary education (MDGs), improvements in all aspects of health care (WSSD) are turned into minimal levels of primary health provision (MDGs), and so on. Both Deacon (2007) and Mathbor and Ferdinand (2008) consider that the MDGs represent limited progress as well as a retreat. Progress is to be seen in the specification of timelines and other concrete definitions of what is to be understood as success. Employment, education and health, all major elements of human well-being, remain central objectives. But all commentators are agreed that there is a step backwards contained in the formulation of the MDGs in that the prevailing dominant political and economic ideology (neo-liberalism) has influenced the way that these objectives have been structured and, at the same time, any claim to universality has largely been overshadowed by a concentration on the poorest countries and sections of the world population. It is not that the poorest sections of the world community do not require the attention of policy and practice, but that moving away from universal principles legitimizes a reduction of scope for development as it applies to other sections of the global population as well as a restriction of a vision for goals and outcomes for everyone. As Midgley (1997, p. 181) puts it, social development 'seeks to enhance the well-being of the population as a whole through harnessing the power of economic development and social ends'. What is done ought always to assist those most in need, but by focusing only on certain aspects of poverty this continues to treat extreme poverty as a 'difference' rather than emphasizing the human right to well-being that is shared by all. Focusing the goals of international development aid solely on the promotion of the global economy, in which the highly developed 'donor' countries benefit most, not only continues to marginalize the poorest sections of the world population, but also treats them as a means to the economic ends of others and not as autonomous human agents in themselves (compare with Rawls, 1972).

In addition to the way in which some national participants appear to have considered the economic gains in meeting specific goals rather than the benefit of setting targets, it is also possible to consider the way in which international debate about many of the issues that are addressed by the WSSD and the MDGs will be impacted by the different value systems pertaining in various parts of the world. In other words, at the level of practical policy-making it may well be that the MDGs represent a level of agreement wider than would have been possible for many countries who are the primary beneficiaries of attention to poverty reduction, and the improvement of social as well as economic infrastructure. In that sense, for example, there may be some modest consolation in the way in which references to gender equality continued to be expressed, such as in Goals 2 and 3. Both these goals emphasize that education is a core component of human development and that the world community should aspire to this being equally available for girls and young women as much as for boys and young men. Indeed, the access of girls and young women to education, particularly with regard to literacy, has been shown to be one of the most robust factors in the achievement of human development in both social and economic terms (UNDP, 1999; UNICEF, 1999). In other words, women's literacy is both an indicator and a driver of human development in all its dimensions. At the same time, the barriers to girls and young women accessing education must not be underestimated and for this goal to succeed will require considerable changes in some parts of the world.

So, on balance, while Correll (2008) is correct in his assessment that the bold ideals of the World Summit on Social Development (UN, 1995) have been diluted so quickly, and for reasons that act against the overt intent of aid and development, Deacon (2007) also makes a very plausible point that the MDGs (UN, 2000a) have more successfully attracted world attention and, in any case, are now the official policy. In that sense the MDGs create a terrain on which international social work, along with other practices, is required to operate.

Implications for Social Work

In so far as the MDGs tend to focus on economic and structural development it may be asked what significance they have for the larger part of social work. To begin this process, a summary of the underlying principles that can be seen in the MDGs may be useful. They are the following:

1. the importance of employment and addressing issues of hunger and poverty;
2. the way in which issues of gender inequality cut across other aspects of human development;
3. the centrality of education and health in the pursuit of human development;
4. the relevance of the environment for responses to other key areas in human development;
5. the idea of partnership at various structural levels (including between socio-economic classes, economic sectors, families, communities and nations, as well as between organizations and institutions).

While some implications of these principles may appear intuitively obvious for thinking about social work, other aspects may require further consideration.

As we have already noted in previous chapters, many of those who are concerned with development issues have argued that social work tends to focus on micro-level issues and policies and consequently to focus on the provision of remedial services, as compared to addressing the well-being of communities and thus their capacities to support individuals and families within them. So, in order to examine the implications of the MDGs for social work in more detail we need to look also at their relevance for macro-level social development practices and policies in which social workers may be involved, and consider the connections between this and the way in which the MDGs also create opportunities and constraints for social work at the more individual or micro-level. It is also the case that the five broad underlying principles that have been noted here are themselves also closely interconnected, for example with gender inequalities observable in the incidence and experience of hunger, poverty, lack of access to education and health, and so on (compare with Mapp, 2008, p. 156).

HIV/AIDS

One example of the way in which the MDGs are both interconnected and relevant for social work can be seen in the way that HIV/AIDS has impacted in sub-Saharan Africa (Heimer, 2007; Chama, 2008; Demmer & Burghart, 2008; Laird, 2008). In this context, understanding the spread of HIV/AIDS cannot be separated from an analysis of access to education, institutional arrangements for health care (including public health and health education), poverty, and the practices of international pharmaceutical companies, as well as social relationships, sexual practices, breast-feeding and other child-care practices, and so on (Heimer, 2007).

In a detailed qualitative study Demmer and Burghart (2008) make the point that the experience of living with HIV/AIDS compared between the United States and Southern Africa is affected in every way by differences between the economic and the political situations in different nations, and the way in which these translate into institutional health care practices including health education, the economic status of individuals and communities, other aspects of the social welfare system and cultural factors in dealing with stress and bereavement. Yet, in many respects, some of the most important variations are seen in matters of degree rather than in totally different experiences. For example, this research compared the United States and South Africa and found that in both countries there was considerable stigma reported in terms of supporting a dying friend or relative and also the individual's own HIV/AIDS status. Similarly, in both countries the people interviewed in this study reported high levels of unemployment and need related to problems in 'making ends meet on a daily basis' (Demmer & Burghart, 2008, p. 365). At the same time, the extent of available supports in the United States was considerably greater than that in South Africa, with implications for major differences in the impact of HIV/AIDS related bereavement and life issues. While American participants in this research reported having difficulties in accessing the assistance and services that are available, in South Africa such assistance often simply does not exist. Likewise, American participants reported stigma and the sense of exclusion, but this must be compared with

South African experiences of being physically ejected from family homes, criticism and ostracism for caring for relatives and friends, and the sheer scale of the extent to which children are becoming orphans or parents are losing children.

Several of the factors identified in the MDGs combine in the issue of HIV/AIDS, of which alleviating poverty and combating major health problems are the most explicit. Nevertheless, the intent of goals around gender, childhood and maternal health and education are all relevant, as is target 4 under goal 8 of improving access to expensive pharmaceuticals for those in greatest need. While it may be the case that these implications are international in the sense that individual people, institutions, ideas and the virus itself moved between countries, there are subtle differences of the way in which social workers in different countries can effectively respond. This is not simply a matter of the greater institutional resources available in the more highly developed countries of the global North, although this is a factor that must be recognized, but also that there are different traditions of coping and helping to which social workers must be sensitive. As both Demmer and Burghart (2008) and Laird (2008) have identified, practice in sub-Saharan Africa will continue to be less effective than it might otherwise be if social work does not take account of the ways in which there are extensive patterns of coping and survival in African societies. In some situations this requires that social workers develop knowledge and skills in relation to assisting people affected by HIV/AIDS to construct alternative ways of gaining a livelihood, coping with the demographic impact of high mortality rates and particular problems such as the incidence of children living on the streets (Chama, 2008; Laird, 2008). Laird (2008, p. 148) argues that in such contexts social work practice needs to embrace the tasks of supporting skills transfer, promoting intermediate technology and micro-finance and other community development practices that are rarely seen in more highly developed countries. She illustrates this point with concrete examples by looking at the recent practice of INGOs such as Plan International and Oxfam, to engage whole villages, communities or extended families with a focus on practical tasks to accomplish development ends. This seems entirely appropriate, but at the same time, Demmer and Burghart's (2008) findings suggest that this social development perspective should be in addition to, rather than instead of, an awareness of and capacity to respond to the personal and interpersonal impact of HIV/AIDS.

Health and the Family

In addition to the specific issue of HIV/AIDS, which in regions such as Africa and Asia may be an issue that increasingly concerns women more than men (Mweru, 2008), the MDGs also refer to health issues concerning women, child-bearing and child mortality (goals 4 and 5). While agreeing with the criticisms that these definitions of issues are considerably narrower and more restricted than the reference to women's equality in the WSSD (see discussion above), it is also helpful to note that in many parts of the world human development continues to be impeded by the way in which women's subordinate social status is closely connected with reproductive health, childbearing and children's health. For example, there is a close correlation between health generally and women's health in particular and both poverty and education (Mathbor & Ferdinand, 2008; Sepehri et al., 2008). At the time of writing, the UN (2008a, p. 24) has noted that the figure for maternal morbidity and mortality remains high, with as many as half a million women dying each year as a consequence of childbirth or complications in pregnancy. This figure seems remarkably durable as it is still the same as that recorded in the mid-1980s (compare with Seipel 1992, p. 201). As many as 99 per cent of deaths in or associated with childbirth occur in the global South, with 86 per cent in sub-Saharan Africa and South Asia – in other words maternal morbidity and mortality is directly correlated with the incidence of hunger, poverty, lack of employment, and slightly with lack of educational opportunities. So, we may reasonably conclude, we are concerned with a social rather than a strictly biological model of health in which, for example, the differences between the health status of those who have next to nothing and those who have nothing at all can be quite stark (Zimmer, 2008).

In a discussion of the role of social work in maternal health in developing countries specifically, Seipel (1992) argues that there is a distinctive role for the profession. First, he suggests that social work can make a strong contribution to the development of health care infrastructure. Noting that there is a massive disparity between the lack of health care for pregnant women in developing countries compared to the level of care provided in the highly developed countries, this argument points to programme planning and implementation as an important task. Second, Seipel suggests that social workers should provide health education and information. He notes that social workers already do play this type of role in the global North, working alongside colleagues from other professions. Third, social workers should be actively involved in advocacy for the status of women within societies and especially within health systems. The contribution of social workers to policy development and advocacy in this area is an important application of professional skills. Fourth, where appropriate, social workers should work in partnership with local women's organizations to support them in the achievement of improved maternal health. Seipel (1992, p. 205) notes that many of the gains in maternal health made in recent years in regions such as Africa have come from local women themselves playing significant active roles in the improvement of circumstances for women, improved knowledge and cultural changes alongside the development of health facilities. These arguments go beyond maternal health as, in many ways, they relate to women's health issues more generally. However, in the contexts with which

Seipel is concerned questions of pregnancy and childbirth are a particularly crucial phase in the lives of women regarding high levels of morbidity and mortality.

An illustration of this approach can be seen in Juliá and Kondrat's (2005) description of a women's health organization in El Salvador, in which all aspects of health care were shared by the women themselves in partnership with health care workers. This included both the definition health problems and the assessment of health needs. This project also emphasized the use of Indigenous approaches, in the sense of drawing on the knowledge already possessed by the women about their own health and also training local women as health workers. The result was that levels of women's health improved along with community self-reliance. As Juliá and Kondrat (2005, p. 545) note, '[g]oals were achieved and skills and capabilities were acquired for sustained use over time'. These gains were made not only by the local women themselves but also by the professionals who worked alongside them.

Literacy and Gender

We may note here again that the strong statements of the WSSD regarding gender equality appear to have been diluted somewhat in the MDGs. At the same time, the education of girls and young women is prioritized in places, notably goals 2 and 3, suggesting that aspects of this broader concern have been maintained. Research showing that literacy among girls and young women is among the most powerful drivers of human development has become conventional wisdom (UNDP, 1999; UNICEF, 1999). As with issues of women's health, there is a high degree of correlation between girls' literacy levels and the economic status of the household in which they live (Rao, 1996; Muno & Keenan, 2000; AMK/CEDPA, 2004).

In situations in which the relationship between social work and education is highly institutionalized, the role of social work in this regard is often in assisting girls and young women to gain access and to remain engaged with education as a normal part of everyday life. This can be achieved in working as school counsellors, as well as in responding to family or other difficulties that may encourage girls and young women to under-achieve in school or absent themselves from a compulsory education system in the global North as well as the South (Rao, 1996; Muno & Keenan, 2000; Farmer et al., 2005; Leve & Chamberlain, 2007). However, in the context of less-developed countries, the role of social work in relation to education is often much wider and less focused on individual girls. For example, although it may at times comprise similar work to that undertaken in the global North, it is also likely to incorporate health and social education, and community development. Examples of issues that may be addressed include gender relations, the position of women in society, as well as women's health issues such as female genital mutilation and reproductive and sexual health more generally (CEDPA, 2005). Indeed, in many situations girls' literacy is not separated from education concerning women's health, child protection (including the risks of human trafficking – see Chapter 3) as well as literacy for adult women (AMK/CEDPA, 2004; Acharya & Koirala, 2006). It is often said that women ensure the health and well-being of families and communities but their own personal health may be ignored in the process, partly due to cultural reasons and partly because of lack of resources (Seipel, 1992). Combining literacy work with development action in these other areas is effective both in the short term and also in the way in which literacy in itself creates conditions for sustainable development and participation of people in local communities.

This is illustrated by a project undertaken in Egypt by the Centre for Development and Population Activities (CEDPA), a US-based NGO that provides education-based development support with partner organizations in countries in Africa and Asia (CEDPA, 2005). This project, undertaken with the Egyptian National Council for Women, linked girls' literacy education with the training of staff and volunteers from local NGOs to:

> advocate for gender issues in their local communities [and to address] a wide range of issues including early marriage, school dropout, illiteracy, female genital mutilation, street children, lack of social and sports activities girls, unemployment, discrimination against women, shortage of schools and lack of medical care (CEDPA, 2005, p. 1).

In addition, girls themselves were trained as community advocates along with 240 representatives from the local NGOs and other community leaders. The skills that were learned by the participants included such things as the assessment of needs, ways of collecting and analysing data to assisting advocacy work, ways of being effective and strategic in communication, planning and monitoring action and the necessary skills for evaluation. Following this project, and building on it, the Egyptian National Council for Women and other local NGOs further developed a network of experienced volunteers and professionals who could continue to advocate for girls and women in regional and national policy (CEDPA, 2005, p. 2).

In this and similar projects social workers are engaged alongside teachers and health professionals, as well as administrators and members of the local communities in question (Acharya & Koirala, 2006, p. 38). Practising in such contexts requires the capacity to work across micro-, mezzo- and macro-approaches, because there must be flexibility to move easily between direct involvement with the girls and young women and other community members (working with individuals and groups), through to programme planning and evaluation, policy development, project management and so on. This multi-level approach also demands that social workers are able to work in partnership with local NGOs and community members as well as other professionals. Combining a focus on literacy for girls and women with education and advocacy concerning the wider issues in their lives in this way not only has an immediate impact but also contributes to longer-term sustainability in community development as literacy forms the basis for the girls and young women themselves to be equipped to take on future action.

Employment and Environment

One of the central ways in which the MDGs are directed to poverty allevia- tion is through the promotion of conditions and opportunities for employment (goals 1 and 8). At the same time these goals cannot be separated from the implications about the environment and sustainability that contained explicitly or implicitly in goals 7 and 8. As the impact of industrialization and urban- ization on the natural world become increasingly evident there are growing calls for improved employment opportunities to take account of environmental sustainability (Seitz, 2008). This in turn is also linked to questions of social sus- tainability and the impact on communities of particular types of industrialization and other changes in patterns of economic activity.

Kuruvilla (2005) describes the impact of an economic development pro- gramme on coastal communities in India. Beginning in the 1950s, the 'inte- grated fisheries' project saw many professionals and volunteers from the global North intervening with the traditional fishing communities in Kerala and then subsequently in other regions of India (Kuruvilla, 2005, p. 47). The profession- als included technical experts in fishing and economics as well as community development experts. Subsequent research on the long-term effects of this project on local communities has demonstrated that, rather than enabling the development of a modern industrial-scale fishing industry, the impact was actually to make matters worse through the impact on fish stocks and other envi- ronmental factors as well as negative changes in the daily lives of people in these communities (Kuruvilla, 2005, p. 48). In particular, overfishing and related fac- tors have disturbed the ecological balance. In addition, the traditional fishing communities found themselves marginalized, with declining employment and economic opportunities, as changed policies and practices in the fishing indus- try led to increased access for foreign fishers as well as the inward migration of fishers from other regions and countries. In addition there was a negative impact on associated lifestyle issues for local communities such as, ironically, being unable to afford to eat fish.

In response to this situation the role of social workers, together with other professionals and volunteers involved in social development, has focused on assisting these communities to respond in different ways to the impact of the earlier 'development'. These include acting as mediators between the fishing communities and external bodies and interests (including state and national government departments as well as international firms), enabling these communities to access alternatives to develop new occupations, assisting state and local government efforts to encourage micro-financing of the locally based economic activities, encouraging and enabling children to gain from the formal education system, conducting community consultations and education programmes with respect to health and other local issues and providing assistance to community-based social movements (Kuruvilla, 2005, p. 49). Although it is acknowledged that the end result remains likely to be a transition from the more or less traditional lifestyle that had existed for a long period of time into a more modern lifestyle, using these approaches that end result will be achieved in partnership with the local communities rather than being imposed upon them in a distorted and marginalizing way. For Kuruvilla (2005, pp. 51–2) this requires international social work, which in this situation might have included both social workers from other countries working in NGOs and local social workers working with international organizations, being informed by the political economy of 'aid' and making this an explicit topic in international and national debates within the profession. It also necessitates a profession that deals in non-hierarchical ways with social power, working in partnership, 'for an on behalf of' local communities and seeking to avoid imposing expertise from outside. Finally, we might add, it also suggests that social workers become more aware of the interconnections between our practice and the relationship of human society with the natural environment.

What of 'Poverty Alleviation'?

It might appear from the discussion so far that there is a disjuncture between Midgley's (1997) argument concerning the need to focus on social factors in development, or of Correll's (2008) criticism concerning the way in which the MDGs represent a retreat from the WSSD, and the tangible connection between poverty and the lack of equity and equality, whether on grounds of socio-economic class and/or caste, gender, ethnicity and 'race', culture and religious beliefs and so on. The MDGs are very clearly oriented towards poverty alleviation with an emphasis on addressing the material dimension to poverty. Yet, as we noted above, those who are critical of the MDGs do not actually deny this connection. The issue concerns the ways in which it may most appropriately be addressed and that it should not become the sole or dominant way of addressing questions that are much wider than a matter of resource or income distribution alone.

Morazes and Pintak (2007) review key theories of global poverty, noting that although many may have become more sophisticated and inclusive of social as well as economic measurements they still tend to reflect the concerns and perspectives of the global North. For example, they argue that this encompasses a debate between an understanding of poverty as the consequence of the normal working of industrial systems and the market economy and theories of individual deficiencies (which they summarize as 'social versus individual blame' [2007, p. 109]). This leads in Northern analysis to a concentration on theories about inclusion/exclusion, universal or selective responses, resource distribution and the institutionalization of welfare in the form of benefits. Even those who attempt to look at the issues in developing countries do not escape this problem. In contrast, it is suggested, theorizing poverty from the perspectives of the poor themselves produces a very different set of solutions (2007, pp. 115–16). Morazes and Pintak cite the work of Ayittey (2005), which makes the claim that 'economic freedom' (as opposed to 'economic security') is what is required. Such an approach would require that economic issues are dealt with together with political, social, cultural and other factors and not treated as if they were separable. This would lead to a 'pro-poor' approach in defining poverty (including critiques of globalization and the effects of colonialism), a community focus on questions of measurement, treating resource issues inclusively (recognizing the links between trade imbalances, internal corruption, basic needs such as access to food, water and medicines) and basing interventions on developing human capital and participation (instead of often simply focusing on 'infrastructure') (Morazes & Pintak, 2007, p. 117).

Recognition of the social dimension of absolute poverty is part of Morazes and Pintak's argument. This is supported by Townsend's (2006) critique of the World Bank reliance on a measure of $1 (US) income per day to define absolute poverty and $2 (US) to determine relative (or socially based) poverty. Not only, he argues, should the $1 per day be increased to $1.50 because of the shift in real prices and costs globally, but the inclusion of social measures in determining what it actually costs simply to maintain a human life (promised but not delivered by the World Bank) would raise the figure further (Townsend, 2006, pp. 5–6). As Morazes and Pintak note (2007, p. 108), even the classical economist Adam Smith (usually, perhaps sometimes unfairly, seen as the originator of theories that now form part of global neo-liberal orthodoxy) allowed that a concept of poverty ought to include those things that are necessary to live at a basic level in the society of which one is part and not only those that are minimally necessary to avoid death. On such a basis, even the $1.50 (US) per day figure sees well over one-third of the world's population as being in poverty while $2 (US) per day takes the figure over two-fifths (Townsend, 2006, p. 5; Morazes & Pintak, 2007, p. 113). This latter figure means that 40 per cent of the global population has access to only 5 per cent of the world's income.

The conclusion that may be drawn from this, for Morazes and Pintak, is that poverty alleviation is not simply a matter of finding a technical solution to problems of income or resource distribution. This is part of the picture, but it must be connected to social and cultural factors. It is not possible to have 'development' that is solely economic; rather, the goal is *social* development in which the alleviation of poverty is a part. Issues of human capacities and skills (human capital), participation and local control, education and access to knowledge as a resource and so on are all necessary. This has implications for social workers involved in poverty alleviation programmes to rethink their relationships with those who they seek to assist, pointing to the importance of working in partnership. It also suggests the centrality of practices that enable this to happen, which are 'bottom-up' rather than 'top-down' in their focus (Ife & Tesoriero, 2006). Theorizing, including understanding poverty, therefore becomes a matter of learning *from* rather than *about* the people and communities in question (Morazes & Pintak, 2007, pp. 118–19). As Morazes and Pintak point out, such principles apply as much to American professionals responding to the aftermath of hurricanes Katrina and Rita as it does to any others, local or international, working in any other part of the world (compare with Chapter 3).

Broadening the Role of Social Work?

Using a framework of core issues evident in the MDGs, this chapter has examined particular aspects of social work practice in contexts where impoverishment, defined broadly, is the underlying question. The examples that have been used focus on countries of the global South, but as we have just noted these issues can be found in the more highly developed nations. They are not confined, therefore, to situations in which international social work consists of taking knowledge and skills from one country to another in a single direction, namely from the global North to the South. They not only include social work that may include some movement of practitioners or programmes between countries, and of exchange and partnership, but they also include the impact of international issues and economic and structural relationships.

Exploring issues raised by the MDGs leads to several implications for international social work. The first of these is the necessity of recognizing the connections between social structures (such as economic and politics systems and institutions), the physical world (natural and human-created resources), social relationships and cultures. In previous chapters we noted the debates in social work that occur between a focus on the person and on the social environment (notwithstanding the attempt to overcome this in the 'international definition' of social work, see IFSW/IASSW, 2001), drawing on arguments about the connectedness of these factors. Yet, as we have seen, questions of health, family, gender, education and literacy, employment, the relationship between human life and the environment and so on cannot be understood in terms of only one or the other of these perspectives, but only through their interconnection. From this we may conclude that effective practice and theory responding to the issues presented in the MDGs must necessarily take a broad view of the focus, methods and goals of social work.

This in turn again raises the requirement for international social work of the integration rather than the separation of macro-, mezzo- and micro-concerns, analyses, practices and so on. In the examples that have been quoted in this chapter the roles of social work included programme planning, management and evaluation, community work including the organization of meetings, negotiating between different interest groups within communities, identifying and mobilizing resources and negotiating with various levels of government, advocacy, direct work with families and individuals. In other words, in responding to the issues identified in the MDGs social workers must utilize a full range of roles and tasks. This is as true for the social worker practising in the global North with service users or with issues that have international origins as it is for the social worker practising in the global South who comes from elsewhere, who is working for an international organization or who, again, is dealing with issues that have international origins. If the MDGs, and the arguments about the need for social development that lie behind them, are applied to the global North as well as to the global South, then this point stands as a critique of the tendency for social work in some parts of America and Europe to focus on individual clinical practices to the exclusion of mezzo- or macro-considerations. Furthermore, in the description of programmes to address girls' literacy or maternal health in these parts of the world it cannot be forgotten that these all provide clear evidence of the close connections between poverty, gender, 'race' and culture and other issues that are grounded in social systems and relationships. In this way attention to what has come to be known as 'anti-discriminatory practice', especially in the United Kingdom (Thompson, 2006), can be seen to be highly relevant in all national contexts (even though, as we will see in the subsequent chapters, this may be disputed in some situations on cultural grounds).

In some respects this understanding of social work in response to the MDGs may be seen as extending the boundaries of the profession. Some issues that have been described here encompass working in roles that are often perceived to be outside the domain of social work. For example, assisting young people with issues of literacy is often regarded widely as being the province of professional teachers. Similarly, health education, especially in countries of the global North, has developed as a profession in its own right or as a branch of nursing. In contrast, however, a broader understanding of social work developed from an international comparative consideration of attention to systemic inequality and of poverty alleviation as a key goal sees such boundaries as unhelpful. In situations where highly developed resources are available this can lead to close partnership working with other professionals (Muno & Keenan, 2000). In less well-resourced contexts, social workers may need to take on such diverse roles and, at the same time, share with others those roles that they have previously claimed (Andhari, 2007). Where social workers are not available others may simply be expected to undertake such tasks and there may even be doubts as to which roles 'belong' to social work (Kreitzer, 2002, p. 55; Claiborne, 2004, p. 217). (We will pursue different aspects of this point in Chapters 5 and 6.) At other times they may be the only professional around. In all situations this includes working in partnership with the members of the communities with whom they are working. The consequences of professional flexibility may be that social work is practised in unusual places or in ways that do not conform to the self-images held by colleagues in other contexts. Nevertheless, without a capacity to adapt and to respond to what is required there is a greater risk, not only in that social work may cease to be relevant in and of itself but, more to the point, that by doing so it will fail to be effective.

In this chapter we have considered the implications of the MDGs (UN, 2000a) for social work. Although it can be argued that these goals are a shift away from the more far-reaching commitments of the WSSD (UN, 1995), nevertheless they do still provide a basis for considering important issues for international social work. Arising from this we can identify a number of themes that require further analysis. First is the apparent tension between macro-, mezzo- and micro-levels of practice and theory. To what extent are these best understood in relation to the degree of development of both social work as a profession and the wider society in which it is contextualized? Or, alternatively, does a critical analysis of international social work point to a different approach, in which these distinctions are an obstacle to more creative and effective practice? These questions will be pursued in greater depth in the next chapter as we consider the extent to which thinking about international social work creates the challenge of asking 'what is social work anyway?' Second, we can continue to see the issue of cultural relativity and neo-colonialism, at least implicitly embedded in many of the aspects of social work that have been explored in this chapter. These concerns continue to be important in the following chapters and will be picked up in several ways in thinking about international organization, social work education and in a discussion of the critique of 'professional imperialism' (Midgley, 1981).

5

Different Forms of Social Work: A Pluralistic and Inclusive View

What is Social Work?

In the previous chapters a very broad understanding of social work has been presented, ranging from the micro- to the macro-level of theory and practice[1]. So far, however, we have not addressed the debate that has existed within social work concerning the identity of the profession and whether it should most appropriately be focused on intra- and inter-personal issues or on questions of social systems and structures. To what extent can it be argued that post-trauma counselling and therapy with refugees settled in a country of the global North, poverty alleviation among slum dwellers in cities of the global South and environmental management programmes in Asia and Africa all appropriate sites for socials work practice? In order to understand the way in which a consideration of international social work can assist the analysis of social work as a whole, the discussion now turns to a question with which social work has struggled since its early development in the nineteenth century. That is, should social work focus on social issues and human needs at the micro- or the macro-level as defining its core nature?

Attempts to produce a workable definition of social work that can be applied internationally have proved somewhat elusive. At a combined meeting in 2000 the IFSW and the IASSW agreed the following statement:

> The social work profession promotes social change, problem solving in human relationships and the empowerment and liberation of people to enhance well-being. Utilising theories of human behaviour and social systems, social work intervenes at

---

[1] Elsewhere in this book I have identified the distinction between micro-, mezzo- and macro-levels of theory and practice (also see the Glossary). However, in this chapter I am following the terms of a debate that has been long established between casework as micro and community work or community organizing as macro-level concerns.

the point where people interact with their environments. Principles of human rights and social justice are fundamental to social work. (IFSW/IASSW, 2000/2001)

These three very complex sentences communicate several important ideas about social work internationally. First, they assert that micro- and macro-perspectives are both key to the definition of the goals of practice. Working to help people resolve problems in their relationships is as much a part of social work as is achieving changes in social structures, provided that both are focused on the goal of people becoming empowered and liberated from whatever obstacles they face in the achievement of well-being. Second, they state that the theories which inform practice include both micro-level perspectives (human behaviour) and macro-level theories (social systems).

Despite the attempt to be inclusive, this definition was highly contested within the international organizations at the time that it was drafted (personal communication) and it continues to present some difficulties for colleagues who consider that it fails adequately to deal with the requirements of social work in their own national context. Moreover, especially for the discussion of international social work, it may be unclear how this definition may assist in considering social work between countries as opposed to practice within any particular national setting. So, having addressed the debate about micro- and macro-perspectives, this chapter will then turn to the way in which our understanding of social work itself relates to understanding international social work.

Different Forms of Social Work?

As was mentioned briefly at the beginning of Chapter 1, the professionalization of social work is widely seen as having its origins in countries of the global North towards the end of the nineteenth century (Lundy, 2004; Olson, 2007). In that period there were two distinct forms of developing practice that together contributed to the emergence of the social work profession as it is now seen. These were the Charity Organization Societies and the Settlement House movements (Parry & Parry, 1979; Payne, 2005). The legacy left by these early forms can be traced through to the current ways in which we may think about the micro- and macro-approaches respectively.

The work of charity organization developed out of the application of the emergent scientific approach to society that characterized European and American thought in the late nineteenth century to the provision of charitable assistance for individuals and families that faced problems of poverty, the breakdown of relationships, inadequate housing and related issues. Although many of these problems were understood to have emerged from the very rapid urbanization and industrialization that saw the massive growth of cities and the impoverishment of rural areas, it was also perceived that while some individuals coped with such circumstances others experienced extreme difficulties and hardships. Moreover, it was believed that the provision of charitable relief to assist people in poverty largely failed because of a lack of a systematic approach either in directing such relief where it would be of most use or in providing the additional support for individuals and families which would enable them to make best use of this help. In response, therefore, efforts were made to create such an approach. This was based on the use of the relationship established between people who receive charitable assistance ('clients') and the individual 'caseworkers' working in behalf of the Charity Organization Societies. The theory behind this approach was that people in the receipt of charitable assistance would be enabled to develop better coping strategies and to make best use of the resources provided to them. Thus, at least in a general sense, the emergence of this 'scientific' approach to charity can be seen as representing the origins of micro-level approaches in social work. In summary, its work was predominantly concerned with individual functioning and questions of social order and many commentators regard it as having been politically conservative (Jones, 1983; Lundy, 2004; Payne, 2005; Olson, 2007).

In contrast, the Settlement Houses were based on a structural approach to the same social issues. The Settlements can be regarded as a social movement, in which people from more wealthy and formally educated classes moved to live and work in areas where poverty was endemic. The underlying theory was that such people possessed social resources, not only those of finance but also of knowledge, and the ability to negotiate the demands of a very rapidly changing society. (Such an idea can be seen as a precursor to the more recent concept of social capital; for example, see Cox, 1995.) The goal was that by sharing the benefits of education and other forms of knowledge that whole communities, including the families and individuals who comprise such communities, would be able to develop the capacity to resolve social problems and to improve their own lives. In this sense, the settlement house approach can be seen as representing the early stages of macro-level practice in social work, because it was based on a structural understanding of social issues and was focused on social change (as opposed to focusing on change in and between individuals). For this reason, commentators are widely agreed in regarding it as having been politically radical (Parry & Parry, 1979; Lundy, 2004; Olson, 2007).

It is important to recognize that these two ideas, that is 'charity organization' and 'settlement', arose as responses to the escalation of the same social issues that followed from the processes of industrialization, urbanization and modernization that constituted what has come to be known as the Industrial Revolution across northern Europe and North America. Another phenomenon that is closely identified with this period is that of the development of the modern profession, for example seen in the growth of law, medicine, nursing, the allied health professions and teaching (Freidson, 1994). Social work, in both the forms that have been identified here, was also part of this growth of professionalism (Hugman, 1991; Payne, 2005). To emphasize the point, where these approaches to early social work differed was in their understanding of the most appropriate ways in which social issues can be addressed and people assisted.

However, underlining the way in which these two approaches developed around ways of responding to social issues, there were also divergent ways of explaining the causes of social problems. On the one hand, the casework method of the charity organization societies effectively tended to concentrate on personal failings, understood in terms of both social skills and moral orientation, while, on the other hand, the settlement house approach was grounded in the view that social problems arose primarily from the inequalities endemic in social structures. This in turn produced the different focus between personal and collective forms of intervention. From this point of view, it can be seen that the two approaches effectively provide the foundations for the division between micro- and macro-levels of theory and practice in contemporary social work.

Although historically these two different strands of early social work united in the founding of university level professional education and training, for example in Denmark, the Netherlands, the United Kingdom and the United States, the distinction between the micro- and the macro-perspectives also clearly created the debate concerning the identity of social work that has been ongoing ever since (Drakeford, 2002; Payne, 2005; Mendes, 2007; Olson, 2007). In some senses this debate could be considered to be comparable to those in other professions about which branch or aspect of the occupation should be considered pre-eminent. However, unlike most other professions, in social work the differences between micro- and macro-perspectives can assume the character of a struggle to define one as authentic and its alternative as 'not really social work'. Recognition of this debate is crucial for understanding international social work for several reasons. In particular, in so far as the development of social work profession in the global South can be seen in terms of the export of ideas from the North and corresponding struggles to create an Indigenous or authentic social work for new contexts, the debate between the micro- and macro-perspectives has also been part of these processes.

The View from the (global) North

Approaches to social work in the countries of the North do not form a unified whole. In particular, we should note that the development of social work in the United States is distinct from the other English-speaking countries (Australia, Canada, New Zealand and the UK) and European countries. Social work in the United States is located in diverse sites, compared to the tendency for the profession to have developed in the other countries through its increasing location within welfare state institutions. Beyond this, the discourses of social work (i.e., the sets of concepts and language that are used to grasp the nature of social work) differ between specific countries and between different parts of Europe as well as between Europe and North America. One example of this it is the extent to which the language of 'anti-racist and anti-discriminatory practice' belongs quite distinctively to the United Kingdom (e.g., see Dominelli, 2008; Clifford & Burke, 2008), even though the issues to which such ideas refer apply across the global North as a whole (and, we might suggest, the entire world).

In terms of the long-standing debate between micro- and macro-perspectives, Olson (2007) has recently argued that the current situation has grown out of a continuing dominance of the micro over the macro. He states that this stems from the mistaken subordination of the value of social justice within the pursuit of professionalization. The goal of social work, he suggests, should be to promote a more just social order. However, Olson sees contemporary social work as preoccupied with the discovery of skills and knowledge which will make social work 'truly' a profession. Referring to key figures in the settlement movement and charity organization in the United States, Olson claims that this has led social work to 'talk Jane Addams and do Mary Richmond' (2007, p. 60). (This view reflects a long-standing analysis of the professional orientation to the professionalization of social work in the global North, especially the USA, in terms of an emphasis on micro-level practices – see, e.g., Elliott, 1993, p. 22.)

Olson's analysis implies that the professionalization of social work, at least in part, is a consequence of conscious reflection on the part of leaders within the profession. Yet this seems, somewhat ironically, to explain the history of the occupation in the global North in terms only of individual action. However, while this may accurately describe the intentions of some individuals, we can also consider some more structural explanations as to why the project of professionalization has become tied to the micro-level perspective.

First, as we have just noted, the development of social work as a profession in these countries has predominantly been located in state welfare institutions. Even in the United States, which differs from other Northern countries in this respect, it is also the case that social work has a large component based on various types of welfare organizations. Although in the United States in recent decades there has been the emergence of a sizeable private practice sector, social work has historically had a tendency to be concerned with people experiencing social needs of a kind not normally found amongst those who have the capacity to pay full professional fees.

Second, because social work is usually agency based, it is necessary to think about what such agencies will employ social workers to do. Although some organizations, particularly those in the non-government not-for-profit sector, will employ people to work on social justice projects, to undertake research, to advocate and conduct campaigns, or to assist communities to address collective issues, it is often the case that they are as likely to hire lawyers, social scientists or people with other professional training (or even no professional training) for such tasks as they are likely to employ social workers. Where social workers have been employed in large numbers it is most often the case that this is to undertake the provision of various forms of welfare services at the level of individuals and families.

Third, social work has taken the same path as other occupations that are engaged in addressing human needs, in that they have sought to have appropriate knowledge and skills defined and recognized so that it is plausible that they should be mandated to act. The processes of professionalization, which this understanding implies, are historically bound up with the modernization of society. In a world in which values and broad intentions are not seen as a sufficient legitimation for the exercise of authority in the public arena, all such occupations lay claim to such authority on the grounds of systematic knowledge and skills. Moreover, professionalism has proved to be a relatively uncertain status to claim as, in recent decades, the impact of neo-liberalism has led to the commodification of welfare in which social workers along with other professions have been reconstructed from providers of services into producers of welfare, and service users have correspondingly become consumers (Hugman, 1998). In countries such as Australia, Canada, New Zealand and the United Kingdom the remaining elements of macro-level practices focused on community have often been largely abandoned as the notion of 'community' has become a location of micro-level practice in the form of 'community care' (Butler and Drakeford, 2001).

Yet, although this argument is substantially correct, it is not the case that structural analyses of social issues or attention to macro-level practices have necessarily been abandoned. Two examples of argument from Australia serve to illustrate this. The first of these is Fook's (1993) development of the theory of radical casework. Fook's approach shows that working at the micro-level, in the sense of interventions directly concerned with individuals and families, can be informed by structural understandings of the causes of social need and that interventions can be developed to take account of this. A parallel development is that of anti-racist and anti-discriminatory practice in the United Kingdom, in which practices based on advocacy and empowerment at the micro-level of intervention also illustrate ways in which structural analysis can be integrated (although some critics, such as Butler and Drakeford, 2001, p. 16, remain sceptical about their actual impact). The second example is that of Mendes' (2007) research into the extent to which structural approaches influenced direct practice, in which he found that social workers employed in a variety of welfare service agencies continue to undertake tasks that included policy development, research, community development, and advocacy and structurally informed interventions with individuals. Although Mendes (2007, p. 42) acknowledges a limitation in his study, that he did not include workers in statutory agencies in his sample, this evidence does point to the continued relevance of questioning a rigid binary distinction between the micro and the macro.

In addition, we should also question the extent to which arguments about the distinction between the micro- and macro-perspectives also make assumptions that macro-level practice is necessarily informed by a critical understanding of social systems, or that it is 'progressive' or pursues social justice. What we should ask when looking at any particular form of social work practice, therefore, concerns the extent to which it engages with such critical understandings or pursues social justice rather than whether it is micro or macro in its focus (Lundy, 2004).

The View from the (global) South

As we have already noted in previous chapters, in many ways the development of social work in countries of the global South can be seen in terms of transmission or export from the global North. In countries such as Egypt, India and South Africa the early stages of social work development were marked by an introduction of an individually focused welfare services model (Walton & El Nasr, 1988; Nanavatty in Billups, 2002; Patel, 2005). However, as Walton and El Nasr (1988) argue in relation to Egypt, as the prevailing social realities challenged early practitioners what followed was a process of adaptation to the new cultural context. This process they call 'indigenization' (p. 148). Yet they go on to assert that this notion is insufficient to describe the process that is necessary for forms of social work to fully be integrated in different cultural contexts. Therefore they argue for a process of 'authentization', which is:

> [the] creating or building of a domestic model of social work in the light of the social, cultural, political and economic characteristics of a particular country (1998, p. 149).

The crucial difference is that whereas the former represents a translation that remains couched in terms of the country of origin, the latter process responds to social needs arising from specific issues in the structural and cultural realities in the country in which it is being developed. Thus, in relation to Egypt specifically, they argue that an initial process of the transmission of ideas from the United Kingdom and the United States was followed by a period of 'indigenization', but this then led to a phase of 'authentization' in response to problems that were encountered in trying to transplant these forms of social work from other parts of the world. The important element in their analysis is that in developing a social work appropriate for Egypt both micro- and macro-perspectives were necessary. They also noticed that although Egypt has developed its own form of secular social welfare there is still a powerful and a distinctive role of formal religion such that developing the relationship between social work and Islam continues to be necessary (Walton & El Nasr, 1998, p. 154). In addition, they emphasize that the integrating concept has been to construct social work primarily as social development rather than to be overly concerned with institutional service provision.

Similarly, Osei-Hwedie and his colleagues in Botswana have argued that a localized approach to defining and developing social work is required, which they say should be 'defined to suit the African [social] environment' (Osei-Hwedie et al., 2006, p. 570; also see Osei-Hwedie, 1993). Silavwe (1995) also makes the same argument about Zambia. This analysis is based on the understanding of African societies as communal in their ethos. From this, it is seen that the focus of social work should be on the integration of individual, family and social strengths and resources in order to resolve whatever social needs are identified (Osei-Hwedie, 1993). It is worth quoting the definition of social work used at the University of Botswana in full:

> [s]ocial work aims to understand and change different situation contexts that affect people socially, culturally and politically. It also seeks to prevent, ameliorate, and manage undesirable social and environmental situations; develop appropriate interventions to meet the needs of people and their communities; design and implement appropriate policies for development; manage and supervise others in the pursuit of development objectives; and undertake research and apply findings in relevant settings (Osei-Hwedie et al., 2006, p. 573).

This definition of social work in Botswana arose in a situation in which a gap was perceived between the imported American/European models grounded on individual skills and the rural and community development plans of the government that set the foundation for social work in Botswana and emphasized the building of social capital. As Osei-Hwedie and his colleagues acknowledge (2006, p. 573), this definition actually has many similarities to those used in countries in the global North. However as with the approach to social work in Egypt (see above) and that described by Silavwe (1993) in Zambia, it seeks to combine the micro and macro in contrast to the separation of these perspectives highlighted by the long-standing debate in the North.

Similarly, in South Africa from the 1940s through to the end of the apartheid era in the early 1990s social work was almost entirely constructed as micro-level practice focused on remedial concerns and operating within an institutional framework (Patel, 2005). Attention was confined to issues such as family functioning and youth delinquency, with a casework model that tended to concentrate on personal and relationship deficits. Patel argues that since the achievement of a democratic government there has been a significant shift in social work (and more generally in the social welfare field) to a developmental model in which micro- and macro-concerns and practices are combined. Alongside social support and care services for families, including child protection, South African social work now also includes community organizing ('mobilization'), home and community-based care in which formal and informal contributions are combined, education and prevention in response to issues such as HIV/AIDS and drug misuse, poverty reduction and the promotion of livelihoods, restorative justice, social planning, policy and advocacy (Patel, 2005, pp. 178 ff.; Maker, 2008; Wilson, 2008; Graham, 2009; Selipsky, 2009). As well as the broadening of social work to integrate the micro- and macro-levels, there is also the very important commitment of social work as a profession to overcoming the legacy of apartheid through the process of reconciliation (Patel, 2005, p. 78).

In other parts of the global South different responses to this debate has emerged. For example, social work was introduced at a relatively early stage to China but was then abandoned after the revolution of 1949. (Here we are considering the People's Republic of China, as under British colonial rule social work continued to develop and professionalize in Hong Kong.) Since the shift in policy towards a market economy, China has restored social work as a profession and is in the process of developing new educational programmes and patterns of employment and social work (Yan & Tsang, 2005). A similar development is also occurring in Vietnam (Hugman et al., 2007). Yan and Cheung (2006, pp. 64–5), in one of the few analyses to engage directly with Walton and El Nasr (1988), argue that 'authentization' (they call it 'authentication') has to be explained primarily as a political process in which different discourses are appropriated and combined in particular relationships. Within this process there will be a struggle for the way in which ideas are reproduced and reconfigured a local context, a process that they call 'recontextualization'.

Two elements to the recontextualization of social work in China can be identified. First, since 1949 social welfare in China has been provided through a government bureaucracy, delivered as an administrative service. The reintroduction of social work to China has been sought by this bureaucracy as a means of improving and professionalizing the technical delivery of these services. The mandate for social work within this framing is to support economic development and to play a role in ensuring social stability and prosperity (Yan & Cheung, 2006, p. 68). The professionalization of social work in China has effectively been achieved through university-level education. Yan and Tsang (2005) studied the orientation of the Chinese social work educators and found that the predominant approach to social work that they emphasized included 'raising the quality of life and fostering harmonious family relationships', 'maintaining social stability', 'resolving social problems', 'social security and satisfying social needs' and '[promoting] social participation' (pp. 892–3). Yan and Tsang conclude that these data demonstrate that the developing professional goals are being framed in a micro-perspective on the function and techniques of social work.

Second, however, there is also a developing focus on macro-approaches evident in rural community development work described by Ku and his colleagues (2005). This approach is based on the definition of the core function of social work as capacity building, which they describe as:

> [...] all people have the right to share in the world's resources equally, and to control their own development; and at the rejection of such rights is at the heart of poverty and suffering. Strengthening people's capacity to determine their own values and priorities, and to act on these, is the basis of the development (Ku et al., 2005, p. 217).

In this way, social work in rural China is seen both from macro- and micro-perspectives, in combination. This approach quite explicitly challenges tradition and culture, both the understanding of the people in the communities that are being assisted and the expectations of those providing assistance, about what it means to be a professional in this field. At the same time, this approach continues to show Chinese characteristics, as the explicit goals of practice include the establishment of harmonious relationships in the community, strengthening social cohesion and participation and so on.

Two factors are common to these different patterns of development. First, both approaches are being developed by Chinese social workers, many of whom are based in Hong Kong SAR, who have education and practical experience derived from countries of the global North (especially the USA, the UK and Canada). Second, differences between these models may be understood as a reflection of the varying social, political, economic and cultural needs and constraints of major urban centres (Beijing, Shanghai) on the one hand and the marginalized and poorer region in a relatively remote province (Yunnan) on the other. This is not to suggest that this mixed pattern of development is inappropriate, because, given the geographic size of China, it is at least plausible to ask whether the demands of appropriate social work in the urban centres and the regional periphery are necessarily different. Appropriateness, or, to adapt the local term, 'authenticity', has to be determined by Chinese social workers for China.

What can be seen from these examples of social work departments in countries of the global South is that the meaning of the goals and tasks of social work can vary according to the context in which they are located. The micro-focus of practice that predominated in the forms of professionalism introduced through colonialism is not necessarily rejected outright, but in each of these contexts has to be placed alongside the development of structural and communal perspectives as a necessary part of the core of social work. Yet, in contrast to the global North, the understanding of structure and community in these countries is grounded in the values of social harmony and social cohesion as crucial objectives. It is not that the social workers are unconcerned about issues of inequality and the structural causes of social need, but that the ways of addressing these have to be constructed in ways that are relevant to these situations. Consequently, the separation of micro- and macro-perspectives on the causes and appropriate ways of addressing social needs is not evident in the same way as in countries of the global North. Rather, these African and Asian approaches emphasize connections between the micro- and the macro-levels (although, as with the North, there are also important differences between these countries).

Is Social Development the Missing Link?

One possible solution to the polarization implied by this debate, proposed by Midgley (1995, 1997, 1999), is that we should rethink the goals and techniques of social work in terms of 'social development'. His definition of social development is:

> [...] a process of planned social change designed to promote the well-being of the population as a whole in conjunction with a dynamic process of economic development (Midgely, 1995, p. 25).

Although this approach is not always recognized in the global North as part of the range of social work perspectives, Midgley (1997, p. 183) notes that the caseworkers of the Charity Organization Society in England included job finding and assistance with the development of small businesses as part of their interventions. Midgley argues that in so far as critical histories have concluded that this strand of social work was inherently conservative, this may be a misapprehension of the intentions within such practices in so far as they sought to facilitate what we would now understand as 'capacity building'. Rather, the problem lay in the extent to which they failed to challenge the exploitation of people in poverty or to address the conflict between such interventions and the more punitive social values of the times that resulted in an ethos that has subsequently come to be seen as 'victim blaming'. For Midgley, this problem was then amplified in the export of social work around the world, in that colonial administrations focused on the provision of remedial programmes (such as those dealing with crime amongst young people or people with mental health, disabilities and problems arising from old age) that was based on a limited view of casework separated from an understanding of and response to economic and structural needs. It was only when this was recognized and programmes such as mass education and related forms of community development began to be introduced that macro-perspectives became more integrated with micro-level responses. In turn this led to the adoption by organizations such as the United

Nations of 'unified socio-economic planning' as a central perspective (Midgley, 1997, p. 185). This was then undermined in the 1980s with the rapid shift to neo-liberal policies on the part of the IMF and the World Bank and the introduction of structural adjustment that emphasized the responsibilities of the recipient countries over those of international donors (Hall and Midgley, 2004, pp. 273–7). Although subsequent criticism led to a modification of these policies, it is still not clear that the IMF and World Bank have actually abandoned such notions altogether (Cammack, 2002; Deacon, 2007).

The importance of global policy for social work is that in many cases countries of the global South have been unable to afford either the residual or institutional welfare programmes that had developed, while at the same time the need for a social development focus was exacerbated but not supported. In the North, the same neo-liberal approaches emphasized individual responsibility and led to a consolidation of approaches in social work that is inimical to communal or structural responses (Ferguson and Lavalette, 2005; Lundy, 2006). For these reasons, a social development approach to social work has been both necessary and at the same time extremely difficult to pursue.

The potential of social development as a way of considering a common approach to social work between different national and cultural settings can be seen in a summary of its core features. Drawing on Elliott (1993), Midgley (1995, 1997, 1999) and Cox and Pawar (2006, p. 35) we can see that these characteristics are:

- combining attention to structural and economic aspects of need with community, family and individual aspects;
- attending to realities of the social and physical environments and the connections between them;
- focusing on capacity building through attention to human resources and social as well as economic capital;
- being concerned with process, including participation, for example seeing the way in which outcomes are achieved as an essential part of ensuring that existing strengths are incorporated and new capacities developed;
- addressing matters of equity, such as questions of gender, ethnicity, centre-periphery and other structural issues that can lead to disadvantage and discrimination.

As Burkett and McDonald (2005), writing in Australia, make clear such an approach within social work is applicable to countries of the global North as well as of the South. Picking up on Midgley's recognition that early Charity Organization Society caseworkers in practice incorporated structural responses as well as interpersonal interventions in their work (and, although not explicitly addressed, we might add that Settlement House workers also addressed interpersonal issues), Birkett and McDonald show that social workers practising in institutional welfare contexts can adopt a social development approach to work that might otherwise be defined as administrative or as a form of social control.

An example of a recent challenge to social work in a country of global North, Australia, is that of rethinking social work explicitly in response to the profession's obligations to Indigenous Australians (Briskman, 2007; Green & Baldry, 2008). A social development approach has much to offer in this process. As Green and Baldry argue, more than two centuries of colonization have seriously damaged an ancient culture and compromised the capacity of communities to address their own developmental needs. Social work has been implicated in these processes, in the form of its role in the removal of children from their families and their country (very often on the grounds of their Aboriginality rather than for what would now be regarded as plausible welfare needs) and in the incarceration in very large numbers of Indigenous young people in today's criminal justice system. In Chapter 3 we looked at the particular needs of Indigenous peoples in countries such as Australia, Canada, New Zealand and the United States of America. The same historical processes can be seen in all of these countries, suggesting that the underlying causes were systemic, that is structural and cultural, rather than arising from the practice of individuals (Weaver, 2002; Blackstock et al., 2004; Briskman, 2007; Green & Baldry, 2008).

As critical commentators in Australia and elsewhere have identified, it is essential for the profession to respond to these needs and to produce new and appropriate ways of working. A social development perspective offers a way of responding to this legacy, not only because it has features that are congruent with Indigenous worldviews but also because in combining macro- and micro-analysis and ways of intervening it would enable social work to be more flexible, more subtle and more responsive in creating appropriate ways of working. Instead of delivering services from a 'mainstream' model, a social development approach suggests that social workers (as well as other professionals and administrators) should listen carefully to Indigenous communities and service users in order to understand the links between culture and ways of resolving problems and seek to work in partnership with Indigenous communities, with the goal of promoting the growth of capacity and community-based self-reliance (Green & Baldry, 2008).

Cox and Pawar (2006) argue that social development is one of four component parts to international social work, together with a global perspective, an ecological perspective and human rights. Healy (2008a) likewise connects social development with human rights and sustainability. This means that even when social work is appropriately concentrating on local issues the context must always be seen in relation to a wider understanding of the causes of and potential resolutions for human need.

Combining the Micro and the Macro: Implications for Professionalization

Although arguments about different ways in which social work can be understood, especially those from the global North, can appear to suggest that it is not possible to talk in an integrated way about micro- and macro-level practices, the social development approach suggests that this is not the case. Moreover, as we noted previously, there has been a tendency in the Northern debates to present one or other of these approaches as that which 'truly' describes social work. The ideological character of this debate has, we might conclude, tended at times to obscure the complexities of social work and the plural possibilities for the way in which social needs can be understood and addressed.

The terms of this debate have also generated the question of whether the goals of social justice and professionalization can coexist (Mendes, 2007; Olson, 2007). The argument is whether social work has lost its 'core' identity. However, on a comparative international basis, it also raises questions about the emphasis in countries of the global South on questions such as 'social harmony' and 'social cohesion', which combines with an explicit interest to see social work develop as a profession in much the same way that it has in countries of the North. Ironically, we have to recognize that the terms of this debate are couched in the value system derived from the European tradition, in which the post-Enlightenment notions of human rights and social justice are understood predominantly in a very individualistic way. Phrases such as 'social harmony' or 'social cohesion' may well be heard by social workers in the global North as invitations to support the status quo against the interests of people who are marginalized or oppressed. However, as we have noted, in countries of the global South traditional ideas of family and community still hold considerable importance as central aspects of a just social order. For social work to operate only with an overly individualistic notion of how these values are to be achieved in such contexts may be both practically counter-productive and also constitute an implicit form of neocolonialism. This does not mean that social workers in Africa, Asia, the Pacific or South America, or indeed Indigenous social workers in Northern countries, fail to hold the same values about the unacceptability of participation in demeaning or harmful practices as to their colleagues elsewhere. What it does mean is that assumptions about what constitutes oppression have to be reconsidered relative to the circumstances of those making the judgement, especially where these involve ways of reconciling individual wishes or interests to those of a group such as the family or a community

(Silavwe, 1995; Yip, 2004; Mafile'o, 2006). These questions will be addressed in greater detail in a deeper discussion of professional values and ethics in Chapter 8.

From this international comparative consideration of how social work might be perceived, we can ask whether it is feasible to define a common core to the profession. However, for such a definition to be seen as relevant it needs to be broad and allow considerable flexibility, so that it makes sense for and achieves the purposes of people in different contexts, while at the same time upholding that which the profession is able to agree is foundational. However, this in turn has implications for the project of professionalization (Mendes, 2007; Olson, 2007). If Olson (2007) is correct and the professionalization of social work has been inextricably tied to the development of highly technical micro-level practices, then a broader and more flexible understanding may indeed compromise this historical project. To put this another way, classic scholarship on the professions has emphasized key traits or characteristics that permit professions to distinguish themselves from each other and to make claims about their boundaries (Freidson, 1994). A broad and flexible view of social work, especially one that incorporates the notion of social development, still leaves us needing to discover what social work is and what other emerging 'social professions' might be (to paraphrase the words of Katherine Kendall, cited in Billups, 2002, p. 163). However, more recent studies of the professions, including in relation to social work (see Hugman, 1991), have emphasized that professionalization is a process in which occupations make claims around particular practices and theories and use these to gain social status and authority. In so far as the definition of social work with which we started this chapter lays claims to notions of social justice, and the associated value of human rights, and then our struggles to professionalize do not address all aspects of the world in which we work and the needs that we seek to address, the project becomes inherently self-defeating. Such a conclusion is uncomfortable, because it means that social work must continue to live with a high degree of ambiguity, as indeed it has now for well over 100 years. However, in pursuing this alternative way of understanding social work, the view of Meher Nanavatty that social work is necessarily 'both counselling and social action' (developed out of many years of experience in promoting a social development perspective in Indian social work) appears to be the strongest position (cited in Billups, 2002, p. 203). Only such an inclusive and plural understanding can provide the required breadth and flexibility of theory and practice.

Implications for International Social Work

Seeing social work in this inclusive and plural way has several implications for international social work, whether this involves social workers practising in countries other than their own, working with service users who have come from other countries, working with international organizations, in professional exchanges or in local practice that responds to internationally generated issues (see Chapter 2). In each of these dimensions it is not possible to rely on 'either/or' thinking about whether we should focus on the micro or the macro, or to put it another way whether social work is about counselling or social action to the exclusion of the other (compare with Cox & Pawar, 2006; Healy, 2008a).

First, this way of seeing (international) social work requires practitioners to be capable of working in ways that are appropriate to context, whether this be at the level of individuals, families, communities or service systems. It suggests that a high degree of specialization in whatever methods or approaches is likely to be less relevant than the capacity to practice flexibly. This is not to argue that there are no situations in which specialized types of work are not required, but rather it points to the need to see such specialism in context rather than as the core defining feature of the profession. It suggests that a generalist approach that is adaptable and responsive is at the heart of international social work.

Second, this in turn has implications for the ways in which social workers are educated for international practice. In addition to sufficient education in theories and methods of direct intervention (including counselling, casework, group work and community work) it is vital that indirect theories and methods are also sufficiently addressed (including social policy, organization and management and research). These questions are addressed in more depth in Chapter 7.

Third, taking an inclusive and plural view of the nature of social work has implications for international debates about values and ethics. As we have noted above, the profession's strongly declared commitment to principles of human rights and social justice raises many questions about the way in which these values may be perceived differently according to cultural and national context. Social workers engaged in international practice therefore need to be capable of addressing these issues and, as we will see in Chapters 8 and 9, of being sufficiently self-conscious concerning their own values and the ways in which these can be reconciled with the values of others without compromising those principles that the profession has widely affirmed.

Fourth, the arguments presented here raise questions about the ways in which international organizations perceive social work and who they might employ to undertake particular tasks (Claiborne, 2004). As we will see in the next chapter, social work can often be seen in terms of particular practices rather than its breadth being recognized. This not only has implications for the opportunities available for individual social workers, but it also suggests that the profession as a whole has a responsibility to reconsider the way in which we are understood by other professionals, administrators and decision-makers, as well as those people who use these services.

This chapter has considered the polarization of claims to define the core nature of social work and has argued, to the contrary, that the lessons of international social work demonstrate the need to think in flexible, inclusive and plural terms. On this basis, the question of whether post-trauma counselling and therapy with refugees, the management of inter-country adoption, poverty alleviation or environmental management programmes are appropriate sites in social work practice should be answered in the affirmative in each instance. An international perspective shows us that social work is all of these things and more.

6

The Organizational Contexts
of International Social Work

International Social Work Organizations

Social work is overwhelmingly an agency-based profession. This is as much the case in the international field as it is in domestic practice. Consequently, to understand international social work it is necessary to examine the agencies and organizations within which social work is practised or which represent the profession of social work at the international level. In this chapter, therefore, we will examine three different types of organizations that are particularly significant for the field.

The first type of organization to be considered is that of service providing INGOs. Social workers are employed in many of these organizations, in varying numbers, and much can be learned by considering the roles and tasks performed by social workers and which organizations they work in relative to which human needs. The second type of organization is the quasi-governmental or inter-governmental domain largely represented by the agencies of the UN, as well as the UN in itself. As we will see, social work has had a long and at times influential relationship with the UN although this has waned over time. The third type of organization to be considered is that of social work's own international professional bodies, the IASSW, the ICSW and the IFSW, along with their regional associated organizations such as the Asia-Pacific Association of Social Work Education (APASWE). These latter organizations have been the site of the practice of international social work (understood in the various ways that have been presented in previous chapters), as well as representing the interests of social workers to governments and to international quasi-governmental and NGOs.

Not only will this chapter examine the types of international organizations in which social work is located and the forms of practice within them it will also consider the way in which these organizations shape the profession internationally. It is not intended to provide a detailed history of these organizations and the role of social work within them as this is already available in Lynne Healy's (2008a) extensive study (to which the interested reader should turn for such an account) but rather to focus on recent issues and contemporary debates.

International Non-government Organizations

International service-providing organizations can provide an opportunity for social workers to practice 'in another country' (Lyons et al., 2006, p. 193), although they also include working with service users form other countries and partnerships between countries. They range from those that provide micro-level interventions, such as ISS, which was discussed in Chapter 2, to those engaged in social development, research, policy and advocacy, such as Oxfam. Other organizations may have a broad range of types of interventions, such as Save the Children or International Red Cross, whose programmes include micro- and macro-levels of intervention as well as various combinations. Yet the relationship of social work with the INGO sector is problematic.

Taken as a whole, there is a predominant focus in INGOs on social development or humanitarian or related types of action, compared to what might be understood as 'clinical' practice as this would be seen in the context of the global North. This has, at least in recent decades, had an impact on the location of social work within such organizations. Studies of social work have paid very little attention to the relationship between the INGOs and social work, which may reflect both the level of interest many social workers have in such work and the lack of attention to social work as a potential source of knowledge and skill within such organizations. One detailed survey of social workers in INGOs has been undertaken by Claiborne (2004), based on 20 organizations[1]. This study identified that there were 37 per cent of the total workforce surveyed who held social work qualifications (16,616 out of 44,608 full-time equivalent), although 'most' (exact figure not stated) worked in just four of the organizations. Of these social workers, 97 per cent were employed as 'program directors' and a further 2.5 per cent in 'direct services' (with the remaining 0.5 per cent divided between management, 'country director', 'development' and 'consultant' positions) (for full figures, see Claiborne, 2004, pp. 210–12).

---

[1] Fifty-seven organizations were invited to respond, selected from those registered with the UN. The response rate may indicate a lack of regard for the importance of this topic by the organizations, or it may also reflect the limited resources of many INGOs. Of the 57, all but three were headquartered in the United States, and Claiborne does not indicate whether any of the responses were actually from parts of the world other than the United States.

Claiborne raises two particular concerns from these data. First, almost all the social workers in this sample were employed in 'program director' roles (and mostly by four large INGOs). This, she argues, suggests that the potential for social work to contribute in other areas is being missed. Such a conclusion leads to the question of why social workers are not employed in direct service, management, development and consulting roles in greater numbers (Claiborne, 2004, p. 213). Second, six of the INGOs stated that social work was not appropriate for their focus, although their goals variously included leadership development, human rights, education, community development and hunger and poverty alleviation. Yet those who did employ social workers actually had very similar objectives. So, Claiborne concludes that these INGOs had a perception of social workers as skilled in counselling or grassroots activism but not in more macro-level work. Given evidence from other not-for-profit organizations, where social workers 'commonly hold administrative and development positions' (loc. cit.) this seemed surprising (compare with McDonald, 2000).

However, this set of perceptions may not be so remarkable if we consider that the predominance of 'clinical' and 'remedial' approaches (which may not necessarily be the same thing) has increased rather than decreased in the last 50 years, especially in the global North (see Chapter 5). If social work is regarded as overwhelmingly concerned with counselling, casework, child protection investigations and so on, and INGOs are defining their objectives in terms of humanitarian work focused on macro-level interventions, then a view that social work is not an appropriate professional base from which to engage in such practices might be quite plausible. The other important factor here is that although many INGOs undertake action that social workers may claim as 'social work', they are often led by non-social work qualified people (whether they are qualified in other professions or not). Not only were many of the pioneers of social work themselves not social work qualified as it is now understood (but included lawyers, medical doctors, nurses, teachers and so on – see Healy, 2008a), but the boundaries of social work have also continued to be especially blurred in these fields of practice.

In order to examine how these points affect the visibility of social work, in early 2009 an informal survey was undertaken of vacant positions listed on the websites of four major INGOs (Save the Children, ICRC, CARE International and Oxfam) and volunteers needed (for Medecins Sans Frontières [MSF]). These organizations were selected because I am aware of social workers employed by them (or volunteering for MSF) (personal communications). No examples of any position that *specifically* required social work qualifications were found, from information about positions in disaster relief, work with survivors of conflicts, various programmes with refugees, community development and poverty alleviation, and disease management and prevention. All these job descriptions used generic terms such as 'a degree in a relevant field' or 'relevant knowledge and experience' to define criteria for positions that would be relevant for social workers (i.e., specifically excluding those that demand medical or nursing qualifications, engineering or similar, languages and translation, or finance and business). MSF also provides a list of specified professions from which it seeks to recruit volunteers that does not include social work, although they have social workers volunteering with them. Other than this, an emphasis on applicants demonstrating capacities to undertake tasks or roles that are independent of any one recognized profession is common across all the agencies. Nevertheless, of these five organizations, only Oxfam did not have links on its website to pages indicating that social workers are employed (or volunteering in MSF); the other four all clearly appeared to have social workers engaged in various roles in different parts of the world. For MSF, some of these are professionally qualified as this would be regarded by the international social work professional organizations and were working internationally (as defined in Chapter 2), while others were locally recruited workers with very short on-site practical training, in a role that in some places might be termed 'barefoot social worker' (see discussion of UNICEF Vietnam below). (The tasks undertaken by the latter group include those that would be done by university trained social workers in many countries, such as counselling or administrating social assistance, but in other cases appear to include domestic work such as cooking and cleaning that in different contexts would be understood as an 'aide' or 'assistant' role.) We might conclude, therefore, that a lot depends on how different professions are perceived or whether they are categorized separately in such roles (compare with Welbourne & Weiss, 2007). So we might agree with Claiborne (2004) that others do not always regard social work in the same way that members of the profession see ourselves.

At the same time, as noted in the previous chapter, we also need to remember that we disagree among ourselves about the nature of social work, its objectives and the roles that it should play, as well as the theories and methods we should use in pursuing these. So we must also ask whether Claiborne's (2004) findings are affected by the emphasis on particular types of practices by the profession as whole and, following this, the choices made by individual social workers themselves. In other words, how do we perceive our own skills and knowledge in the international arena, what do social workers actually want to do and are social workers being turned away from such positions as opposed to not seeking them? Lyons (1999), Lyons et al. (2006) and Healy (2008a) all cast doubt on whether large numbers of social workers actually choose to work in such organizations. So, in so far as social workers are not seen as appropriately engaged in or adequately trained for the types of work that INGOs undertake, then this may be a product of the way in which social workers (individually and collectively) present ourselves, at least as much as the way in which decision makers select or reject social work for particular roles[2]. This points to the conclusion that social work as a profession world-wide often fails to recognize the role that it could play in such work. In turn, such a failure is influenced by and influences curricula in professional education, choices made by entrants to the profession and so on.

Another way in which international social work plays a role in NGOs is through the support that may be given to such organizations at the national or local level by international donors. One example of this is described in a study of a particular NGO in the development of the 'third sector' in Croatia after independence from the former Yugoslavia (Despotovic et al., 2007). Following the rapid upheavals of the 1990s, expectations of government provision of social welfare in that country gradually have changed sufficiently to accept the emergence of a civil society sector (p. 176). INGOs have played an enormous role in these changes, including as funders and as providers of expertise. This in turn has promoted the growth of 'intermediate' NGO support organizations that are themselves NGOs. Despotovic et al. (2007) examine the work of one of these, the Centre for Civil Initiatives (CCI) based in Zagreb but working throughout the country. Initial input came from a psychologist, a social worker and a teacher (p. 183). The focus of the organization has been on assisting local NGOs to organize and to obtain funds and access to expertise for specific projects that include restoring a bridge in the centre of a town, building a new medical clinic, advocating for residents' civil rights so they could access health services, promoting rural economic development and supporting 'citizen's advisory councils'. Despotovic et al. conclude that while interdisciplinarity has been a key to the success of the CCI, the underlying approach is that of social work (2007, pp. 186–8). This has been recognized in the location of relevant professional training in the social work faculty at the University of Zagreb.

The way in which social work has been a major influence in this example parallels the role that the profession plays in the 'third sector' in some other countries and it accords with the ethos of the INGOs that have supported the development of the CCI (compare, e.g., with McDonald, 2000). Social work in Croatia has also been influenced by international links and exchanges, so that the community development model that is demonstrated in the CCI has connections with this approach to social work in many other places.

---

[2] It is also plausible to read Claiborne's figures (2004, p. 212) as suggesting that 79 per cent of the positions in the INGOs she surveyed that can be regarded either as social work roles or as appropriately including social work in the pool of potential recruits actually were occupied by qualified social workers (i.e., 16,616 employed out of a total of 20,993 such positions). However, given that we have already noted that almost all of these were employed in just four organizations, these findings suggest that tangible links between social work and this field are patchy at best. Data from other parts of the world might help to expand our understanding of this point but as yet this appears not to be available.

The United Nations and its Agencies

Social work played a strong role in the emergence of the UN in the 1940s and its subsequent development (Healy, 2008a, 2008b). Following the global conflict of the early 1940s the initial work of the UN was through the UN Relief and Rehabilitation Administration (UNRRA) in which many social workers, particularly from the United States, played leading roles. As the UN continued to grow social workers have also been involved in the development of UNICEF, the UNDP, the UNFPA (United Nations Fund for Population Activities), the UNHCR, the WHO and the World Food Program. Each of these agencies has a major role in the promotion of human development as well as in the coordination of humanitarian and relief work in response to particular situations. All of these agencies come under the umbrella of the ECOSOC which reports to the General Assembly.

Again, readers interested in the history of these organizations should consult Healy's (2008a) detailed study. For the purposes of this discussion, we will focus particularly on UNICEF and UNHCR. The work of UNICEF promotes human development through a concern with the well-being of children and young people. While its approach as an organization may be described as holistic, it particularly seeks to support the development of primary health care, clean water, education, nutrition and social services. All of these activities are conducted within the framework of the *Convention on the Rights of the Child* (CRC), which was adopted by the General Assembly in 1989 (UN, 1989).

As with other UN organizations, UNICEF works predominantly in partnership with national governments and national NGOs. Its various programmes include a focus on the development of policy and services as well as direct provision. UNICEF focuses on the needs of children affected by war and conflict, various forms of exploitation of children including in hazardous work and in sex work (including those who are trafficked), children with disabilities, children living in extreme poverty and those whose families are affected by HIV/AIDS (Cox & Pawar, 2006). As Healy puts it (2008a, p. 109) the focus of UNICEF on 'child protection', understood broadly, is of particular interest for social workers. Examples of UNICEF's programmes include post-conflict trauma recovery projects in countries of Africa and Asia, projects to assist children orphaned by HIV/AIDS in several countries of eastern and southern Africa, rehabilitation projects for children who have been trafficked from countries of Asia and Africa, children living on the streets of cities in South America, Africa and Asia, and a programme to promote access to primary health care among Aboriginal children in northern Australia. It should be noted that UNICEF tends to operate in the global South and in this context the meaning of child protection is more extensive than it has become in countries of the North. However, it also does include attention to the harm or neglect of children within domestic situations that parallels Northern concerns (UNICEF Vietnam, personal communication).

Through these various programmes UNICEF has also played a significant role in the promotion of social work as a profession (Hall & Midgley, 2004, p. 214). Hall and Midgley comment that the social development approach in social work is particularly relevant in this context, but at the same time it should be noted that UNICEF has also sought to promote psychosocial interventions in social work, for example in the way in which the care of children living on the streets, those orphaned by HIV/AIDS and those who have been trafficked involves counselling and other micro-level responses as well as the provision of effective social services and the development of relevant government policies. One example of this integrated approach has been the work of the child protection section of UNICEF Vietnam to develop 'barefoot social workers' in remote areas (UNICEF Vietnam/MOLISA, 2005). In this project, members of local communities (all women) have been recruited and given short-course training in basic social work concepts and methods. They are then employed on a part-time basis to provide advice and counselling to families in their local communities who are experiencing difficulties in relation to the care of children. In addition, these workers may provide direct assistance, for example in taking care of a child in order to give a mother with mental health problems some respite, or providing advice and psychosocial support as well as links to formal services for a family where the father has just been diagnosed with HIV. From the evidence of these demonstration projects, the Vietnam government has been encouraged to engage more rapidly with the official recognition of social work at a profession (UNICEF Vietnam/MOLISA, 2005; Hugman et al., 2007).

Turning to the work of the UNHCR, we can note the involvement of social work at varying levels. In direct work with refugees, forced migrants and asylum seekers, social workers are represented among the fieldworkers of the organization (Cox & Pawar, 2006, p. 282). Whether living in large camps, as many refugees and forced migrants have to do, or in situations of resettlement, what is often needed is a combination of psychosocial and practical assistance (see discussion in Chapter 3 above). As Cox and Pawar note, social workers and others in these roles seek to:

> humanise conditions, developing as far as possible sense of community, facilitating a range of social and recreational activities, introducing health and education services, and providing psychosocial programmes, as well as assisting in the running of such centres in ways that are not deleterious to well-being while consistent with other accepted objectives of the centres (p. 284).

The staff of UNHCR are also involved in repatriation. This may be voluntary and organized, in which UNHCR staff assist refugees in returning to their countries of origin with some resources and initial assistance for resettlement being provided. Sometimes refugees may also independently return to their home countries of their own volition, and there may even be situations in which repatriation occurs under duress due to circumstances in the country of asylum. In these situations it is much more difficult for UNHCR staff to provide assistance. Especially when refugees have been absent from their home country for extended periods of time, further development work is actually needed if those returning to be reintegrated and reconciled in their own countries.

Cox and Pawar also point to the process of local integration (2006, p. 285). As the majority of refugees and asylum seekers live in countries close to their country of origin to there may well be strong cultural ties with the local communities. However, Cox and Pawar note that social work seems to have had little involvement in this type of response.

At a different level, the example of the work of the Centre for Refugee Research based in the social work programme at the University of New South Wales in Australia that was discussed in Chapter 3 demonstrates ways in which social workers can be involved in research and policy development. Using a sustained series of action research projects focused on the specific needs of women and girls at risk in refugee situations, the Centre for Refugee Research has been able to provide policy advice to the UNHCR headquarters in Geneva (Pittaway & Bartolomei, 2005). This is also an area in which other professions are closely involved, especially lawyers specializing in human rights. The particular contribution of social work has been in the capacity to integrate direct experience in the field, based on a methodology that provides a voice for refugee women themselves, and assisting refugee women to make representations about their own situations.

Of particular concern to those who have worked with or studied the needs of refugee women is the almost ubiquitous phenomenon of rape (Pittaway & Pittaway, 2004). Not only is rape used as a weapon in conflict, in which the objective is to denigrate, shame and terrorize those who are attacked, but there is also much evidence that women continue to be at risk in contexts such as refugee camps. It is even the case that in many situations such acts are perpetrated by other refugees or by people exercising authority such as camp guards and administrators (Cox & Pawar, 2006, p. 308; Pittaway et al., 2007). In these circumstances social workers can make representations about the truth of the situation within the policy and decision-making levels of the UNHCR, as the example of the Centre for Refugee Research demonstrates.

Just two examples of the UN agencies have been used in this discussion, focusing on specific areas of practice. However, it is also necessary to note that social work as a profession has both had an historic role in the development of the UN as a whole and continues to play a role through the recognition of the key international organizations as having 'consultative status'. This is a mechanism whereby the UN accredits NGOs to participate in its work. 'General Category' consultative status gives an organization the authority to attend ECOSOC meetings, to communicate with members and to address committee meetings. Of the international social work organizations only the ICSW holds the 'General Category' consultative status, which is regarded as the highest level because it enables an organization to be involved in most or all aspects of ECOSOC's work (see, e.g., Healy, 2008a, p. 183). Since their founding the other organizations (IASSW and IFSW) have held 'Special Category' status that recognizes their capacity to engage in selected areas of ECOSOC. This difference in level of recognition enables ICSW to represent a range of INGOs in the field of social welfare. At the same time, it points to the fact that the Council has an identity broader than that of social work as a profession, which suggests that the IFSW and IASSW are regarded as having specialized or sectional points of view in the way identified in the discussion above about social workers employment in INGOs. Given the close involvement of many of the founders of the social work organizations in the development of the UN this may seem somewhat ironic. However, it is also a reflection of the path to professionalization taken by social work in many parts of the world (Welbourne & Weiss, 2007); that is, social workers have struggled to create organizations or services that then come to be defined in terms of another profession or service area (such as health and medical services, legal services, government administration and so on).

Nevertheless, social work professional organizations can make a variety of contributions to the business of the UN. Between them, the IASSW and IFSW have representation in many relevant areas, including migration, refugees, ageing, children, human rights, education, the status of women, mental health, Indigenous peoples, peace, social development and also the environment. In some cases both organizations have representation, in others it is only one. For example, in May 2007 a delegation was convened by IFSW to address the Permanent Forum on Indigenous Issues sub-committee undertaking work for the draft of the document which was accepted later in the year as the *Declaration on the Rights of Indigenous Peoples* (UN, 2008b). This delegation comprised social workers from different parts of the world, including countries of the global South and North, most of whom were Indigenous people of their own countries. The presentation addressed the connections between culture and identity, land and active participation in social development. In this way social workers were able to provide input to the process that combined personal experience with knowledge derived from practice and research.

As with the point about the presence of social workers in INGOs, in considering the presence of social workers in the UN and its agencies we need to ask if there is an issue about involvement and commitment or whether the question actually relates to one of identity and visibility. It is more relevant to look at the contributions that social work can make and how these might be achieved then to focus on whether the profession as such is recognized in formal ways. Of course, it may be entirely appropriate to be concerned if voices are explicitly excluded *because* they are those of social workers, but given the evidence of participation by social work across the UN sector this appears not to be the case in practice. As with INGOs, discussed above, there appears to be a combination of social workers not recognizing this as a field of practice and of others not recognizing the potential of social work to contribute. So, on this basis, we should direct our attention to ensuring that social workers continue to be involved in positive ways in these sectors.

We also need to consider what would constitute a 'positive' contribution to the UN sector. Although the work of the UN and its constituent organizations can be seen as promoting development, peace and so on (indeed, these are stated as explicit goals), there is also criticism that the sector pursues the interests and values of the global North. For example, the Universal Declaration on Human Rights, while being widely supported is also criticized from some parts of the world as being a reflection of cultural values specific to the global North (Gasper, 2006; Giri, 2006). It has even been suggested that the UN can be a violator of human rights, for example through peace-keeping interventions and the way in which it selects those issues in which it will intervene (Mégret & Hoffman, 2003). (The implications of this type of criticism for social work ethics and values will be pursued in Chapter 8). Aid and humanitarian programmes, such as those of UNDP, UNICEF and the World Food Program, are also regarded by some critics as being driven by the interests of the powerful, rich countries (Hattori, 2003). At its worst, this type of relationship can be seen as a vehicle for donor countries to force their ways of dealing with issues onto disadvantaged countries for whom there is little choice (Cammack, 2002).

Given these criticisms, we must ask whether there is actually scope for social work to play a role in the UN system. The examples cited above, of social work researchers engaging with UNHCR to seek to support the empowerment of refugee women, of social workers in UNICEF promoting better social welfare for children in a country in transition or of social workers from around the world participating in the formation of the Declaration on the Rights of Indigenous People, point to positive possibilities. However, at the same time, criticism of the UN system as neo-colonial indicates the need for a critical awareness and appropriate approaches by international social workers. It is the ideas and values that support this which form the basis of the discussion in the following chapters.

The International Professional Organizations

So far in this analysis reference has been made many times to the IASSW, the ICSW and the IFSW as the international professional organizations of social work. As such, they provide vehicles for social workers to engage in debate and to work together between different countries to develop the profession. As well as separate and conjoint conferences they also collectively auspice the journal *International Social Work*. However, as Lyons (1999), Cox and Pawar (2006) and Healy (2008a) all note, these organizations also constitute the basis for international social work practice understood in the other ways that were defined in Chapter 2. So to analyse the contribution of these organizations to international social work we need to consider both aspects.

It is significant to note that although these three organizations now have separate identities, and may even be perceived as pursuing differing agendas, they actually have grown from the same set of actions by founding social workers in the early part of the twentieth century (Healy, 2008a, 2008b). The pivotal moment was the First International Conference of Social Work, held in Paris in 1928. The Second International Conference took place in Frankfurt in 1932, followed by the Third in London in 1936 (Healy, 2008b, p. 4). However, as Healy also notes, the most active area associated with these conferences was the Committee of Schools of Social Work, which initially brought together 46 members from a total of 10 different countries, which grew by 1939 to 75 members from 18 countries (loc. cit.). This became the IASSW in 1954 and now includes members from all continents and regions. Membership is predominantly that of schools (536 at the end of 2008), although individuals can also become members. In Chapter 1 the origins of social work as a profession were dated by the initial establishment of education and training programmes in higher education institutions. As historians of social work internationally have identified, the impetus for professionalization has frequently been led by such the elements in the educational field (Parry & Parry, 1979; Midgley, 1981; Healy, 2008a).

The First International Conference of Social Work also saw the establishment of the Permanent Secretariat of Social Workers (Healy, 2008a, p. 177). After a hiatus during the 1940s, the Secretariat was revived during the 1950s and subsequently became the IFSW. Whereas the IASSW focuses on social work education and training, the IFSW concentrates on the promotion internationally of social work practice. As does the IASSW, the IFSW both addresses issues internal to the development of social work by promoting dialogue and interaction between countries and at the same time provides a means by which social work can have a voice internationally in social welfare planning and policy development. The IFSW can also represent the wider community of social work in dialogue with national governments. An example of this work is the Human Rights Commission that was established in 1988. In addition to a Commissioner who is a member of the overall board, there are also similar positions in each of the regions and, in addition, there is a formal link with the organization Amnesty International. This role in particular has provided a strong basis for the Federation to engage with the work of various bodies of the UN. At one stage both the IASSW and the IFSW had paid positions of General Secretary. In the early 1990s, however, financial support from the government of Austria was withdrawn and due to increasing costs the IASSW was forced to close its office in Vienna (Healy, 2008b, p. 14). IFSW continues to maintain the position of General Secretary in Berne, Switzerland, which enhances its capacity to co-ordinate the involvement of member or affiliate associations from 90 countries (as at the end of 2008). Only representative professional associations, normally one per country, are recognized as members, although individuals can also identify with the work of the Federation by joining the 'Friends of IFSW'.

The third organization to grow from the First International Conference of Social Work was that of the International Conference on Social Work. The shift of name (with the same initials) to the International Council on Social Welfare in 1966 was highly significant. Whereas in its original form it was concerned with social work, it grew broader from the original scope of understanding of social work so that it now is characterized by a focus on social development and social welfare policy while the other two organizations became more narrowly concentrated on issues of increasing professionalization. Membership of the ICSW is now largely comprised of major national social welfare peak bodies as well as some practice agencies such as International Social Service and the International Organization for Migration. The ICSW is also supported by the permanent office of General Secretary, based in Utrecht, The Netherlands, in the offices of the Netherlands Centre for Social Development; it also maintains an office in Kampala, Uganda.

A fourth organization must also be noted, that of the International Consortium on Social Development (ICSD). Originally called the Inter-University Consortium for International Social Development, it was founded in the 1970s by social work educators. It now aims to advance the field of social development through interdisciplinary study and action by bringing together academics and practitioners from any discipline concerned with social development. ICSD has close links also with the other three organizations and, like them, participates in the UN in various ways although as at the end of 2008 it did not hold representative status in ECOSOC. Membership is comprised of both educational institutions and individuals and the membership of the Consortium remains overwhelmingly North American, with office holders drawn very largely from social work in Canada and the Untied States (with some notable exceptions). Major areas of work include biennial conferences and a scholarly journal, *Social Development Issues*.

Some aspects of the practice of these international organizations have already been identified above, for example in relation to human rights, Indigenous peoples, the promotion of social work as a profession and so on, especially as these have impacted on the development of the UN and its agencies. In each case we can say that these organizations provide both an organizational basis and a legitimation for social workers to be involved in these types of practices at an international level. Another example, highlighted by Healy (2008a, p. 184) is that of the involvement of the ICSW in the debates at the UN in the mid-1990s regarding social development. These debates culminated in the Social Development Summit of 1995. The ICSW played a pivotal role in organizing NGOs, developing data and briefing organizations, disseminating material from debates on policy proposals and ensuring that NGOs were able to participate. (Documents on this activity can be found at the ICSW website located at http://www.icsw.org.) Following the shift of emphasis at the UN to the MDGs (see discussion in Chapter 4) the ICSW has maintained a highly critical position with regard to the much more restricted understanding of poverty that these goals contain (Correll, 2008).

The international social work organizations are not themselves immune from criticism. That they have succeeded in providing a strong voice for different facets of social work (however broadly or narrowly defined) in international forums and succeeded in bringing together social workers from all parts of the world in dialogue is not in doubt. However, in recent decades a more explicit debate has emerged about the extent to which it is actually either possible or desirable to create 'single' voices in this way (see, e.g., Gray & Fook, 2004). In so far as social work necessarily addresses the needs of people in their social environments, this argument points to the necessity of being able to ground theories and practices in the realities of each different situation. In other words, how we understand the nature of social problems and how we construct the most appropriate ways to intervene and assist people will be affected by the cultural and national contexts of those practices. In particular, the work of the IASSW and IFSW together in developing global concepts around social work education and the ethics and values of professional social work have been quite contentious. Each of these particular areas is of crucial importance to the historical professionalization of social work and also to our understanding of social work as a whole; therefore each will form the basis for discussion in the following two chapters.

Another aspect of this particular criticism is evident when we consider who actually has exercised leadership in social work as it has professionalized and internationalized over the last century. As we have acknowledged elsewhere in this book, professional social work has its origins in the countries of the global North. Nevertheless, as other parts of the world have increasingly become involved in these professional structures it can be observed that the leadership has tended to remain in the North, especially in North America and Northern Europe (including Scandinavia). Although the membership of the boards or committees of management of each organization are comprised of representatives from each region, the presidencies of both IFSW and ICSW remain in the North, as do the roles of General Secretary. In 2004 the IASSW elected its first president from the South, Professor Abye Tasse from Ethiopia; then in 2008 Professor Angie Yuen from Hong Kong succeeded him. As Lyons (2008, p. 205) has noted:

> one of the greatest achievements in this period has been in shifting internal and external perceptions of 'who can lead': [Tasse] has demonstrated that 'people other than white Europeans' have the experience, skills and expertise to 'manage' a major professional association [...] and to represent the interests and mission of social workers globally to others inside and outside social work education.

It may be that the previous presidency of Professor Lena Dominelli, from the United Kingdom, opened up the possibility of this change (Lyons, 2008, p. 202), as Dominelli is a leading social work scholar and practitioner who has addressed issues of anti-racism and anti-discrimination widely in her work (see, e.g., Dominelli, 2007, 2008). In many ways this development can be seen as setting a challenge to IFSW and ICSW also to think broadly about sources of future leadership.

Locating Social Work in Organizations

Another issue that is raised by the different foci of these three organizations goes to the heart of the identity and character of social work (see discussion in the previous chapter). The divergence of the ICSW from a specifically 'social work' identity recognized that the field of social welfare (also variously referred to in particular countries as 'human services' or 'social services') is wider than one profession. In the national and local organizations that employ social workers, as well as the INGOs and the UN agencies discussed in this chapter, social work practice is overwhelmingly found in multi-disciplinary settings (see, e.g., Payne, 2000; McDonald, 2006; Hughes & Wearing, 2008). Of course, the same must be said for all other professions, including medicine, nursing and allied health, lawyers, teachers and so on. The main difference is that in health services and hospitals, courts and other legal institutions, or schools, colleges and universities, it is usually the case that particular professions predominate. In this sense, social work is almost uniquely characterized by having relatively ill-defined, permeable (and even 'fuzzy') boundaries. This is reflected in the extremely wide variation between countries regarding the right to title of social work and, consequently, whether there is formal state recognition such as registration, licensing or some other statutory regulatory mechanism that defines what social work is and who may practise it (Barnes and Hugman, 2002).

Because of this distinctive feature of social work, the successes of international practitioners and organizations have largely been as a consequence of the vision, determination and capacities of particular individuals and groups. However, history is not simply the actions of individuals. It is also the case that particular world events and the course of development of particular national societies provided the basis on which such actions could take place. Indeed, it might be observed that one of the talents of the early social workers in the Charity Organization Societies and in the Settlement Houses, as well as those who created the international social work organizations, was that they sought to apply knowledge and values gained from their social work experience in situations where the profession did not have a ready-made mandate. There may be a paradox in asking whether the successes in professionalizing social work, especially in the global North, have actually resulted in it now being seen as having a more restricted potential, in addition to the fact that as the INGOs and the UN agencies have expanded, they have tended also to seek particular expertise in a wide range of other professions. For these reasons, the particular pattern of representation of social work in the INGOs studied by Claiborne (2004) or the different understandings of social work evident on the web pages of Medecins Sans Frontières are entirely explicable. The question that this observation poses is whether by continued debate social work will resolve such matters so that we are able to provide a single clear definition to others of 'who we are and what we can do' or whether the strength of social work lies in its diversity and its capacity to employ this in making use of opportunities, even of creating them.

This is not to argue that the pursuit by professional organizations of objectives that benefit the profession is necessarily inappropriate. What matters is whether these are the primary or even the only concerns. We ought to be able to say unequivocally that those who seek to (re)establish a role for social work in INGOs, UN agencies or to engage in the international professional bodies do so with the explicit goal of furthering the aims of the social work as a whole and addressing issues of human rights and social justice. Such claims, first and foremost, relate to meeting human need. In that sense, all these actions ought to be an expression of the same objectives as seen in any other aspect of social work. What is at issue is the way in which these objectives are pursued, the ideas held about human need and how it may be addressed and whether or not social work lives up to its own values in these actions. In particular, in different ways it has been noted that these different types of organizations are not necessarily, or not always, benign. Most have their headquarters in the global North and their actions and organizational structures often reflect this. Both the goals that they pursue and the way that they pursue them can reflect Northern perspectives and interests. Of course, they can also be involved in working hard towards positive, humanitarian outcomes. Just as there are aspects of which we must be critical there are also aspects of the organizations that reflect the core claimed values of human rights and social justice. The point is that these aspects must be recognized, at least, as contradictory in the sense that both exist in the same structures and practices. This creates challenges and choices for social workers that we need to ensure are made more explicit and debated more widely within the profession internationally.

The questions that have been identified in this chapter follow from those discussed previously, in that they concern the identity of social work and how the profession might continue to have debates internally concerning these things while at the same time relating to other professions and being involved in various types of organizations. The practices of social work that have been identified in this chapter, including humanitarian aid and relief, human rights, social development and so on, characterize the positive goals of international social work in these various organizations. That these organizations are as yet still grappling with questions such as the legacy of the colonial era, cultural diversity and so on points to the need for continued analysis, debate and action. In the following two chapters we will address particular instances of current concerns, namely social work education and social work values and ethics before proceeding to revisit Midgley's (1981) charge of 'professional imperialism'.

7

International Perspectives on Social Work Education and Training

The 'Global Standards'

In 2004 the IASSW and the IFSW together approved a document to establish global standards for education and training in the profession (Sewpaul & Jones, 2004). The process of producing the global standards (as the document quickly came to be known) was through a joint committee of the two organizations, with representation from each of the regional groupings within both. This document was intended to identify common features in social work education around the world, and to make these available as guidelines that will facilitate the further development of appropriate national standards (Sewpaul & Jones, 2004, p. 503). Sewpaul and Jones note that the possibility of identifying any universal position on this aspect of the profession was contested. As we will see, the eventual document itself and the process have continued to be criticized from several different standpoints.

The purposes for the development of the global standards can be summarized as: the protection of service users; the facilitation of relationships between universities and colleges around the world, and of the movement of social workers between different countries; to draw a distinction between social workers and other social professions; to facilitate the development of social work education, and to give the international organizations the basis for supporting schools of social work in different countries (Sewpaul & Jones, 2004, p. 503). Surprisingly, the people who chaired this process themselves questioned the feasibility of some of these objectives, such as drawing a clear distinction between social workers and other social professions. They also acknowledge the contentious nature of most of the other objectives. Nevertheless, they argue that the creation of these standards can form the beginning of an international dialogue that may lead to some of these objectives being fulfilled (p. 504).

The global standards consist of nine key sections, which specify standards regarding:

1. schools' core purpose or mission statements;
2. programme objectives and outcomes;
3. programme curricula including fieldwork;
4. core curricula (including material relating to the social contexts of practice, the skills of the practitioner, methods of practice and paradigms of a professional orientation);
5. professional staff (including the nature of qualifications possessed by those teaching in programmes);
6. social work students (including admission, retention and examination);
7. structure, administration, governance and resources;
8. cultural and ethnic diversity and gender inclusiveness;
9. social work values and ethical codes of conduct.

Each of these sections then goes into great detail concerning the way in which schools of social work should seek to provide social work education and training. (The term 'school' is used here to include whatever is the organizational unit within a given educational institution, such as 'faculty', 'school', 'department' or 'programme'.) In producing the detailed standards the committee was concerned to avoid the fragmentation or trivialization of social work skills and knowledge (compare with Lorenz, 2008, p. 19). Moreover, the idea of defining the standards as 'minimum' was rejected on the grounds that this might inadvertently also make them 'maximum' and that social work schools in disadvantaged locations might be jeopardized as a consequence (Sewpaul & Jones, 2004, p. 505). Against possible criticisms that these standards would constitute the hegemony of the global North attention was paid to the composition of the committee to seek to be regionally inclusive, as well as attempting to word each standard to allow for flexibility that would facilitate responsiveness to national and cultural contexts (pp. 506–7).

Healy (2008a, p. 177) regards the global standards as 'a major step forward in defining quality social work education'. Her discussion suggests that it might be seen as a means by which the struggles in regions such as Africa, Asia, the Caribbean and Eastern Europe could be strengthened and the goals of human rights, social justice and social development be achieved more effectively. This, Healy considers, will enable social work to 'rightly claim to be a global profession' and to be able to focus on 'efforts to strengthen its role in international action as a force for human social change and development' (2008a, p. 357). From this, social work should be better equipped to address the issues and problems that have been discussed in Chapters 3 and 4, including making a contribution to tackling the deficiencies of the MDGs and in meeting the targets they set.

In a similar vein, Noble (2004, pp. 528–9) cautiously argues that the debate about global standards has the potential to promote stronger links, dialogue and exchanges while at the same time challenging the hegemony of the global North by opening up attention to a variety of cultural perspectives and historical relationships between countries and regions. Moreover, globalization in social work education may force social workers to theorize the profession in ways that look outside national borders and established assumptions. In short, there are ways of seeing this aspect of the globalization of social work, through education and training, as having many positive dimensions.

Against the Global Standards

There is, however, another perspective on the idea of a global vision for social work education. Despite the conscious attention of those involved in the debates to the risk of simply reasserting global Northern perspectives, there has been a considerable questioning and criticism of both the process and the document on precisely these grounds. As Noble comments, despite the positive aspects of the internationalized perspective that could be developed within the 'global standards' approach, countries such as Papua New Guinea and many Pacific Islands have developed social work education in a more vocational way compared to most other countries, with non-university programmes 'preparing students to work in government community development [...] and NGOs' (2004, p. 530). Noble's review of several countries (The Philippines, Hong Kong and China, Sri Lanka, India and Korea) noted concerns about whether the 'global standards' would have a negative impact on countries where social work is new, where it has developed in different ways and where financial restraints present concrete barriers to meeting the standards for administration, staffing, governance and so on (p. 531). In many countries of the global South social work educators face low salaries and problems with inadequate infrastructure, including buildings, books, computers and Internet access and so on, all of which are taken for granted by Northern colleagues.

Questions and criticisms can be divided broadly into two distinct types. First, there are those who are concerned about the specific ideas that are contained in the global standards document. Second, beyond this there are also those who challenge the very idea that the universal perspective on social work education and training is either possible or desirable. We will examine these positions in turn.

Against Specific Ideas

A very clear criticism of the detail of the global standards document has been made by Yip (2004). Explicitly identifying his position as that of traditional Chinese culture, Yip asserts that many parts of the document emphasize the value system of the global North and, consequently, what follows in relation to the nature of social work and how it may be learned and taught is couched in these terms. Although Yip addresses the global standards, much of his criticism actually concerns the ethics and values of social work and so will be addressed in more detail in the following chapter. However, in relation to the global standards we can note that this criticism primarily concerns the value of human rights and the way that this is treated as an overarching principle. This can be demonstrated, for example, in one of the standards regarding the social context of social work within the core curricula. This stipulates that curricula should aspire to promote:

> [a] critical understanding of how social stability, harmony, mutual respect and collective solidarity impact human functioning and development at all levels, including the global, insofar as that stability, harmony and solidarity are not used to maintain the status quo with regard to infringement of human rights (Sewpaul & Jones, 2004, p. 498).

For Yip, the phrase 'insofar' effectively functions to negate Chinese, and other Asian and global Southern value systems, by subordinating them to what he regards as the culturally relative values of the global North. The alternative that Yip proposes is that we should seek an integrated understanding of social work, and therefore of social work education and ethics, that values Afrocentric and Asiacentric cultural positions along with the Eurocentric (2004, p. 600). In turn, this might then lead to a sharing of ideas based on greater cultural exchange (p. 610).

Against the Very Idea

There have also been a number of critiques of the global standards that question whether such a document is valid at all. For example, Payne and Askeland make the comment that 'what is valued academically, epistemologically and ontologically varies between countries and cultures' (2008, p. 60). Consequently, they question whether attempts to create standards contain the inference that any differences imply poor quality rather than other perspectives. Payne and Askeland therefore regard the global standards as 'too prescriptive and detailed to permit the kind of cultural flexibility' that they argue is necessary for social work to develop appropriately in different contexts (2006, p. 80).

In a more sustained critique Gray and Fook (2004) and Gray (2005) ask why there has been such a strong emphasis within social work internationally to create a single universal understanding of the social work profession in such detail. They note that although there are some broad similarities to enable us to speak of social work in different locations, the differences in forms and degrees of professionalization, the academic status, the extent to which social work is effective in meeting human need and the extent to which social work can contribute to social improvement vary enormously between countries (Gray & Fook, 2004, p. 629). Thus, at the very least, they suggest that the purpose of creating a single universal set of standards appears to come from a belief in the benefits rather than a recognition of the difficulties. This also raises the possibility that such a move derives from continued implicit professional imperialism, even if this is not a conscious motivation (see Gray, 2005, pp. 233–4). From this Gray and Fook argue that international social work as an explicit area of the profession does not require universal standards but rather requires attention to the skills, knowledge and values that enable people to work in other countries, to work with service users who have come from other countries, to engage in exchanges and partnerships and so on (Gray & Fook, 2004, pp. 630–2; Gray, 2005, pp. 234–6). This suggests thinking about curricula and structures of education that are relevant for different contexts, as well as restoring macro-level practices especially in countries in the global South where social development may well be more appropriate than social casework.

The common feature of these two types of critique is that of professional imperialism, in the form of the implicit hegemony of ideas from the global North, which are seen as representing a 'universal' position. For these critics, the tendency to seek universals runs against the dynamic of 'indigenization' or 'authentization' (see Chapter 5). This, it is being argued, will be greatest in those countries where cultures and social structures are most different from the Northern ideas that are being taken as 'global' standards. The risk is that instead of being seen as 'appropriately different', some educational structures will simply be regarded as 'sub-standard'.

Recent Developments in Social Work Education: Three Examples

To consider this issue in more detail we will turn to some specific recent examples of social work education developments. Of these, one is from Africa and two from Asia. In some ways they can all be considered as 'of the global South', with histories of colonization and recent 'modernization'. They have been selected because they represent some broad issues that are relevant to understanding these debates.

Botswana

Osei-Hwedie and his colleagues (2006) describe the recent development of the MSW at the University of Botswana. This programme was specifically geared towards an indigenization of the curriculum, reshaping it so that it would more effectively address the social needs of Botswana and also educate social workers in theories and practices that are relevant to the national context (pp. 573–4). Thus the programme was centred on a community-based approach, not in terms of 'community organization' as such, but rather in the African sense of beginning with the idea that the community is the focal point of society (also see Graham, 2002). The MSW extends the range of social work qualifications, which had been created in the 1980s, from certificate (now phased out), through a two-year diploma and four-year bachelors degree (BSW).

While the Diploma programme focuses on front-line staff needs, the BSW provides a broad social work education for those who will progress to leadership roles, including communication skills, theories and methods of practice, social policy, management and supervision and research; students are also required to take courses in law and the social sciences (Osei-Hwedie et al., 2006, p. 575). It also includes field education. The MSW is intended to provide a higher level of education, enabling practitioners to specialize in social policy and administration, clinical social work or youth and community practice. It also seeks to equip practitioners to engage in research and evaluation and to 'promote equality and social justice at a national level' (p. 578). The description of these programmes emphasizes their community and developmental orientation.

As other writers have also noted, the issue for developing 'authentized' social work education in Africa is primarily about content and focus (Muleya, 2006; Anucha, 2008). The questions are whether the social worker can understand and respond to the local context appropriately, whether relevant values can be put into practice and so on. The actual structures, even the range of topics, considered very generally, may be quite similar to those of other parts of the world. Field education may also be a key part of the process, as it is in the global North (Anucha, 2008). But when the adaptation of these ideas is grounded in African perspectives then 'authentic' social work can develop.

China

The (re)development of social work in China has, in many ways, been driven by the growth of university level programmes (Yuen-Tsang & Sung, 2002; Yan & Tsang, 2005). There are two dimensions to this, however. In the major cities of eastern China there has been growing concern on the part of regional and national governments about the management of social services and responses to social problems after the introduction of the market economy (Ku et al., 2005, p. 214). This led the Ministry of Education, in co-operation with the Ministry of Civil Affairs, to approve the establishment of social work programmes, with a national curriculum. By 2006 there were over 200 schools authorized to teach social work (Yan & Tsui, 2007, p. 642).

One of the major debates among social work academics in China, which has also involved colleagues from Hong Kong, has been the extent to which a 'recontextualization' (or 'authentization' as we have previously considered it) can be achieved. For Tsang et al. (2008, p. 73) there are several poles to this dynamic, namely: the nature of modern China (rapid change, and a tendency for people to oversimplify Chinese culture in debates, even among Chinese colleagues); the relationships of insiders and outsiders in the context of global–local debates; social work as an academic discipline and as a set of practices; and the plausibility of attempting to predict the future course of development. As Yan and Tsui note, one of the major factors that affects the growth of social work is whether it can contribute to social stability within the context of rapid change (2007, p. 649). This leads this group of critics to suggest that it is most appropriate for China to integrate both local and foreign forms of knowledge and practice. Consequently, social work education in China has tended to draw heavily on influences from the global North, especially from North America and via Hong Kong from the United Kingdom.

However, Tsang et al. (2008, p. 82) note that social work education may have developed faster than practice. At the national level, the demand for social work has been greatly influenced by the Ministry of Civil Affairs. At the same time, the imperatives in practice between the big cities of eastern China and the provinces, especially in the west, differ markedly. This has seen two different forms of social work developing at the same time, with a focus on practices such as casework in the major urban areas and a social development focus in regional areas (Yuen-Tsang & Sung, 2002; Ku et al., 2005). Of particular note is that the latter emphasizes practice-based learning, through intensive field education. The goal of this approach is 'capacity building' both for the residents of the rural areas in which groups of students work and for the students themselves (and their teachers, also), which they call a 'triple capacity building model' (Ku et al., 2005, p. 230).

Vietnam

As with China, after reunification in 1975, Vietnam abandoned social work because it was considered unnecessary under socialism (Nguyen Thi Oanh, 2002). Then, after the decision in 1986 to create a market economy in order to deal with serious economic stagnation and widespread poverty, there was also a growing awareness that social problems remained and were taking new forms as prosperity grew rapidly. In the late 1980s permission was given for one subject on social work to be taught in the women's studies degree at the Open University of Ho Chi Minh City, following which it was adopted as an entire degree programme in 2000 (Durst et al., 2006). The discipline was also introduced in Hanoi at what is now the University of Labour and Social Affairs (ULSA), which was then the staff college of the Ministry of Labour, Invalids and Social Affairs (MOLISA). In 2004 the Ministry of Education and Training (MOET) approved an increasing number of universities to teach social work (Hugman et al., 2009). The number has grown rapidly and by 2008 as many as 36 universities had been approved (UNICEF Vietnam, personal communication), but as there is no formal recognition of social work as a profession, graduates find it difficult to gain employment. MOLISA employs many staff who undertake roles that are, in effect, forms of social work but the requirement in Vietnam is for a profession to be recognized by the government and this process is still under way. Moreover, many of those who undertake these roles are regarded as 'para-professionals' in that they have in-service training; the numbers of staff required in the system are unlikely to be met by university graduates in the next decade (UNICEF Vietnam/MOLISA, 2005; Hugman, et al., 2007, 2009; Taylor et al., 2009).

In 2004 the Canadian International Development Agency (CIDA) funded a project for lecturers from ULSA to train in social work in Canada and by 2008, 12 had completed an MSW. A further three academics have trained in the Philippines. There have also been several projects to develop curricula and train university teachers, with consultants working at individual universities, and with MOET, MOLISA and UNICEF Vietnam. Consequently, the influences on the development of social work and social work education have come not only from Canada and the Philippines but also from Australia, Hong Kong, Korea, New Zealand, Singapore, Sweden, the United Kingdom and the United States. That the MOET approved curriculum closely resembles programmes in many of these countries therefore may not be surprising. However, the combination of social work theory and methods (including working with individuals and families, group work and community development), social policy, research, law and foundational social sciences all contribute to the forms of practice that are being debated with MOLISA and other government organizations (UNICEF Vietnam/MOLISA, 2005, 2007). In other words, the strong resemblance of social work practice to other countries where employment in large government agencies predominates can be seen as a crucial factor in the shape of social work education (Taylor et al., 2009). Moreover, there is a clear recognition by Vietnamese academics and others involved in these debates that social work in Vietnam must develop appropriately for the needs and the culture of the country (Vietnamese Expert Group on Social Work, 2006). This includes creating Vietnamese texts and other educational materials. As with the situation in China (see above), the pattern of development is one of a conscious combination of global and local ideas and practices.

International Issues in Social Work Education

These brief vignettes of recent social work education developments in three countries connect with many of the debates that have already been identified. As we will see, this not only concerns these countries but also has implications for others where social work education is long-established. In particular, the issues raised are: the contextualization of social work (knowledge, skills and values); differential access to resources and influence; who plays what role in developing social work education; and how social work education can itself be understood as part of international social work.

First, the question of contextualization has to be addressed not only for countries of the global South, but for all countries. It should be emphasized here that the term 'contextualization' has been used deliberately, in order to point to the way that this process affects *all* social work education. It is relevant not only in situations where ideas and programmes are being adapted in a new way, but also in those where social work education is apparently well entrenched but in which there are continuing struggles with the tensions between theory, practice and values. There is also wide variation in who sets curriculum and other standards for schools of social work, variously including professional associations (as in Australia and Canada), social work education councils (as in the USA), government bodies (as in the UK, China and Vietnam) and relative autonomy guided by consultative committees made up of these three interest groups (as in Botswana) (Osei-Hwedie et al., 2006; Welbourne & Weiss, 2007; Healy, 2008a; Tsang et al., 2008; Hugman et al., 2009). In China it appears that different forms of social work are developing in different regions. However, if Payne and Askeland (2008) are correct in their assertion that what is required is flexibility, with sensitivity to culture, access to resources and so on, then it must be recognized that these factors also affect schools of social work in the global North. The setting of national standards may well disguise the extent to which this is also the case in countries such as Australia, Canada, New Zealand, the United Kingdom or the United States, although in each of these (as noted elsewhere in this book) there are debates about education to equip social workers for appropriate practice with Indigenous peoples and/or other ethnic minorities (Dominelli, 2008; Green & Baldry, 2008; Clifford & Burke, 2008). Another exception to this is the recognition of 'regional and rural social work' as a distinct form of practice requiring specific education in countries such as Australia and Canada (Cheers & Taylor, 2007). But in other ways there is little evidence to suggest that the debate about contextualization in the exchange of ideas between countries has yet had any impact on the consideration of provincial differences within countries.

Second, it must be recognized that the resource base is vastly different between each country and also between regions within them, in economic terms and in relation to skilled and experienced personnel. These disparities in resources and infrastructure affect the ways in which different parts of the world can meet the 'global standards' and, furthermore, the extent to which they can engage in the professional formation of social work in ways that can be shared internationally (Payne & Askeland, 2008, p. 143). Access to books and journals, both as readers and as authors, access to the Internet (or even having functioning computers and consistent electricity supplies), the possibility of attending international conferences and meetings and so on all tend to favour the participation of colleagues form wealthier countries and to effectively exclude those from more disadvantaged locations. Thus it is not only the case that in some countries simply studying social work is more difficult than in others, but also that the very ideas that are learned about what constitutes social work and how it ought to be practised tend to be dominated by perspectives form the global North (and especially those from English-speaking countries). Some efforts are made by organizations such as IFSW and IASSW to deal with this point, in the form of differential fees and support for travel costs (the 'solidarity fund'), but in other areas differences are not addressed. There are also regional differences within countries. As Tsang et al. (2008, pp. 75–6) remark, although a country such as China generally has significantly less educational resources available than a country such as the United States, there may be parts of China where resources now are rapidly approaching the levels of the global North. At the same time, universities in countries such as Australia, the United Kingdom or the United States differ widely in their resources and in the curriculum demands placed on them, within those countries as well as internationally. So, in this way, the possible implications of 'global standards' universalizing standards that can only be achieved by wealthier countries might mirror differences within each country, in which some universities can easily meet their national standards while others find it difficult.

Third, these brief summaries point also to the question of who plays what role in developing social work education. The evidence appears to be that this is always some form of interaction between professional bodies, the schools of social work and employing organizations (which in many countries, as we have noted, are often government agencies). The room for 'the profession', which or may not be seen as including both associations and schools, to set curriculum and the structures of education is limited by the necessity of working with employers and governments. In some cases this can even result in social work schools being closed by hostile governments, as has happened in countries as diverse as Chile, Hungary and Spain (Welbourne & Weiss, 2007, pp. 234–5).

In most countries, however, it means that some accommodation is often made to the employment of graduates and the tasks that agencies wish to use social workers to accomplish. Again, in some situations this can become an attack on the integrity of social work, and it is under these circumstances that international documents (on education and training, on ethics and on the definition of social work) can be used as a defence or as a means of building up the profession in more favourable times through critical analysis (Welbourne & Weiss, 2007, p. 243).

For these reasons, it may well make sense to those involved in developing social work education to make use of experience in other countries, even where those countries have different cultures and social structures. The role of international consultants can be useful, especially in circumstances where local stakeholders have not yet formed a common discourse in which to engage in national debates about the shape and content of social work and social work education. What may matter more is whether both international and local participants in these processes recognize that there is not a single model of social work education that must be adhered to in every way in every place. What this requires is that international exchanges of ideas and expertise in social work education seek to model the goal of empowerment in social work practice by being reflexive and open to the needs and interests of all stakeholders in a way that gives different positions a voice, with the type of humility identified by Gray (2005, p. 235) in which those from the global North question their own assumptions. This is not simply a matter of welding on to the structure of social work education a skill of 'cultural sensitivity' (compare with Dean, 2001) but of integrating that sensitivity into the way in which we think about and practice social work education in our own national and cultural contexts as well as across borders.

Fourth, therefore, social work education also has to be considered as part of international social work. This follows from the previous points because they indicate that the internationalization of social work education informs the way in which social workers may consider moving between countries, be better equipped to work with service users who have moved between countries, and to engage in professional exchanges. The development of policies and services internationally also is closely tied to the internationalization of social work education, because of the role that social work academics play in research. As we have noted repeatedly throughout this book, the spread of social work around the world has often been based on the establishment of educational programmes. For this reason it may be appropriate to recognize the development of social work education as a contributor to social development (Hugman et al., 2007, 2009). However, in order for social work education to be seen in this way it has to be focused on the development of skills, knowledge and values that are relevant to the local–national context. In other words, not all social work education can be regarded as social development, but only when it contributes positively through the contextualization of curriculum content and programme structure.

It is from this point of view that Noble's (2004) positive remarks about the potential in the globalization of social work education must be understood. That is, we must seek to ensure that a local–global dialogue is facilitated. It is only when this happens that the dominance of perspective from the global North can be challenged and in social work in all parts of the world can engage in the processes of appropriate contextualization. This in turn will provide the most fruitful possible basis for identifying the common core of social work as an internationalizing discipline. However, as Noble (p. 535) warns, this can only happen when the processes of debate and decision-making are more genuinely inclusive.

International Social Work Education

Beyond the question of the contribution that social work education can make to international social work, we must also ask whether it is plausible to think in terms of international social work education. There are two aspects to this. The first of these relates to the way in which social work education may be provided across national borders. The second concerns the content of international social work and other related material in the various curricula of social work programmes around the world.

Studying between Countries

There are now many social work programmes that are explicitly focused on the training of students from different countries and for students to work in a variety of countries (Lyons, 1999; Payne & Askeland, 2008). Most of these programmes are located in universities in various parts of Europe (including Scandinavia and the UK) and have, at least as part of their rationale, a goal of promoting greater integration of social work across Europe. In that sense, from other points of view such development might be regarded as regional rather than international. Nevertheless they do have the capacity to educate social workers in many of the crucial ideas and skills that are necessary to create a more positive internationalization.

Added to this, the financial pressures on universities combined with the interest of social work academics in international and cross-cultural issues have also led to universities offering their programmes in other countries (as stand-alone programmes, not as partnerships or exchanges). Examples of this include universities from Australia and the United Kingdom who provide social work degree programmes in Africa, Asia and Eastern Europe. In addition, as Payne and Askeland (2008, p. 137) point out, the growth of information and communication technology (ICT) has fuelled a rapid growth in 'distance education'. Through this mode, students in remote areas of a country can access higher education based in metropolitan or regional centres (Chenoweth & Steklik, 2002; Smith, 2007; Darkwa, 2008), and using distance education technologies can make social work learning more accessible for disabled students, such as those who are deaf (Smith, 2007), and this mode of programme delivery also provides access for students from other countries (Askeland & Payne, 2007).

Darkwa (2008), writing about social work education in Ghana, argues that there are both benefits and problems in incorporating distance programmes in countries where resources are relatively scarce. The benefits are that this type of provision addresses the issues of large distances and the social implications of students having to leave their homes, families and local areas to study. Problems include the lack of access to technology, appropriate styles of learning and the educational support that can be made available. Yet the same benefits and issues can be seen in a country such as Australia (Napier & George, 2001). Assumptions about access to ICT cannot be made simply because of the general levels of wealth and material development of a country, nor should questions of how people learn most effectively. As we have noted above, students may lack access to computers or the Internet, for example, as well as finding the lack of interaction with other people to be a challenge in learning (especially in a discipline such as social work) (Askeland & Payne, 2007; Smith; 2007; Darkwa, 2008). So this type of development answers some questions while raising others.

Distance education between countries also poses a problem of relevance and appropriateness. If we hold that at least some social work knowledge, skills and values are linked to culture and other local factors, distance education access by 'international students' creates challenges for both learner and teacher. If it is to be done effectively, it requires that both students and academics recognize these factors and respond carefully to the process of contextualization at the level of individual practice. In turn, if the programme and its teachers have not incorporated a recognition of the need for contextualization, then this will be difficult. The risk is that students fail because they are trying to deal with this process without support and in turn academics may be reluctant to work with 'international students'.

Integrating 'International Social Work' in the Curriculum

The inclusion of international social work as a specific subject in the social work curriculum has been widely advocated (Lyons, 1999; Cox & Pawar, 2006; Lyons et al., 2006; Healey, 2008a). Cox and Pawar note that this is increasingly happening but at the same time caution that the extent and quality of the material on international social work varies greatly between specific programmes (2006, p. 366). Just as many of the issues in the international social work are contested, so to is the way of defining the curriculum that would best prepare social workers for this aspect of the profession. For Cox and Pawar, drawing on their own analysis and that of other writers, this should include comparative material on social policies and social welfare institutions, cross-cultural practices and values including international perspectives on ethics, international law as well as local legislation and teaching on poverty that addresses this issue in various locations around the world. And they also advocate that international social work material should not be confined to electives but should also be integrated (they use the term 'defused') throughout curricula. At the same time, they appear to recognize that the amount of material that is seen as essential for learning in the social work curriculum may mean that some teaching on international social work might only be available as a specialized option.

In addition to class-based teaching, preparation for international social work also raises questions about field education (also variously called 'practicum' or 'practice placement'). As we have already noted, this is a common feature of social work education that can be observed all around the world. There are a variety of ways in which programmes can incorporate appropriate experience that addresses international social work. These may include ways in which students can work in another country as part of field education, but they can also include working in agencies that serve refugee or other migrant communities. In addition, inclusion of international exchanges within locally based field education can also provide useful learning opportunities. Although relatively rare, when field education involves working on research or policy issues this may also provide opportunities to undertake internationally focused practice.

In the light of the critiques of neocolonialism that have already been discussed, it is necessary to sound a further note of caution about international field education, especially where this involves students from the global North going to work in the global South (Noble, 2003). As Wehbi (2009) observes, there is a risk that such arrangements can easily be exploitative. Great care must be taken to ensure that students are adequately prepared and that support is available throughout their placement in another country. To permit, or even encourage, students to undertake their education overseas without such preparation and support can result in risk for the student, as well as in damaging practice that harms people in the contexts within which the student might be placed. At an extreme, it reduces field education to a form of tourism and service users to objects who serve the interests of the student.

In order to counter the tendency to construct international field education programmes in this way, schools can look at the exercise as one of developing their own international practice. The most suitable way of providing international education in this way, according to Tesoriero and Rajaratnam (2001), is through bilateral or multi-lateral relationships with social work schools or service agencies in other countries. This returns our attention to exchanges and partnerships as forms of international social work as well as emphasizing that internationalization not only concerns students and individual academics but also schools as institutions (Dominelli & Bernard, 2003). This in turn requires that schools identify what they can offer to colleagues and service users elsewhere as well as the benefits of such arrangements for their own students. This encompasses not only the expectations that a school might have for its own students but also a careful appraisal of what it can offer in return. This might take the form of providing opportunities for students from another country also to undertake field education internationally, or it may consist of some other contribution that such a school could make to the work of colleagues elsewhere. Especially when relationships are between countries of the global South and North, attention needs also to be paid to the problems that students in the global South may have in accessing resources to undertake an international learning experience (Razack, 2000). Bursaries and other forms of assistance may be necessary to ensure a genuine reciprocity in such relationships and in addition schools need to consider the amount of support that needs to be provided to ensure that international students gain positively from the experience.

'Global' as a Contradiction in Social Work Education

This discussion has implicitly emphasized that the international vision for social work education contains a set of ideas that appear to form a contradiction. (In this sense, a contradiction can be seen when two mutually exclusive ideas must necessarily coexist.) For clarity, the elements that make up the contradiction between the positive and the negative aspects of such a vision can be summarized in the following way.

1. So that social work can grow as more than an isolated series of local or national practices, it is essential that a global understanding and definition of the profession be developed.
2. In order for this to be achieved we need to have internationally shared ideas about education and training for the profession.
3. At the same time the same problems of disagreement about the nature of social work also relate to thinking about social work education. In particular, the dominance of thinking from the global North is regarded by some critics as undermining the appropriateness of social work education in other settings.
4. However, it might also be argued that the experience and resources of social work education in the global North can provide a means to assist colleagues

elsewhere in developing relevant curriculum and programme structures – which returns us to point 1.

The way of resolving such challenges, it has been argued, is through relationships of partnership and exchange in which attention is paid to ensuring a balance and the appropriate interchange of ideas. This resolution also applies to the contradiction that is presented by the idea of international field education, which can be an excellent way of developing social workers who have greater awareness and capacity in international social work but in which the same problems of neocolonialism and exploitation are a risk.

The 'global standards' with which this chapter started can also be seen in this way, that is as a concrete expression of these contradictions. Some commentators emphasize the positive aspects, while others concentrate on the negative elements and yet others note that there are two sides to the debate. It is this latter position, I suggest, which offers a way forward. However, this will only avoid the problems that have been identified if they are made explicit and a conscious effort is made to form more genuinely equal, flexible and open working relationships between institutions in different countries. Consideration of social work education from a global perspective points us to two further issues. The first of these is that of values and ethics in social work, as these were seen to be an important part of the detailed critique of the 'global standards' document. The second is that of the problem of professional imperialism, which continues to be a critical part of the way in which ideas and practices in social work are shared around the world. Therefore in the following two chapters we will consider each of these topics in turn.

8

The Possibility of an International Social Work Ethics

Social Work Ethics and Values

Since its earliest days social work has been defined not only in terms of the knowledge and skills that it brings to social issues and problems but also in relation to the values that are regarded as core to its identity. Indeed, for some social workers it is the values of the profession that are its defining feature (e.g., Reamer, 1999). However, such a position runs the risk of overstating the place of values in understanding social work, in that without being able to identify the knowledge and skills that social workers bring to their role(s) we are unable to say what it is that we *do*. Furthermore, all professions make claims to particular values. This can be seen both in the codes of ethics that are espoused by professions in health, education, law, science and so on, as well as in the wider notion that professions 'pursue values' (Koehn, 1994). By this, Koehn is referring to the idea each profession is formed around a goal that can understood as a 'non-moral value' (that which is valued, but is good in itself and not as a moral issue). For example, in the case of medicine, nursing and the allied health professions it is the value of 'health' that is sought, or for teachers the value sought is that of 'education'. In this sense we may say that the value pursued by social workers is that of 'social well-being', and indeed this notion is contained explicitly in the international definition of social work (IFSW/IASSW, 2000/2001). The 'values' of social work that are stated in the IFSW/IASSW definition to include 'human rights' and 'social justice' can therefore be seen as ideas that help us to understand what might constitute 'social well-being'. Indeed, many social work scholars identify these, especially human rights, as the foundational, if not absolute, values of social work (Ife, 2001; Reichert, 2003; Mapp, 2008).

Seen in this way the values of social work represent one position among many, although by definition for social workers these values are of primary importance. At the same time, social work is not the only profession to incorporate notions

121

of rights and justice in its ethics. These values are widely referred to in many 'caring' professions (Gallagher, 2003; Hugman, 2005). What may differ is the way in which these values are interpreted and used – in other words, how they can be recognized in practice. Banks (2006, p. 44) suggests, for example, that the way in which social work emphasizes 'social justice' differentiates the profession from medicine, nursing and allied health or teaching (at least formally). From this we can add, therefore, that the values of social work are an expression of *how* we perform our roles, or at least aspire to, rather than a definition of the profession as such.

The international definition of social work thus contains a claim that a commitment to the values of 'human rights' and 'social justice' are an essential aspect of how we can understand the profession. Although not using these precise terms, the earliest clear statement of this position can be seen in the work of Jane Addams (2002 [1907]) in the United States of America, although in this respect she was also voicing the ideas held by many social workers in northern Europe (compare with Forsyth, 1995). In more recent times these values have formed the guiding ideas of the codes of ethics of the profession's associations in different countries (such as Australia, Canada, the UK and the USA) (NASW, 1999; AASW, 2002; BASW, 2002; ACTS/CASW, 2005). They were also used quite explicitly for the framework of the document *Ethics in Social Work: Statement of Principles* that was agreed between the IFSW and the IASSW in 2004, precisely because they are contained in the international organizations' definition of the profession.

Yet, how such values are expressed in action has been contentious from those early days and continues to be so. In particular, critics have argued that in the process of professionalizing social work has largely abandoned these values in practice, as it has had to accommodate to the pragmatic concerns of employment in government agencies that are largely concerned with managing social welfare systems and controlling those groups within the community that are most in need (Olson, 2007). As we noted in Chapter 5, this debate is often couched in terms of a dispute between micro- and macro-levels of practice but it is more plausible to see it in relation to questions of the way in which social work is practised. In other words, questions of value begin with the goals towards which action is oriented and issues of how such goals are pursued follow from this (Hugman, 2005).

Banks (2006) provides a very wide-ranging international comparative review of codes of ethics from 31 national social work associations. Banks notes that the common features of these codes include statements about the underlying values of the profession, together with a framework for the application of these values to an understanding of the ways in which practice can be regarded as (morally) 'good' or 'right'. Only one code in the sample considered by Banks takes the form of an 'oath', that of the South African Black Social Workers

Association; the remaining 30 state values and/or principles (such as 'integrity, 'rights' or 'justice') then spell out the ways in which these can be applied (Banks, 2006, p. 83). Banks also comments that several of the codes specify particular moral qualities ('virtues') that should be demonstrated by social workers (p. 85). In addition, she demonstrates that those countries that produced codes of ethics earlier in the twentieth century have provided models that have been used, whether explicitly or implicitly, in other places. The international statement of principles also provides a model, as is its intention (IFSW/IASSW, 2004, section 1). Consequently, although the sample in Banks' survey included countries from the global South, such as Hong Kong, Singapore, South Africa and Turkey, as well as new countries of Eastern Europe, such as Bulgaria, Croatia, the Czech Republic, Romania, Russia and Slovakia, there is a relative uniformity at least at the general level of the form and broad content of these codes. This may reflect the fact that the associations included in this review are almost entirely from Europe, North America, Australasia and three locations that were formerly British colonies (only Japan and Turkey do not fit these criteria).

However, it might also be said that all of these codes of ethics are grounded in the international statement of ethical principles and that a degree of uniformity follows from the shared characteristics of social work around the world. Because it was the intention of the international statement to provide a framework that would enable social workers in each country to develop their own codes of ethics, the document is based on an assumption that differences will occur in the ways that the principles are applied to suit local cultures and institutions, rather than in the creation of entirely different sets of principles. In this sense we can observe that the discourse of the international organizations on values and ethics is built on the understanding of social work as a single entity, even though wide variations in detail may be expected. As we have already seen, this explanation might describe how things are but whether this is how they should be requires further investigation.

The ethical principles that provide the foundations for the international statement and national codes of ethics can be summarized as follows:

- duty – including the duty to respect each human person as a moral end in himself or herself, on which the idea of human rights is constructed, and which derives from the philosophy of Kant;
- consequences – especially in the way formalized in the notion of 'utilitarianism', in which an act is 'good' or 'right' according to the extent to which it produces human well-being and which can be seen as the foundation of the value of 'social justice';
- virtue – the moral characteristics which are seen to be important for social workers to demonstrate;

- relationship – that the extent to which the good of other persons is promoted through the way in which social workers act in relationship to
  them.

These ideas have been widely identified as key principles in analyses of social
work ethics (Reamer, 1999; Clark, 2000; Reisch, 2002; Hugman, 2005; Banks,
2006; Bowles et al., 2006). Although the way in which such values are combined in different national codes varies, the degree of commonality supports
Banks' assertion (2006, p. 41) that social work around the world can be
regarded as having a 'common morality' approach. Such an approach is based
on ordinary shared beliefs and it assumes that no value is absolute but each
must be seen in balance with others. While there are strong similarities between
such ethical thinking in social work and that of colleagues in other professions,
for example in medicine and other health professions (Beauchamp & Childress,
2001), in social work the balance tends to emphasize a more radical interpretation of questions such as rights and justice (p. 44). The notion of radical
here refers to a recognition that human identity includes social relationships
and structures, so that the moral claims of individuals cannot be regarded as
absolute but must be seen in context.
    The types of practices that are suggested by this approach to ethics not
only bridge any perceived divide between micro- and macro-levels, but also
point to ways in which social workers might be regarded as morally com-
pelled to consider particular ways of understanding social issues and problems
(Reisch, 2002). Examples include the focus in the United Kingdom on 'anti-
racist and anti-discriminatory practice' (Thompson, 2006; Clifford & Burke,
2008; Dominelli, 2008) and the development of ideas of 'structural practice' in
Canada (Mullaly, 1997) or of 'critical reflective practice' in Australia (Fook &
Pease, 1999). In each of these approaches a balance between the promotion of
human rights and the pursuit of social justice is contextualized in a radical critique of the social structures of the contemporary world. From this perspective,
social work ethics must attend to questions of social class, of sex, gender, sexism
and patriarchy, of 'race', ethnicity and racism, of age and ageism, of sexuality
and heterosexism, and of the social construction of the divide between ability
and disability with various forms of discrimination that arise from that.

Social Work Ethics, Universalism and (Cultural) Relativism

An irony in debates about social work ethics is that, despite recent emphasis on critical approaches such as 'anti-racist and anti-discriminatory' values
(Clifford & Burke, 2008), all these approaches to ethics have been criticized as
reflecting the dominance of the global North in ideas about social work. These

criticisms have come, in particular, from Africa, Asia and the Pacific Islands (e.g., Silavwe, 1995; Yip, 2004; Mafile'o, 2006). Similar arguments have also been made by Aboriginal Australian, First Nations Canadian, Maori and Native American social workers (e.g., Weaver, 1997; Green & Baldry, 2008). In short, these criticisms see social work ethics, especially as expressed in the statement of principles of international organizations, as inherently 'Eurocentric'. The underlying values, principles and the detailed discussions of application are regarded both as deriving from the European philosophical traditions and as embedded with the social assumptions of the global North.

This debate must be understood in terms of the difference between 'universalism' and '(cultural) relativism' in ethics (Hugman, 2005, pp. 16–21). Universalism is the position which states that core values apply to all human beings, irrespective of their identity (including cultural background or personal preferences and so on). Relativism is the position which holds that values are necessarily formed and sustained in relation to matters such as identity and context, of which culture is a particular instance (although this might for some relativists include individual circumstances or characteristics). The critique of universal statements about social work internationally, therefore, is primarily a tension between those who hold that the same values are essential for the nature of social work as a profession wherever it is practised and those who argue that the values of social work must be appropriate to the cultural context in which practice occurs.

Silavwe's (1995) critique of social work values, that he argues had been imported into Zambia through an emphasis on social casework, is primarily focused on the applied principles of 'self-determination' and 'confidentiality'. The term 'applied' is used here because these principles themselves rely on more generalized notions of human worth and how this might be sustained. Silavwe argues that it makes no sense to attempt to operationalize these principles in a society in which more traditional values of co-operation, shared responsibility, mutuality and openness define what is good and right. For example, he considers the way in which Social Casework and Remedial Services Committees in local areas operate (p. 82). These committees comprise people of influence within the local community (which may include social workers along with clergy, traditional healers, political leaders and so on) and their business is conducted through interviews at an open gathering in which other members of the community may take part in the discussion. Silavwe asserts that a notion such as confidentiality makes no sense in this context. Similarly, self-determination has little meaning in a culture in which one's life choices are deeply interconnected with the other members of the social group. As a consequence, social work in Zambia has become more concerned with community development.

Mafile'o's (2006) analysis of social work in Pacifika society (the Pacific Islands) makes a similar point. Here too the right ways of proceeding and good outcomes are reflections of appropriate social relationships. Again we can see that the interpretation of principles of human worth, dignity, rights, social justice and so on is quite different to that found in North America or northern Europe. For example, a younger person deferring to the views of an elder in their wider family grouping may be regarded positively and supported by a Pacifika social worker in a way that would be regarded as a breach of the younger person's rights in European or American situations.

A recent critique that has sought explicitly to challenge the dominance of Eurocentrism in international social work in the form of the international organizations' documents on education and on ethics is that of Yip (2004). Writing explicitly from the basis of Chinese culture (which he broadens out to encompass Asia as a whole), Yip argues that the international ethical statements of social work continue to ignore the importance of cultural expectations in how people act in relation to social issues and problems. For Yip, the tension between the universalist assertion of values in the IFSW/IASSW documents and the culturally diverse values that can be observed around the world is best expressed in a series of dual values. Where the universalist (for which we should understand 'global Northern') position is grounded in the values of rights, equality, individual autonomy, change and empowerment, traditional Asian (and other 'global Southern') cultures value responsibility, social norms, family, stability and relation (Yip, 2004, pp. 604–5). Although IFSW/IASSW recognize 'diversity' as a value (subsidiary to 'social justice'), the way in which they do this, according to Yip, is to construct variations from the universalist position as 'what happens in multicultural countries' (p. 604) – in other words, cultural difference is seen as representing a 'minority' position that has to be accommodated within a 'majority' cultural context. This does not address the endogenous cultures of those countries that do not share these value assumptions. Thus, in so far as international social work ethics are constructed as universalist, they remain a form of professional imperialism. This is not simply a matter of interpreting these values in different countries but of accepting that they may well be inappropriate.

In a series of case vignettes Yip (2004, pp. 606–9) considers the five particular points of tension between the Eurocentric and traditional Asian values that he identifies. These demonstrate that the way in which a social worker may successfully assist someone can depend on modifying the values that he sees as endemic in the international documents.

1. Responsibility vs. rights. The notion of rights originates in Western philosophy and there is no comparable term in Chinese (for example). In contrast, Confucianism, which underpins ethics in many Asian countries, emphasizes responsibility.
2. Social norms vs. equality. The underlying value of communal cultures is one in which orderliness of actions that are based in the recognized social norms

takes precedence. Higher status brings with it obligations to promote the well-being of others and should be acted on with humility.

3. Family vs. individual. In cultures in which well-being is perceived as the property of families and not individuals the Eurocentric emphasis on the individual as the basis for moral consideration simply does not make sense. Silavwe makes a similar point about African values when he identifies the importance of family and community (1995, p. 81).

4. Stability vs. change. Where the global Northern position is that problems should be dealt with by seeking change (thus change is a goal and hence a value), Asian philosophies emphasize acceptance, endurance and stability as important values (which may sometimes take the form of personal virtues).

5. Relation vs. empowerment. Compared with the pursuit of the capacity to exercise power appropriately in resolving one's problems, Yip suggests that Asian values stress achieving harmony and interdependence in relationships..

It is important to note that in Yip's analysis, the point is that the Eurocentric position adopted in the international ethical statements (in the guise of universalism) actually negates one side of each of these tensions. In contrast, he argues that the Asian philosophical position is to hold each of these pairs in tension. The goal is a balance between them, rather than a counter negation.

However, Yip's argument also assumes a particular interpretation of the way in which human rights and social justice are demonstrated through principles such as 'self-determination'. (We might add that 'confidentiality' is often regarded in this way as well.) Indeed, such assumptions are widespread in the way that many social workers understand such concepts as core values in themselves rather than as particular ways of achieving the values of human rights and social justice (Banks, 2006; Bowles et al., 2006). To understand this point, it will be helpful to look in more detail at the issues raised regarding human rights and social justice.

The Particular Issue of 'Human Rights'

The IFSW/IASSW (2004, section 4.1) *Ethics in Social Work: Statement of Principles* amplifies the value of human rights as including: respecting the right to self-determination; promoting the right to participation; treating each person as a whole; identifying and developing strengths. Each carries a short explanatory note that explains the principle. The third and fourth of these explicitly refer to the family and community relationships and norms of service users. This section explicitly draws on the UN Declaration of Human Rights (UN, 1948).

Of the several different situations and associated values that Yip presents, that which best demonstrates the challenges to the value of human rights raised by his arguments is that of a situation in which a woman seeks help with how she may respond to domestic violence perpetrated by her husband (Yip, 2004, p. 606). In the first instance the social worker (Chinese, but trained in Euro-centric theories and methods of practice) attempts to encourage this woman to consider her rights not to be abused and, if necessary, to leave her husband. The woman is unable to respond to this approach as it causes a deep conflict with the traditional Chinese cultural values she holds concerning the role of women in the family and what it is to be a wife. She is also concerned for the well-being of her daughter should she make the choice to leave. Eventually the situation is resolved by the social worker helping the woman to look instead at her respon-sibilities to her daughter, an approach which accords with her cultural values, and the woman is then able to seek safety for her daughter and herself by them together leaving her husband.

The thread of Yip's argument is that instead of focusing on the achievement of a value such as human rights, defined in abstract philosophical terms, we should instead focus on the good outcome for the service user. This, he is saying, can only be understood in culturally appropriate terms, which in this context are built on the value of responsibility. The service user was helped to examine her own responsibility to protect her daughter in comparison to her husband's failure to exercise his own responsibilities of caring for his wife and daugh-ter. Because the value of rights made no sense to the woman in this situation, practice that was trying to achieve it was inappropriate and thus ineffective.

A similar argument can be read in Healy's (2007) discussion of a compara-ble situation concerning a Vietnamese migrant settled in the United States of America. Here too she portrays a woman dealing with an abusive partner. As in Yip's vignette a social worker's use of the concept of human rights as the basis for articulating the choices faced by the service user is ineffective. It is only when the woman considers the needs of her daughter that she is able to take action to protect herself and her daughter and leave her abusive husband.

Although this results in the woman taking the same action as in the previous example, Healy's comments on this situation are somewhat different to those of Yip. Healy begins from a commitment to a more robust defence of the notion of human rights as an underlying value. The problem for Healy is how we may do this in situations where cultural values are used as a reason to deny another person's rights. So, her conclusion is that while we ought to promote human rights as a core value we should do so in ways that are more culturally sensitive. The question is not *whether* human rights are a core value but *how* this value should be used in practice.

It is important to note that these two positions on the cultural relativity of a concept such as human rights come from quite different positions in relation to international social work. Yip is discussing a situation in which a particular perspective on social work has been introduced as set of ideas and practices into a culture in which it is not 'authentic' (as we have considered this term in previous chapters). For it to become 'authentized', this argument suggests, there must be a shift in values and how these relate to actions. In contrast, Healy is looking at a situation in which a locally 'authentic' practice has to respond to the demands of 'international service users'. Such a response includes rethinking the ways in which values can inform practice, but at the same time defending the relevance of those values.

In both situations we can see that the women were assisted in quite similar ways and (this is crucial) both Yip and Healy base their analyses on the view that domestic violence is morally unacceptable. In other words, neither is arguing that the women in question ought to have stayed with their husbands and endured abuse. What is less easy to conclude is whether this apparent similarity of outcomes leads to a resolution about the appropriateness or otherwise of a value such as human rights in informing social work ethics (e.g., providing the basis for saying that domestic violence is bad or wrong). We will return to this point below, but first we need also to consider the other overarching value of the IFSW/IASSW document, namely 'social justice'.

And What of 'Social Justice'?

The value of 'social justice' might also be seen as culturally relative in much the same way as that of 'human rights'. This value concerns the goal of 'fairness' in the way that social structures and institutions impact on members of the society, whether these are individuals, families, community groups and so on (Reisch, 2002). The elements of this value, as defined in the IFSW/IASSW *Statement of Principles* (2004, section. 4.2) are: challenging negative discrimination; recognizing diversity; distributing resources equitably; challenging unjust policies and practices; working in solidarity. As with the principles amplifying the value of human rights, these are expanded to give greater clarity. The second, in particular, emphasizes family and community norms in defining ways in which fairness can be understood differently in relation to different people and situations.

Reference to social justice issues can be found widely in writing about social work from the perspectives of the global South as well as the North. For example, Kawawe and Dibie (1999) challenge social work to grasp the difficult problem of taking a stand on the oppression in lives led by many children, especially in the global South. In particular, they are critical of what they term 'harmful fundamental cultural values and practices [...] that endanger the world's children [and include] child labor, prostitution, infanticide, forced girl marriages, girl genital mutilation and child sexual assault' (p. 79). Similarly,

Moyo and Kawewe (2002) critique the position of women in Zimbabwe in terms of the impact not only of patriarchy but also of socio-economic class, racism and ethnic discrimination. While many aspects of these forms of injustice might be considered to be 'culturally traditional', these African social workers argue that they are unacceptable because of the detrimental impact that they have on the lives of children and women, including those of Africa.

The counter argument is, precisely, that because practices such as child labour, infanticide, forced marriages of girls and female genital mutilation (FGM) are culturally traditional, then to regard them as oppressive and unjust may again be a form of neo-colonialism or cultural racism. Yet a careful reading of such critiques often fails to find any real defence of these practices. What is actually being addressed is the task of finding a more culturally sensitive way of grasping the implications of cultural difference as part of the process of achieving social justice. Infanticide, for example, may be explained in terms of the struggles of extremely impoverished communities that lack access to contraception and abortion, rather than as a preferred method of planned family size (Williamson, 1978). (We should also note that there is, of course, a parallel ethical debate in countries where these methods of controlling pregnancy and childbirth are available, including voices that defend infanticide in certain conditions – see, e.g., Singer, 1993.)

The two practices that sometimes appear to be defended from within the caring professions in the global North are those of child labour and FGM. Child labour is judged in terms of the extent to which it constitutes a threat to the well-being of the child – asking, for example, whether school attendance is always paramount and suggesting that the risks involved in certain work is actually the issue (Balagopalan, 2008). However, the argument here concerns what will enable young people to become integrated members of their communities, rather than advocating for something that could be considered 'unjust'. Similarly, some social workers and other professionals in health services in countries of the global North have also argued for a more questioning approach to FGM, on the grounds that while challenges to the practice in those countries where it originates take place within a mainstream culture, in its own terms, in countries of settlement (especially as refugees) women are a highly visible minority whose situation is highly vulnerable (Berg, 1997; Allotey et al., 2001). So, it is argued, simply stopping FGM through use of law or professional power and authority can be seen as an attack on the minority culture rather than as protecting women. Thus it becomes a social and cultural harm that has to be balanced against the physical impact of FGM, especially for those who regard the practice as a cultural 'good' (Al-Krenawi & Graham, 1999). However, these again are arguments about how such issues should be addressed, suggesting that it is more important to work through changes to attitudes and beliefs than to simply oppose and criticize practices directly. Boyle and Carbone-López (2006) provide an example of this when they note that in parts of Africa women them-selves have come to question FGM not on grounds of human rights or social justice but because they have come to regard this aspect of their culture as no longer relevant or even as 'bad culture'. Al-Krenawi and Graham (1999) observe a similar dynamic among Bedouin-Arab women in the Negev (also see Allotey et al., 2001; Freymeyer & Johnson, 2007).

Those from countries of the global South as much as from the North appear to find the value of social justice to be one that underpins practice and theory in many different situations (Kuruvilla, 2005; Lundy, 2006). As we saw in Chap-ters 3 and 4, social work internationally is often concerned with human needs that stem from the distribution of resources and the actions of other human beings as much if not more than those from the impact of the natural world. This is clearly the case for refugees and forced migrants, those who are trafficked or subject to other forms of gender-based violence, and Indigenous peoples, but it is also true for those who are affected by the natural world in some way, such as in situations of natural disasters, or who are disabled, to take several exam-ples at random. The pursuit of social justice occurs in interventions both with individual and family need and in relation to social policies and institutions.

Human Rights and Social Justice Together

Many of the discussions of human rights and social justice, especially those from countries of the global North, link or even conflate the two principles, despite their separate philosophical origins (Reisch, 2002; Banks, 2006). Some analysts, such as Lundy (2006), actually refer to 'social justice/human rights' as a single perspective. So, to return to Yip's (2004) critique of international statements on social work values, if we regard a concern with human rights as essentially culturally relative (to the global North) what implications does this have for social justice in other parts of the world?

For Lundy (2006), the connection between human rights and social justice is inescapable. She argues that it is not possible to achieve social justice with-out a robust concept of 'rights'. For example, '[a]n understanding of poverty that holds that people have a *right* to food, clothing and shelter has a differ-ent connotation to one that states that people *need* food clothing and shelter' (p. 123). The use of the concept of 'need' in such a context, she states, implies that people are responsible for their own situation and for resolving it; 'rights', on the other hand, point to unjust structural conditions that create poverty and to the necessity of changing those conditions. It is only through this approach that well-being and self-worth can be enabled.

To consider this argument carefully, it is important to consider why some-one might be said to have a right to these (material) goods. The short answer must be that without these things it is not possible for someone to live a human life. In Canadian winter, to use Lundy's home country as an example, lack of clothing and shelter as much as lack of food and drink can quickly lead to someone's death. But in any case, life without these things in any society is 'poor, mean, nasty, brutish and (possibly) short' (to paraphrase the English philosopher Hobbes, 1968 [1651]). However, there is a danger that the argument becomes circular, thus:

1. human rights are those things to which we can lay claim because they are necessary for us to live a human life, that is they are derived from human need;
2. the idea of need is not an adequate basis for claiming them because they might be denied or with-held, for example on grounds of desert (or a lack of it);
3. to have these goods denied or with-held is unjust because it prevents people from living a human life;
4. therefore, such needs ought to be defined as human rights, which are a claim that cannot be denied;
5. so it is necessary to define the concept of 'rights' – return to point 1, and so on.

Social justice may be a sufficient basis for social work ethics if the basic premise of human rights is accepted. However, if we break the circle by arguing that the idea of rights is culturally relative then the whole process becomes highly problematic for social work. For this reason, the debate about human rights is central to the claim that there is a common core to social work internationally, even if it is very circumscribed and there is much that is culturally or situationally relative.

Rethinking Human Rights?

Asad (2000) makes the very telling point that 'rights' are not 'things' but are better understood as ways of thinking and talking about human needs, human relationships and so on. The question we should ask, therefore, is not what human rights 'are' but what they 'do'. Asad goes further and states that although it is necessary, the human rights discourse is not sufficient; it is a rather 'thin' way to address oppression and violation because in the end it relies on law and access to the law to be achieved. So he argues that it is also necessary that values of 'compassion, patience, commitment, selflessness, etc.' are put into practice (Asad, 2000, section 51). These values will appear differently in different contexts, but without ethical relationships human rights become rigid and formulaic. As I have noted elsewhere (Hugman, 2008) this can be the case in countries both of the global North and of the South.

Nussbaum (2000) has proposed a way of thinking about human rights, needs and social justice, which is grounded in a cross-cultural analysis. She argues that, as the basis for what are claimed as rights rests in various capacities to live a human life, we should focus on these, which she calls 'capabilities', as those things that anyone can reasonably be expected to accomplish. From empirical studies Nussbaum suggests the following constitute these capabilities: 'life of normal length'; 'bodily health'; 'bodily integrity' such as being 'secure against assault'; 'senses, imagination and thought'; 'emotions'; 'practical reason'; 'affiliation'; living in relation to 'other species'; 'play'; and 'control over one's [immediate] environment' (2000, pp. 78–80). These capabilities 'exert a moral claim that they should be developed' that does not require justification by reference to any other value (p. 83). For Nussbaum, this approach enables us to avoid getting trapped in disagreement about human rights because:

> [...] the language of capabilities allows us to bypass this troublesome debate. When we speak simply of what people are actually able to do and to be, we do not even give the appearance of privileging a Western idea. Ideas of activity and ability are everywhere, and there is no culture in which people do not ask themselves what they are able to do [...] (Nussbaum 2000, p. 100).

The language of human rights thus becomes one possible form of the moral claim to those human capabilities that can be agreed cross-culturally. In Yip's (2004) vignette of a Chinese woman dealing with gender-based violence as much as in Healy's (2007) discussion of the same phenomenon in a Vietnamese migrant community in America, the same capabilities (such as bodily health and bodily integrity) form the basis for justifying practice outcomes that were good both morally and technically.

How then as social workers may we find our way out of what appears to be an impasse between those for whom human rights is an absolute value and those who regard it as an (alien) imposition? I suggest that the resolution of this dilemma can be found in considering the difference between what can be seen as 'primary' and 'secondary' values. This notion is derived from a position known as 'ethical pluralism' (Kekes, 1993; Hinman, 2003). Pluralism argues that it is inevitable that we will fail to agree on one or more values as paramount in all circumstances. Instead, it points to the importance of distinguishing those values that can be considered 'primary' and those which are 'secondary'. The former are those that are pursued in themselves and can be shown to apply across many different contexts, while the latter are those values that are situationally specific and may be seen as ways of achieving primary values. So, for example, in social work human rights, social justice, virtue, relationship, harmony, responsibility and so on may be seen as primary values. In contrast, self-determination, confidentiality, deferral to elders, the specific terms of a code of ethics and so on are secondary because they differ between contexts and assist in achieving the primary values.

This is not to say that all ethical disputes can be resolved easily by adopting a pluralist approach. Indeed, this approach recognizes that disputes are inevitable, just as in the common morality of everyday life we may agree with others on the shared stock of beliefs but disagree about which values should have precedence in which situation (compare with Nagel, 1979). Yet this does not invite us to adopt a relativist position, in which 'anything goes', justified by culture or expedience. In this respect, it may be that the criticisms from the global South that we examined above are really those of the ways in which the notion of human rights and social justice are imposed through the inappropriate application of secondary values in practices that make no sense in that context. Given that Silavwe (1995), Yip (2004) and Mafile'o (2006) clearly do not wish to see people oppressed or violated, their arguments for the consideration of diverse values contribute greatly to the international debate precisely because we can agree on the opposition to oppression and violation as primary values.

Moreover, cultures are not static (Fook & Pease, 1999). Elsewhere (Hugman, 2008) I have argued that it is helpful to remember that many of the values that social workers in the global North now take for granted may themselves be criticized from within European cultures (or those that derive from Europe) as 'not traditional'. As someone who was born in the north-east of England and trained there as a social worker, and who has now been a citizen of Australia for many years, I am conscious of those people in my own communities who have defended men abusing their wives or using violence to 'discipline' children as 'exercising their traditional authority within the family'. Indeed, as with the global South (compare with Nussbaum, 2000, pp. 7–9) in these situations it is often men who assert definitions of cultural norms which, given the scope to do so, many women in the same communities challenge.

The Implications for International Social Work

This discussion has explored the ways in which we might think comparatively about ethics and values for social work internationally. From this, there are three particular implications for international social work that can be identified.

The first of these is the importance of identifying cultural differences in the way we think about social work ethics and values. This is important in multicultural contexts, such as those which exist in many countries of the global North (remembering also that local communities may also have their own 'traditional culture'). How practice is undertaken with service users whose value orientation is 'international' (which may include long-standing ethnic minority settlers as well as refugees or other recent migrants) must be informed by the capacity to grasp what is 'good' in cultures other than one's own (Dominelli, 2008). Such a capacity is also a requirement for anyone who undertakes social work in a country different to her or his origins. The idea of capabilities may assist here, in that it provides a basis for considering what is important for people to pursue in order that they can live a fully human life in the terms that make sense to them. It is also on this basis, where such values are in conflict, especially when people move across national borders, that we might also raise cross-cultural questions about practices such as forced marriages for girls and FGM. Being able to engage in the processes of dialogue and debate is also part of professional exchanges and international co-operation.

The second implication is that in teaching social work ethics and values, students are introduced not only to particular interpretations as these might apply in a particular country, but also to cross-national and cross-cultural perspectives and debates. The teaching of ethics has to include both information about the principles that are stated in relevant national codes and the international statement. But at the same time, social workers must be prepared to think about ethical issues and to learn to take responsibility for our practice. As empirical studies by McAuliffe (2005), Banks (2006) and Bowles et al. (2006), among others, have shown, when social workers apply ethical principles such as confidentiality or self-determination rigidly (in other words, as if they were primary values) this can sometimes produce very bad outcomes in terms of service users' well-being. 'Good' practice in any context must include the capacity to think carefully but flexibly about the best ways to assist service users to achieve well-being.

The third implication is that the IFSW/IASSW ethical document (2004) must remain under review. This document was produced because the previous document was seen as having been too prescriptive and biased towards the global North (personal communication). However, from my own observations of the debates within IFSW and IASSW (that took place in Adelaide in 2004) and the underlying disagreements that were expressed, as well as from critiques such as those of Yip (2004), I suggest that this is a journey that has actually only just begun. Finding ways of agreeing on and expressing the primary values of social work, together with appropriate ways of defining secondary values (which we might expect to take place predominantly in national codes of ethics), is the challenge that faces social work internationally. If we are to overcome the legacy of professional imperialism it is a challenge that we must face.

9

Professional Imperialism: A Concept Revisited

Midgley's Analysis

Throughout this book a central theme has been that of the question about whether the nature of social work, and therefore of international social work, continues to be defined by its origins in the global North. An early statement of this as an issue that has to be addressed is Midgley's (1981) critique of the way in which social work was internationalized through the transmission of theories and practices from global North to the South, for which he coined the term 'professional imperialism'. Drawing on the wider historical analysis of imperialism and colonialism, Midgley argues that social work is not simply a technical matter that is independent of its social context. Rather, because relationships between countries of the South and the North were defined by colonialism the spread of social work inevitably has been bound up in these relationships. Thus, international social work can only be understood through an analysis that addresses the implicit 'imperialism' in claims to universality. Following from the discussion of cultural relativity and universalism in the previous two chapters we can see that the question of whether professional imperialism has been transcended is one that we still need to consider. Examining this question will also direct us back to the problem of whether it makes sense to think of social work as an international profession.

In common with other histories of social work, Midgley's (1981) analysis of social work in the global South begins with a recognition of its origins in countries of the North. Midgley identifies processes of industrialization, urbanization and modernization (especially as this applied to social welfare) as important factors in this development. The secularization of society and the increasing influence of positivist natural science also played their part (Midgley, 1981, pp. 3–4). As Midgley recognizes, the nineteenth century was a time in which European colonialism, especially that of Britain and France, was at its height.

136

Therefore, the governmental structures and institutions were already in place through which particular models of social welfare were exported by these colonial administrations to Africa, Asia, the Caribbean and South America (p. 40). However, the models of social welfare and the social work practices embedded in them that were taken to colonies in most cases simply replicated the metropolitan thinking, with little regard for the way in which they related to local situations. So by the early part of the twentieth century social welfare in colonized countries tended to be based on residual notions of human need (Midgley, 1981, p. 105). This meant that attention tended to be focused on questions of juvenile crime, child welfare (such as child prostitution and children living on the streets) and basic health provision, seen in terms of the circumstances and behaviours of individuals and small sections of the population, while the overall well-being and human development of the wider population was ignored. Despite subsequent shifts to the approach known as 'mass education' (the forerunner of community development) and other more developmental ways of looking at the needs of such societies, social welfare as a whole, and consequently social work, remained grounded in a set of policies that have been described as 'deliberate under-development' (e.g., compare with Gunder-Frank, 1969). It is not that such questions of individual, family and community welfare do not concern social work in the global South. For example, Elliott (1993) provides a model of the social development approach in which micro- and macro-theories and practices are integrated. But that is the point, the social development approach seeks to integrate in this way, whereas the transfer of social work ideas and techniques historically tended to focus only on the micro-level and on remedial or institutional ways of understanding and responding to social need.

For the most part, the development of social work as a distinct profession in countries of the global South tended to begin in countries that were not under direct colonial rule and spread as countries obtained their independence (Midgley, 1981, p. 57). Some social workers had been trained in metropolitan centres, especially the United States and Britain, and brought skills and ideas 'back home'. Midgley notes that the growth of schools of social work in countries of the global South accelerated from the 1950s when social work was recognized as an international profession by the UN. This resulted in increasing support from various UN agencies, especially UNICEF, for the development of social work education globally. In his discussion of this development Midgley notes (p. 56) that some voices were raised to question the suitability of professional education based on practices in Northern countries (also see Walton & El Nasr, 1988, p. 149, on the origins of this argument in a UN report in 1971). Nevertheless, the majority opinion in many parts of the profession was that in the global South social work specifically and social welfare more generally would eventually conform to the standards of 'developed' countries. The lack of resources in countries of the global South, in terms of both skilled personnel and relevant literatures, meant that reliance on countries of the North for relevant knowledge and skills continued. While some of those who were involved in these processes recognized the issue and attempted to respond to it, others, Midgley argues, did not (1981, p. 102).

As we have already seen in the previous chapter, Midgley's analysis points to the cultural specificity of the values that underpin much social work theory and we do not need to repeat these arguments here. Recognizing this then paves the way for a discussion of the theories and practices of social work, which, Midgley asserts, ought to be formed around the material circumstances of each national context. In short, the predominant needs of the global South are for social development and not for institutional and individualized social services, so it is in these areas that social work should devote its attention (1981, ch. 6). From this, Midgley then concludes that more appropriate forms of social work should be developed in countries of the South, and with this a reformulation of social work education (pp. 151–7). Social work, for Midgley, should be pragmatic (pp. 167–71), which would require that:

- training be concerned with direct practice;
- an emphasis be placed on practical rather than theoretical skills;
- the primary focus of the profession be on the most pressing problems facing communities rather than individual need;
- pragmatic social work be based on the principle of indigenization.

Midgley has subsequently developed the concept of a social development focus for social work with continued emphasis on addressing the large-scale problems of countries in the global South (Midgley, 1995, 1997; Hall & Midgley, 2004).

Indigenization and Authentization Revisited?

If we are to address the challenges of this analysis adequately it will be helpful to return to the concepts of indigenization and authentization that have been identified in previous chapters. To recap, 'indigenization' refers to the adoption and adaptation of theories and practices in social work in ways that are relevant to the local (i.e., Indigenous) context; 'authentization' refers to a process of developing theories and practices for social work which are derived out of the realities of the local context (i.e., are authentic) (Walton & El Nasr, 1988).

There is a clear distinction between these concepts, although it is quite subtle, in the emphasis on the origin of theories and practices in situations other than those in which they are now being developed as compared to the origin of such theories and practices in the current situation. Of course, this is not to say that all reference to the idea of social work and its professionalization, even the very term social work itself, being derived from another context can be ignored. The crucial question that is raised by the debates around micro- versus macro-theories and practices, universalism versus cultural relativism in ethics and values, and so on, is whether social work should be considered as a single entity or whether it is more appropriate to regard it as a looser collection of different ideas, actions and structures. This in turn poses a further question, namely why it continues to be important in countries where it may be argued that social work does not fit well culturally for the notion of 'social work' to continue to be used. As can be seen from the development of social work in Africa, South America, Asia and the Pacific Islands, even those who are severely critical of a 'western' bias in social work theories and methods nevertheless continue to struggle for the relevant growth of something that can still be understood as 'social work' (see, e.g., Mafile'o, 2006; Osei-Hwedie et al., 2006; Yan & Cheung, 2006).

To answer this question we need to consider that the internationalization of social work has not taken place in isolation from all the other facets of colonialism and more recent forms of globalization. Not only was social work taken to many parts of the world from colonial countries to those that were colonized, but also this process has occurred (or is occurring) alongside industrialization, urbanization and modernization that have great similarities with the same processes that lead to the development of social work in the global North. Although these processes can be seen as having exacerbated poverty and other forms of human misery, they have also brought many benefits. Problems of industrial pollution, poor housing, the sharpened divide between rich and poor and so on appear to be interwoven with growing material wealth, greatly expanded access (in many countries) to education and health services and modern concepts of the rule of law.

It might also be argued that the entire concept of 'the professional' in the modernized world has been exported from the global North. 'Modern' schools and universities, hospitals and (in many cases) courts of law and judicial systems around the world have been greatly influenced by such institutions in the North. Within them the professions of teacher, doctor, nurse, allied health professionals and lawyer have developed along the lines that draw substantially on the Northern models. This is not to say that equivalent concepts did not exist in the pre-colonial societies of the global South, or that more traditional practitioners in education, health and law do not continue to exist as important figures in their communities. What is clear, however, is that the modernized notion of professional has become a globalized standard.

However, as distinct from pre-colonial understandings of teacher, doctor, nurse or lawyer, Midgley refutes the idea that a similar construction of the social worker can be found, describing such claims as 'myth building' (1981, p. 94). The idea of the social worker in this sense is a modern construction, he argues; moreover, unlike areas such as education and medicine, the content as well as the form of social work is highly encultured. So claims that the idea of social work in countries of the global South can be shown to originate in traditional thinking, especially religion, are mistaken. Although social work did emerge from religious and philanthropic customs of Europe, it is grounded in those traditions, while its reference points elsewhere can be shown to be forms of 'westernization' (pp. 94–5).

However, although there are some parallels in Northern cultures between social work and the activities of religious or private philanthropy, it can also be argued that the development of social work marks a more substantial break in these contexts as well. That is, the emergence of a profession of social work in the North was as alien to traditional culture as it has been in the South. Pioneers such as Hill, Loch, Barnett, Addams and Richmond had to argue, advocate and campaign for its establishment (Parry & Parry, 1979; Payne, 2005). Therefore, it might be argued that the issue is not that professional social work is an Indigenous concept in one part of the world and an imposition elsewhere. It is, rather, one of understanding the ways in which social work develops in each situation in terms of the range of theories and practices that it embraces and the determination of what is appropriate in each context, within the forces of industrialization, urbanization and modernization.

For this reason thinking about international social work still needs to progress from the concept of indigenization to that of authentization as these were defined by Walton and El Nasr (1988). As has been widely observed, social work differs in very many respects between the countries in which it first developed. For example, the ways that social work is theorized and practised in the different countries of Northern Europe and Scandinavia, North America and Australasia are each quite distinctive (see, for e.g., Lorenz, 1994, 2008; Lyons, 1999; Payne & Askeland, 2008). There are wide variations in the emphasis between micro- and macro-levels of practice, types of micro-practice(s), the institutions within which social work operates, relationships with other professional constructs (such as 'social pedagogy') and the regulation of the profession that gives any discussion of social work a distinctive national flavour. On this basis, expectations that social work in other countries should closely resemble one or more of these models appear totally inappropriate.

At the same time, a common core can be identified that it enables us to continue to speak of social work with a sufficient degree of understanding between all the different forms that it takes around the world. That we continue to meet at international conferences, engage with international organizations and encourage to sharing of ideas through journals suggests that this is possible, at least in principle. But to achieve and maintain such a dialogue requires that colleagues in different countries accept the validity of 'authentized' variations in other places. The determining factor, it may be suggested, is that of the national debates around the different elements which make up a diverse and flexible profession.

An Example of 'Authentization' in Practice: Vietnam

In order to illustrate this discussion, we will consider the contemporary developments in Vietnam to create a profession of social work. That this is only one example means that it must be considered as illustrative rather than definitive. Nevertheless, given the present author's involvement in parts of this process (UNICEF Vietnam/MOLISA, 2005; Hugman et al., 2007, 2009), it also provides an opportunity for me to 'take responsibility' for this analysis by applying it to my own practice.

A form of professional social work developed in the South of Vietnam prior to the unification of the country in 1975 (Nguyen Thi Oanh, 2002). The models of social work practice and forms of professional education at that time were heavily influenced by French and then American sources. In 1975 the Vietnamese government abolished social work as, in common with many other communist regimes, it was regarded as unnecessary in a socialist society. In 1986 it was decided that in order to develop economically, Vietnam needed to shift to a market system within a socialist political structure (compare with Dai, 2008). The impact of this move was that the country began to develop its economy very rapidly. With these changes various social problems emerged, or re-emerged, that were seen to require skilled professional intervention. Some former social workers were then approved to begin teaching basic social work theories and methods at the Open University of Ho Chi Minh City. This in turn led to the establishment of other social work courses, such as that at the (then) College of Labour, Invalids and Social Affairs (now the University of Labour and Social Affairs) (Hugman et al., 2009, p. 179). In 2000 the MOET approved the national curriculum for social work and by 2008, 36 universities had received approval to teach this discipline. Yet, despite this development having received government support, social work is still not recognized as a profession and consequently there are no employment opportunities with this specific name. In response to this situation the MOLISA has initiated the development of a national plan to develop the profession, supported by UNICEF Vietnam (Hugman et al., 2007). In 2009 this plan is still being developed.

One of the major reasons why the development of this plan has taken several years and is still in progress is that the modernization of the social welfare field, of which the development of the social work profession as part, is being carefully considered in relation to the cultural, political and institutional norms of Vietnam. The development of social work in other Communist, or post-Communist, countries has also required a similar process (Yuen-Tsang & Sung,

2002; Namdaldagva, 2004; Ku et al., 2005). Many participants in the debates and discussions, including political and community leaders, have wanted to consider carefully the way in which a formal profession of this kind reflects changes in family and community relationships and the impact of a growing economy on more traditional patterns of dealing with social problems.

In 2005 a national study was conducted to examine the needs for a formal social work profession and the human resource implications of such a development (UNICEF Vietnam/MOLISA, 2005). This study concluded that there is a substantive need for social services in the areas of children and families (including child abuse and domestic violence), mental health, disabled and older people requiring support, and the social impacts of prostitution, drug misuse, HIV/AIDS and crime. It also concluded that a high level of training and education will be necessary to ensure the improvement of services in these areas and that the social work profession can play a key role in this process.

This study, and the continuing developmental work following from it, has explicitly addressed the importance of developing forms of social work that are appropriate for Vietnam (Hugman et al., 2007, 2009). This is seen as 'social work with Vietnamese characteristics'. The Vietnamese Government officials and academics involved in this development have been very keen to examine possible models from a wide range of other countries, but at the same time to create an authentic Vietnamese social work.

Two aspects of the recommendations contained in the 2005 study in particular demonstrate the distinctive Vietnamese approach being considered. The first of these comes from a recognition that the human resource implications in modernizing social welfare services are a vast undertaking, especially for a country in transition. Therefore, the role of university-trained social workers in the coming decade is likely to be in dealing with complex situations, supervising and supporting local practitioners in the wards and communes and to be able to contribute through more senior roles in management, research and policy development. The largest number of local practitioners are likely to be trained at high school level and in technical colleges, building on the existing experience of the 'barefoot social worker' project initiated by UNICEF that has been discussed in Chapter 6 (UNICEF Vietnam/MOLISA, 2005; Hugman et al., 2007). Although referred to as 'para-professional' (in Vietnam a recognized profession must have university level training) these workers are clearly regarded as part of the overall profession of social work and not as a separate occupational grouping. It is planned that their training and education will be carefully linked to the graduate levels to enable career progression.

Second, there is a continued recognition of the need to develop appropriate education and training materials that are suitable for Vietnam (Hugman et al., 2009). In common with other countries the theoretical and practical ideas about social work that have informed debates in Vietnam have largely been derived from countries of the global North, both in the form of over-seas education for Vietnamese social workers and in the form of consultants advising the universities as they develop training programmes. As has happened in many other countries, the lead within the universities has often been taken by academics qualified in other disciplines (particularly sociology and psychology). Nevertheless, this has provided a resource of people skilled in writing and developing curricula within the Vietnamese context. Therefore, there is clearly a process of translation, which Yan and Cheung (2006) call 'recontextualization', as authentic Vietnamese ideas are developed.

The example of Vietnam demonstrates the key features of the development of professional social work that were identified by Midgley (1981) as appropriate in attempting to progress beyond neo-colonialism. That is, there is a focus on direct practice as well as attention to organizational and educational matters, the overall structure of training and education incorporates practice as well as theory and the overall process is being geared towards the current needs of the country. One area demonstrated by the national study (UNICEF Vietnam/MOLISA, 2005) is that the practice of social development may not easily be regarded in Vietnam as a relevant field for social work. This is partly because such concerns are regarded as 'political' in some respects and also because emphasis in development policy is currently still being given to economics. However, this remains open to debate.

Very strong parallels can be drawn between the development of social work in Vietnam and that occurring in countries such as China and Mongolia (Yuen-Tsang & Sung, 2002; Namdaldagva, 2004; Ku et al., 2005). In each case it remains to be seen what authentic forms of social work will come to look like. However, in the process debates about professional imperialism, and indigenization and authentization, have enabled a more critical stance to be taken and the need for variation in the form and content of social work to be accepted positively as a feature of the profession (Lorenz, 2008).

Reversing the Process: 'Bringing it All Back Home'?

Explicitly addressing the notion of professional imperialism also raises another important possibility. If we are concerned with ensuring that the influences from social work in the global North to the global South are appropriate, what of the transfer of ideas and practices in the other direction (Midgley, 1990; Razack, 2000; Gray, 2005)? In other words, should transfer in the reverse direction also be questioned or are there grounds for welcoming the prospect of such influences?

This dynamic has been addressed to an extent in considerations of professional exchange programmes. The different partnerships and models considered by Healy et al. (2003) all contain the goal of mutual learning, with exchanges including the development of ideas across the North–South divide. Each was established in ways that sought to go beyond a 'one-way' transfer. In most of the examples cited, there is still at least an element that the knowledge provided by social workers from the global North enabled the developments of services systems and educational programmes at a relatively broad level, or the training of faculty and service administrators. By comparison, the learning by those from the North being focused on knowledge about the particular other country in question, or of a specific culture or more narrowly defined curriculum developments such as in the teaching of international social work, or social policy and so on (Hokenstad, 2003, p. 139). Several projects described in this collection particularly emphasize a benefit for students from the North being able to undertake practice learning. So, in that sense, learning can proceed in both directions. However, it remains unclear as to whether any explicit gains were intended for the wider development of curricula, or even for social work as a profession more generally, both of which occur in North to South transfers and learning.

Could this have been possible? An underlying challenge to the idea of a transfer of knowledge from the South to the North is that, in many respects, the structural relationship between countries understood in these terms remains that of neo-colonialism. There remains in place a dynamic that has been characterized as 'metropolitanism' (Connell, 2007), in which a subtle and often implicit hierarchy of influence exists. This can be seen also between countries of the global North, for example in the tendency also for social work in countries such as Australia and New Zealand to draw heavily on ideas and practices from the United Kingdom and the United States, while influence in the other direction is much less apparent. Gray (2005, p. 236), for example, notes the relative lack of attention to international ideas by social workers in these metropolitan centres. A measure of being able to progress beyond 'professional imperialism' might be if countries of the North sought consultants from the South to assist in developing services or resolving practices issues. However, most instances of 'learning for the North' continue to relate either to individuals gaining a greater knowledge of specific 'other' cultures or of informing practice about specific minority ethnic communities.

If this is the case, then what potential might there be for a more equal relationship, one that accords with social work's declared values? One answer is that partnerships and exchanges do not need to be 'equal' to be 'mutual' (Mericourt, 2001). Indeed, and it must be remembered that social workers in countries that are in the very early stages of developing the profession may wish to draw on the experience of colleagues in other countries where social work is well established. Problems occur when the post-colonial dynamics are not recognized, where those from the global North operate from the basis that there is only one plausible approach to social work and so seek to control the agenda, whether consciously or not. Therefore, dealing positively with the structural inequalities that are given by history and politics requires conscious attention to what is happening, the roles that each party plays and the choices that each can make about the relationship (Gray, 2005). The alternative answer, that cross-national partnerships and exchanges should not take place, is neither convincing nor practical. So the important factor is whether or not ways can be found to ensure that the relationship is one of equity.

As a corollary, we can also ask a similar question about the work of consultants from the global North advising governments or organizations of the South. Simply avoiding such action is not feasible, in that not all cross-national developmental work can be conducted as exchanges or partnerships of this kind. As an alternative position, Gray (2005) points to the need for an element of 'humility' (p. 235) in such practice when she writes, from the position of the global North, that:

> [t]his requires a different type of seeing and responding when social workers from the West enter into new terrain to advise on the type of social work needed. [...] We need to tread lightly, to learn to listen and to tune into culture lest we too quickly impose our culture on others and hence stand guilty of imperialism (p. 236).

Such an argument resonates with discussions elsewhere about the inherent power dynamics that are found in all aspects of social work (compare with Hugman, 1991). In that sense, it applies a similar consciousness to the generation of solutions in practice. That is, we have to find ways of resolving the tensions and paradoxes created by our shared history and politics by making these dimensions explicit in the way we work. For those from the global North involved in exchanges and partnerships, as well as for those undertaking consultancy, this suggests that the same approaches of addressing power issues and an ethics of service that can inform critical practice with individuals or communities can also be applied to our own profession. For those from the global South, it suggests the need to maintain a conscious grasp of the many different things that social work might be and the importance of questioning the view from the North when it does not fit the local situation (Tsang et al., 2000).

Social Work: One Entity or Many?

Gray and Fook (2004) and Gray (2005) have argued that although there are very many conceptual and practical difficulties in understanding social work in universal terms there are, nevertheless, some good reasons why we might wish to do so. Even a minimal level of a universal approach, they claim, will enable us to '[increase] our knowledge and understanding of human problems, strengthen practice, and further [develop] the profession in raising its profile' (Gray & Fook, 2004, p. 637). By the notion of a 'universal social work' they mean those aspects that show a high degree of commonality in theory and practice between very different countries and regions (Gray & Fook, 2004, p. 627; Gray, 2005, p. 233). Although they agree that these are difficult matters on which to find such agreement, their review of questions of universal versus local concepts, imperialism versus indigenization, universal versus culturally specific values and globalization versus localization is used to suggest five key points for an international dialogue on social work. They suggest that these points will assist in the process of finding enough of a common basis for us to continue to talk about social work as a single entity in widely divergent national contexts (Gray & Fook, 2004, pp. 639–40).

First, a basic level of universal agreement requires a 'grounded approach', in which any overarching ways of understanding and talking about theory and practice are built from the ground up in a comparative way between diverse situations. Within such an approach there is plenty of scope for valuing those differences that reflect what is particular to each local situation. But it also requires that we base our dialogues on realities rather than ideal notions.

Second, even a minimal acceptance of commonality will require a broad and inclusive approach to defining the profession. For example, it may be the case that at the beginning of the twenty-first century the standard entry-level qualification to social work in many countries is now a bachelors degree (Sewpaul & Jones, 2004). However, this is not the case in every country and unconditional acceptance of colleagues in different parts of the world on the basis of what is the defined standard in their country will be much more productive in enabling those from different places to engage in the international professional community. Moreover, it is helpful to value interdisciplinary working and seeking closer allegiance with colleagues in sectors that may traditionally have had their origins as part of social work, such as those who work in organizations that are members of ICSW or ICSD.

Third, we are directed back to the relevance of a social development approach to social work. Again, this needs to be on an inclusive basis. However, especially as the more micro-level practices that predominate in the global North tend to displace wider concerns with poverty and other forms of social deprivation, acceptance of macro-level practices is actually the problem in most situations. At the same time, this is not a call to jettison micro-level practices, but rather to endorse the idea of a breadth of vision in the focus and methods of social work.

Fourth, social work should be regarded as contextual. This not only means addressing people in ways that recognize their situations (the person-in-environment approach) but also, as with the previous point, embracing the idea that social work should also be concerned with social contexts as a whole.

Fifth, localized dialogue that recognizes diversity within as well as between particular contexts has potential to facilitate the development of 'authentic' local (i.e., 'indigenized' in the terms of that debate) social work. This will then provide a stronger base for a more equal international dialogue.

This proposed set of steps has strong parallels with the pluralist approach discussed in the previous chapter, in that it seeks to find what is shared and can be regarded as 'primary' or 'basic', recognizing that this will necessarily be at a relatively high level of generality. In such an approach the specific ways of applying primary ideas may then be seen as 'secondary' or as 'local detail'. It is not that one is more important than the other (as might be implied by the use of ordinal categories) but rather, to use a metaphor, one is the body of the bird while the other is the plumage (Nussbaum, 2000, p. 50). For example, we may find that there are clear differences between countries on matters such as the balance between micro- and macro-level focus, the extent to which social development is regarded as part of social work or a separate entity, the precise meaning of anti-racist and anti-discriminatory practice or the extent to which social workers are employed by government or non-government organizations. Similarly, we may find that while in one country a university masters degree is required for professional recognition while in another country a technical college diploma is the benchmark qualification for professional social work, yet in all situations it is agreed that an appropriate education in relevant knowledge, skills and values is necessary for social work (Barnes & Hugman, 2002). Acceptance of these differences as relevant to each local context can enable a more open dialogue to occur than too great a concern with establishing criteria that are not only difficult for some countries to meet but may actually be irrelevant (or even harmful) to the development of social work there.

We are left, however, with the historical and political reality of the inequalities in the relationships between countries and cultures. The pluralist method of identifying those ideas and values that can be regarded as primary still has to take this into account. Centuries of colonialism and the implicit neo-colonialism that marks many aspects of globalization have to be overcome in both theoretical and practical ways. As Gray and Fook (2004, p. 632) remind us, Said (1978) argued in his critique of 'Orientalism' (an intellectual tendency in anthropology, history, politics and so on to both idealize and at the same time homogenize and denigrate 'eastern' culture) that even 'oriental' people may have absorbed 'western' culture in ways that they find difficult to identify and acknowledge. The process of 'de-colonization' is one that concerns everybody in social work, especially those who are concerned with or involved in international social work (in all dimensions that have either been identified in this book, which includes domestic practice with people from other countries). It necessitates that we identify and respond critically to the influence of colonialism in our theories and practices. This is also true for social workers in the settler societies of Australia,

Canada, New Zealand and the United States, whether they are Aboriginal or First Nations or 'from the mainstream' (to use an Australian term).

Gray and Fook's (2004) recommendations for an inclusive and flexible approach to ideas and actions that enable us to hold on to the idea of social work as a single entity internationally echo Midgley's (1981) call for pragmatism (a point that they acknowledge). Making this the key to his argument leads Midgley to add a cautionary note that the test of appropriateness for different views of social work is that they should have concrete relevance for each specific context. As Midgley puts it (1981, pp. 170–1), not only should theories and practices not be embraced solely on the grounds that they are from countries where social work is long established but, at the same time, new ideas 'should not be adopted simply because they offer an alternative to western casework'; nor should social workers seek to become skilled in other forms of practice if these cannot be integrated within the profession. This argument means that micro-level practices should not be seen necessarily as inappropriate in countries of the global South, only that the question must be asked. In other words, as practices develop they should be pragmatically relevant to their context and not be adopted simply because these are the dominant modes of thinking about and practising social work in North America, Europe or Australasia. This leads us to the conclusion that the arbiters of what social work can be and do should be those who are concerned with its development in any particular context. Thinking in these terms will only be facilitated when there is greater acceptance across the profession of the breadth and diversity of social work within as well as between countries.

10

International Social Work: Issues for the Future

Thinking about International Social Work

Conclusions reached by recent studies of international social work differ in many ways in their implications for future developments. For Healy (2008a) the continued growth of internationalism provides the basis for an open, inquiring dialogue between forms of social work in different parts of the world. The risk for social work in any country, she argues, is that it gets caught up in a tendency to isolationism that follows from too great an emphasis on national and cultural differences and the threats to security that follow from increasing global tensions. Healy is especially concerned that matters of cultural difference and security must not be used as reasons to undermine human rights (p. 360). (It is important to recognize that Healy is writing in the USA and reflecting on the years following 11 September 2001.)

More specifically, Cox and Pawar (2006) enthusiastically embrace the project of international social work but wish to see a shift in focus to a social development approach. This, they argue, will require changes to the way in which we think about social work generally, as well as specific developments in social work education to prepare social workers to practise more appropriately in various contexts. Such a change might be more difficult for those social workers from the global North, because they are educated within frames of reference that are more taken for granted, and less adaptable to a social development perspective, and so they have more to un-learn. It will also demand that international social work is more clearly featured in the professional curriculum, with an emphasis on structural issues and practices (p. 366).

In contrast, Payne and Askeland (2008) appear more sceptical about the idea of international social work. In their analysis the relationship between the various parts of social work in different locations is bound up with the contradictions of globalization. These include the implications of post-colonialism, such as the linguistic and cultural dominance of the global North and the hegemony of neo-liberalism in economics. In such a context they argue that social work is a very minor player, both as a profession in relation to other professions and because of its 'small-scale objectives and focus on interpersonal, small group, family and community relations' (p. 154). So they emphasize the ways in which the differences and changing circumstances require flexibility, contextualization and diversity and argue for a more fluid view of social work that is critically responsive to globalization rather than 'international'.

Dominelli (2007) also emphasizes diversity and a critical stance on globalization and in this regard she also is conscious of the limitations to some of social work's grander claims (such as promoting empowerment or being able to manage 'risk'). Nevertheless, in doing so she also maintains an international perspective in which social work is seen as part of the overall dynamic of globalizing societies. The implication is that we should address international issues in all aspects of theory and practice. For Dominelli, the values of social work in social justice and human rights are embedded in the critical analysis of globalization, which asks who is included and who is excluded by these processes.

Likewise, Lyons notes that although forms of social work may be 'specific to a given time and place' (1999, p. 2), the impact of globalization can be seen in everyday practice around the world (e.g., in issues that are presented in Chapters 3 and 4). This analysis is extended in Lyons et al. (2006), leading to the view that social workers may enhance their local practices by developing a more international perspective (p. 12). This notion was incorporated in the various definitions of international social work discussed in Chapter 2, although it was noted that unlike the other ways of seeing the field this view becomes broad to the extent that it is not possible in this type of analysis to provide detailed examples from the literature. (Such examples are provided by collections such as Ferguson et al. [2005] and some of the papers that accompany Dominelli [2007].)

Underlying all of these analyses of international social work is a basic question about the nature of 'internationalism', in other words about the relationship between ideas and practices connecting different national or cultural contexts (see, e.g., Gasper, 2006). This question concerns whether social work can, in fact, be 'international'. At one extreme is the view that social work is a single entity, with skills, knowledge and values that can be defined across national boundaries. At the other extreme is the position that social work is necessarily shaped by 'local law, culture and welfare regimes in any particular state' (Payne & Askeland, 2008, p. 153). How we answer this question forms the basis on which we can understand 'international social work', if we conclude that such a phenomenon exists.

In reality it appears that even the most severe critics do not actually rule out the plausibility of examining international social work as a field, while the most enthusiastic proponents of international social work as a distinct entity also are critical of failure to recognize issues of national and cultural difference. So, we may say that analyses of international social work tend to sit at various points along a continuum between these two extremes. This can be observed not only in the detail of their arguments, but also in the active involvement of the individuals concerned in international social work in one or more of the ways in which it was defined in Chapter 2 (as demonstrated in these very colleagues' own discussions). Thus, the debates tend to agree that 'international social work' can be recognized as a distinct field but that it can be addressed in different ways.

In Chapters 1 and 2 of this book, it was noted that social work has now developed in at least 90 countries, in the sense of there being an organized professional association in each of those nations. As an activity, it was noted that we might also expect to find that social work exists in other places as well, even if it is not recognized as a distinct profession. International social work was then defined as social work that involves relationships between countries in the form of the movement across national borders of social workers, service users and/or social problems and issues. For service users this includes situations of seeking refuge or asylum, as well as planned migration or even temporary movement. For social workers it encompasses those who are employed by international organizations, those who migrate and work in national or local organizations, partnerships and exchanges, conferences and other cross-national linkages. So in Chapter 3 several major international issues that impact on social work were identified and discussed, which include refugees and asylum seekers, human trafficking, natural disasters, poverty and the impact of globalization. Within these issues it was seen that there are specific challenges for children, women, disabled people, older people, Indigenous people and those from ethnic minority communities. This analysis emphasized the way in which international social work tends to focus on the impact for individuals, families and communities of macro-level issues such as social development, conflict and so on. Chapter 4 addressed the United Nations' MDGs as a particular international focus for some of these key issues and examined issues of the role that social work might play in responding to the targets that have been set. It also reviewed the criticisms that have been made of the MDGs.

These early chapters raised important questions about social work, from the perspective of considering social work in different national and cultural contexts. From this, in Chapter 5 an argument was developed for a broad and inclusive view of social work as a whole. Using a comparison between the global North and South, this analysis emphasized that social work is only adequately grasped if we look at the integration of macro- and micro-perspectives, as these affect the way we understand the objectives, the theories and the practices of social work. The potential of a social development approach for international social work was considered.

In Chapter 6 the specific organizational settings of international social work were discussed. This included both those organizations that employ social workers within the various meanings of 'international' noted above and the international professional bodies of social work itself. Thus we examined INGOs and the agencies of the UN as well as the IASSW, the ICSW and the IFSW. It was observed that social work has had a positive impact in the work of INGOs and UN organizations, although it is not always visible. In Chapters 7 and 8 key issues in the work of the IASSW, IFSW and ICSW were explored, in the form of the *Global Standards on Education and Training in Social Work* (IASSW/IFSW, 2004) and *Ethics in Social Work: Statement of Principles* (IFSW/IASSW, 2004). These discussions considered the arguments for and against such international policies and statements, highlighting problems that had been raised in previous chapters regarding the tension between the idea of social work as a single (universal) entity and the differences between nations and cultures.

In Chapter 9 the questions of universal and specific ideas and practices in social work were brought to the issue of 'professional imperialism'. Identified by Midgley (1981) as the underlying dynamic of the international growth of social work, this concept was revisited to consider the ways in which it may continue to inform our understanding of international social work. In that discussion the chapter began to bring together some of the central themes that had run through the preceding chapters about the ways in which social work can be understood as the product of historically and culturally specific social relationships as compared to seeing it as a single international phenomenon.

In summary, therefore, this book has sought to respond to the question of internationalism and international issues in social work by emphasizing that the varying shape(s) of social work in differing national and cultural contexts can be held together in a creative tension. However, it has also repeatedly been observed that social work is part of the global dynamic of relationships between countries and regions in which the global North exercises hegemony over the South. So, while social work action, including the development of social work itself in countries of the South, has sought to address and ameliorate the problems that have been identified above, it has also often been part of the same structural dynamic, for example in the ways in which it has at some times and in some places been part of colonization. Recognizing this then returns us to the question of whether international social work has overcome the problem of 'professional imperialism', to which the answer must be that we have only partly redressed this historical problem. From a consideration of this question, it has been argued that understanding international social work requires that we identify and address a core contradiction, that of the relationship between universalism and localism (relativism grounded in national and cultural differences) in the definition of social work and its theories, methods and values. This in turn directs us back to the problem of whether social work is one entity or many and, therefore, how we might respond to the challenges of international social work.

Universalism versus Localism

It is, perhaps, easier to summarize the universalist position. Quite simply, it holds that in each location, what we understand as social work is inherently the same. The task is to be knowledgeable and skilful in providing effective responses to the needs of service users (whether individuals, families, groups or communities). Therefore, what is required is that we are able to identify the range of issues that constitute the 'international', to build knowledge about these and to ensure that we are appropriately trained. A universal position does not necessarily rule out matters of culture and diversity, but rather also treats these as the subject of specialized knowledge and skill (Dean, 2001). At its most extreme, Dean argues, 'culture' can come to be seen solely as technical matter. In short, a fully universal position begins with a single view of social work and seeks to apply this across all contexts.

The culturally relativist position is, as we have seen, the opposite. Taken to its full extent, here we find the argument that social work is so different in each national and cultural setting that any transfer of ideas will result in the inappropriate imposition of ideas and practices in an alien context. In this perspective, 'international' practice can only be considered in terms of the difference of requirements according to the specifics in each situation. For example, the social worker going to work in another country is obliged only to think and act in terms of a unique local approach to social issues, including the knowledge and skills required to address them, and so on. Such an argument may even be used to suggest that 'social work' cannot be appropriate outside the context of modernist culture (i.e., that of the global North) (Azmi, 1997).

And yet, as we have also noted in the preceding chapters, both these positions are actually untenable in their extreme forms. To the universalist, we can respond that there are important cultural and other differences that change the shape of social work in different contexts, in the way that knowledge, skills and values come together to form practices and institutions. Social work in New York differs from that in London, and both are different from social work in Sydney, as much as all three locations are different again from Delhi, Addis Ababa, Beijing or Nuku'alofa. To the localist we can observe that, despite these differences, it is still possible for us to talk about social work in all these places, to understand each other in relation to the different approaches to knowledge, skills and values that are evident in each setting, to meet together in conferences, to read published accounts and arguments and make use of these, and so on. This suggests that to understand international social work and to think about its development we need to find a third position.

Is such a third position simply a matter of meeting half way between universalism and localism? To this question, I think that the answer has to be that it is more than this, at least in the sense of not just taking parts of each argument and trying to connect them. It is, I suggest, more a matter of how we hold the competing arguments in a creative tension that enables us to find new ways of proceeding. One way of attempting to do this can be seen in the debates around Nussbaum's (2000, 2006a) *ethical* approach to internationalism, which demands the equitable treatment of all people around the world combined with 'substantive ethical obligations across national boundaries' (Gasper, 2006, p. 1230). As was noted briefly in Chapters 8 and 9, Nussbaum bases this argument on the idea that there are common elements to the achievement of a fully human life (which she calls 'capabilities', in that to achieve full humanity our lives must be so ordered as to provide us with the capability of accomplishing them). However, as Nussbaum emphasizes, the form in which these capabilities are made real varies widely between different cultural contexts.

Although critics have argued that this approach continues to risk the denial of cultural diversity (Giri, 2006; Truong, 2006), Nussbaum's (2006b) response is that it is only by starting with the recognition of common humanity, inclusive of *all* people in *all* situations, that we can begin to work for objectives such as achieving human well-being and meeting basic human needs in ways that make sense in terms of local norms and expectations. Nussbaum also provides strong evidence that such concerns are not culturally specific to the global North, but resonate with the lives of people in many parts of the world (2006b, pp. 1321–3). A similar conclusion is reached by Pittaway and her colleagues (2003, 2004, 2007) in their work with refugee women, and echoed in Healy's quotation of the words of Kofi Annan (who is himself West African), that '[i]t is never the people who complain of human rights as a Western, or Northern imposition. It is too often their leaders who do so' (in Healy, 2008a, p. 239).

I find this compelling both in theory and in practice. Philosophically, the argument that a 'cultural perspective' must be permitted to be free to restrict the freedom of some members of the society in which it pertains is self-defeating, because it demands something that it then denies. This is especially the case, as Annan's remark implies, when these types of claims are made by those who benefit from such arrangements and those who are denied capabilities are forced to remain silent. I accept that some arguments for cultural relativity in this debate are motivated differently, for example as a defence of global Southern cultures from the apparent back-door hegemony of what is seen as a Northern perspective (Azmi, 1997; Yip, 2004; Giri, 2006; Truong, 2006). Nevertheless, although it is only anecdotal, my own practical experience of discussions with colleagues in various African, Asian and Pacific contexts is that objectives such as social justice and human rights are regarded in many parts of the global South as meaningful and important, even if their tangible appearance may be different from my own expectations (compare with Razack, 2000). (This accords with Nussbaum's and Pittaway's conclusions). As we saw in Chapter 8, particularly, when we accept objections to the universality of these values it ought to be as an argument against particularities of interpretation and application and not the central concern of social work for human well-being and basic needs (e.g., see Yip, 2004; compare with Hugman, 2008, and Banks et al., 2008).

Using Nussbaum's (2000) framework of capabilities as a point of reference, McGrath Morris (2002) argues that social work has set itself the very difficult task of addressing those aspects of individual, family, community and social functioning that enable or prevent people from achieving well-being and meeting their basic needs. This includes a recognition that choices and opportunities are 'economically and socially constructed', even that people may choose to restrict their own options out of preference for particular values (McGrath Morris, 2002, p. 369); but the important question is whether people have the necessary capabilities to act as full members of their societies. This then provides a foundation for social work to consider social justice and human rights as basic to human well-being but to see their different detailed expression also as valuable. Indeed, in a socially just world it is necessary that anyone's rights be achieved in ways that make sense to them and not simply as others would define them. McGrath Morris also makes the point that this approach supports the integration between micro- and macro-perspectives, especially in that it identifies that social justice relates to individual and family issues as well as communities and social structures (2002, p. 371).

'Visions' of International Social Work

In Chapter 2 the field of international social work was articulated in terms of five different ways in which some aspect of social work traversed national borders:

1. the practice of social work in a country other than the home country of the social worker;
2. working with individuals, families or communities whose origins are in a country other than that where the social worker is practising;
3. working with international organizations (whether or not the social worker travels outside her or his home country);
4. collaborations between countries in which social workers exchange ideas or work together on projects that cross national borders;
5. practice that addresses local issues which originate in globalized social systems.

However, the analysis presented in the preceding chapters suggests that these cannot be taken as straightforward, but as we have seen must be regarded as contested sets of ideas and practices. How does a position in which we acknowledge the claims of both universal and local perspectives of human well-being and basic needs affect the ways in which we might understand these different aspects of international social work?

In order to answer this question I want to look first at some specific examples of how this analysis might affect the way we consider international social work. Then, in conclusion, I will suggest that this analysis tells us something about social work as a whole.

The first implication of this analysis for international social work is that all colleagues, but especially those from the global North, ought to consider their own positioning in relation to others. This is the case in situations where people cross borders, whether as social work practitioners, service users or in collegial exchanges. 'Considering our positioning' includes a recognition of the cultural influences in the ways in which we understand what constitutes human well-being and basic needs and the ways in which what we 'know' about social work is grounded in a particular national context. I say 'especially those from the global North' because the movement of social workers and social work ideas still tends to be predominantly in the North to South direction, but also because those colleagues from the South may well be more used to experiencing themselves as 'other' in the international discourse of the profession (e.g., Razack, 2000; Graham, 2002; Mafile'o, 2006; Marais & Marais, 2007; Yan & Tsui, 2007). This directs our attention to the idea of 'humility' discussed by Gray (2005) that is cited in Chapter 9. It is not an argument that we (especially those of us from the North) should not engage in international work, but that we should be more self-aware and self-critical in how we view our knowledge, skills and values and how we act in relation to other countries (Doel & Penn, 2007).

Second, following from this, the profession in its various structures would gain from pursuing the idea first proposed by Midgley (1981) that social work around the world has much to learn from the struggles of those in the global South. Again, we might observe that this applies especially to social work in the global North. As has been noted by key writers in this field, the extent of the comparative study of social work and attention to international social work can be limited (e.g., Lyons, 1999; Healy, 2008a). But such attention to other countries needs to progress beyond 'knowing about' for its own sake (which may have value but which, at its worst, can become a sort of 'travelogue' – compare with Ahmadi, 2003, p. 15) and to focus on learning about each other and about difference, as well as learning more about ourselves through the process. Anecdotally, my own experience is that suggesting to colleagues in countries where social work is relatively new that we might aspire to the goal of a future in which social workers in the global North expect to consult colleagues from the South to help resolve problems of the development of the profession often is regarded as a humorous remark. However, unless we can embrace such an idea, the legacy of professional imperialism remains tangible.

Third, international social work organizations can examine their recruitment of social workers. There is a cycle of employing those who are trained in the global North, particularly in key roles, which goes back to the earliest days of the profession internationally. We also noted in Chapter 6 that the international professional organizations have had very few elected office holders or employed staff from regions other than Europe and North America. Of course, the availability of people with the appropriate qualifications and experience is a substantive issue in this respect. But a more conscious attention to this question would assist in effecting change. For example, are the criteria for what is 'appropriate' inclusive or are they defined in terms of regionally specific views about the nature of social work, and what opportunities are provided to enable colleagues to participate?

Fourth, where international social work is concerned with service users or social issues crossing borders, there may well be a case for 'cultural competence' as part of the set of knowledge, skills and values. The point that has been noted about this, however, is that it is not simply a technical matter of adding new knowledge and skills to the existing stock of practices. Rather, it requires that we rethink social work in terms of how we understand our objectives and values as well as developing a more reflexive stance on our own backgrounds, assumptions and capacities. This must, as a central concern, embrace an anti-racist perspective in theory and practice (Dominelli, 2008; Clifford & Burke, 2008). As with the second point above, this ought also have the potential to inform our continued development of all forms of social work, locally as well as internationally.

Lessons for Social Work

The implications of this analysis not only concern international social work as a field within the profession, but goes beyond that to our vision of social work as a whole (Ahmadi, 2003; Healy, 2007). We have noted in this discussion that the relationships of social work across national borders have tended to privilege the global North over the South, because of the ways in which these have been grounded in historical and current economic, political and cultural realties. In contrast, the argument here has been that we need to make a conscious effort to go beyond this unidirectional relationship. In Ahmadi's words, it is necessary to see international social work as 'less an endeavour emanating from one national source than a multi-directional web having the character of a decentred practice' (2003, p. 16).

In Chapter 5 an argument was made for an inclusive view of social work, that embraces micro-, mezzo- and macro-perspectives. The idea of a 'decentred' practice does not mean that we should lose our sense of social work as something that we can recognize *as* social work in its different guises in different places, but instead calls into question the search for a single way of understanding what social work is. Thus, the balance between micro, mezzo and macro may shift between places and over time while we continue to be able to relate each of the various forms that emerge to each other, to be able to exchange ideas and to find ways of working together across national borders.

Following Midgley (1995), Ahmadi (2003, p. 18) calls for a greater emphasis on 'social development' as the international objective for social work (also, see Cox & Pawar, 2006). Indeed, in so far as international practice and exchanges have resulted in the creation of a vision for the profession that focuses only on the micro-level and excludes mezzo- and macro-level concerns, this should be a priority (compare with Olson, 2007). The limitations of this argument, however, can be found in the sense that in many places where social work is in the early stages of development, or where poverty and other material needs seem overwhelming, that a micro-level concern with human need and rights at an individual level is not missing. For example, Lyons et al. (2006) make a convincing case that the issue of 'loss' is one that has great relevance to social work in many different contexts and requires us to be able to integrate the micro and the macro (also see Razack, 2000, p. 88). Similarly, Healy's (2007) concern that social work is facing the impact of a global 'retreat from human rights' contains both individual and structural implications for action.

The same breadth of vision is also called for in relation to the values, and hence objectives of social work (compare with Weiss, 2005). But, at the same time, this is not a call for 'anything goes'. The argument for diversity does not, for example, take us as far as accepting that social workers may reasonably be involved in terrorism or torture. Notwithstanding the ways in which social work has been compromised by repressive and violent political regimes, such as by Nazism and Fascism in Europe in the middle of the twentieth century (Lorenz, 1994), social workers of many different backgrounds have tended to regard the value of human well-being as primary. Where debate can reasonably take place is in relation to the ways in which this objective is to be understood and pursued in any particular locality.

Social work can be seen as the professionalization of responses to those aspects of our societies that are seen as problems of human well-being. In Nussbaum's (2001) terms, social work is grounded in compassion: understood not as 'pity', but as the response of our intellect and our emotions to the plight of others, based on a recognition of our shared humanity. Social work is not unique in this, as this value orientation is shared by other 'caring' professions (Hugman, 2005). What is unique is the particular *set* of knowledge and skills that, together with a certain understanding of values, constitute social work's practices. (I am allowing here that there is considerable overlap between social work and other professions, just as there is also between those other professions.) In these terms we can say that social work, in whatever context, is built on an ethical 'response to "others" ' (compare with Bauman, 1993), while finding its rationale in the common humanity of all.

Yet social work has continually to struggle with the recognition of the 'other', because each of us brings our identity to this encounter, in our sex, age, ethnicity, nationality, sexuality, physical and mental abilities, as well as our religious and political beliefs. Even at the very local level, therefore, social work must attend to 'otherness' in so many ways if it is to be relevant and effective. There is a risk that in focusing on issues and practices that are not dealt with widely in other fields of social work, such as social work with refugees, human trafficking, natural disasters, poverty and social development and Indigenous issues (see Chapter 3), a view may be perpetuated of international social work as concerned with the global South or those parts of the North where 'Southern' circumstances prevail, such as in Indigenous communities of the 'settler societies' (Australasia and North America). Yet, the argument for a multi-directional, decentred focus runs counter to this tendency, in that it points to the fact that consideration of these issues has implications for social work in *all* contexts.

Understanding international social work is important for social work as a whole, because it highlights the question of social work as a response to the 'other' in so many ways. We can see this in the critique of 'professional imperialism' and questions about continuing 'neo-colonialism'. It is evident also in the debates about whether social work is one thing or many things. Some of 'us' are perhaps more used to experiencing ourselves as 'other' in the discourse(s) of social work. A critical analysis of international social work brings further to the foreground the extent to which all social workers, and all forms of social work, have an identity. One particular response to this may be for those of 'us' (including the present author) from the global North to discover ourselves more as 'other', which this analysis suggests is a major requirement for the possibility of a multi-directional, decentred (and thus, we might add, decolonized) profession to develop. So, especially in the context of increasing globalization, understanding international social work is crucial for the ways in which we can understand social work as a richly varied set of theories and practices.

Glossary

Apartheid – Literally meaning 'apartness' in Afrikaans, this term refers to the laws, policies and practices of racial segregation that were implemented in South Africa between the late 1940s and the early 1990s. It led to services and other aspects of social welfare, including social work, to be structured and practised differently for the different 'racial' groups and meant that White South Africans were the most advantaged and Black South Africans the most disadvantaged.

Asia-Pacific Association of Social Work Education (APASWE) – This association is comprised of more than 200 schools of social work from the Asia and Pacific regions, as these are defined by IASSW (see below) of which it is an affiliate organization. Its website is at http://www.apaswe.net/index.asp

Association of South-East Asian Nations (ASEAN) – Formed in 1967, ASEAN is a bloc of ten south-east Asian countries that seeks to promote economic and political co-operation between members. Some cultural exchange is also part of its agenda. This bloc also has formal ties with other countries in the wider Asia-Pacific region. Unlike the EU (see below) ASEAN does not have common governance institutions.

Authentization – A term used by some social workers to refer to the development of forms of social work that are directly appropriate to the local context, in other words 'authentic'. (See 'indigenization' below.) In some discussions, such as those from China, the term 'contextualization' is used to refer to the same process.

Economic and Social Council of the United Nations (ECOSOC) – ECOSOC is the main UN forum that co-ordinates discussion, policy and reporting on economic and social issues. It brings together the work of the specialized agencies, the functional and regional commissions and the various UN funds and programmes. More than 2,000 organizations are registered with the Council and, along with the member states of the UN, have 'reporting status' which means that they can speak at the Council. Some organizations, such as ICSW (see below) have 'General' status, meaning that they can address ECOSOC on all matters, while others such as IASSW and IFSW (see below) have 'Special' status and can only speak on matters in which they are regarded as having special interest and expertise.

European Union (EU) – Formed in 1994, out of the preceding European Community, in 2009 the EU has 25 member states. Although each country is a sovereign state, the EU has moved towards greater integration economically, politically and socially than (for example) ASEAN (see above). It has an elected parliament and a currency (which at the time of writing had been adopted in 16 countries). Although officially social policy is the responsibility of each state, there are mechanisms for promoting discussion and research about such matters.

G8 – The 'Group of 8' was the term used for the eight economically powerful nations who met in Gleneagles in Scotland in 2005 to consider cancelling the debts of highly indebted poor countries. Some cancellation of these debts was agreed, subject to evidence of civil society and the rule of law. The use of the term 'Group of' has also been used for other meetings, with varying numbers of countries represented, such as the G20 meeting in 2009.

General Agreement on Tariffs and Trade (GATT) – A treaty, originally between 23 countries, that ran from 1947 to 1994, that sought the reduction of restrictions on international trade. These included tariffs and quotas on imports. It was replaced in the 1990s by the World Trade Organization (see below).

Global 'North' and 'South' – These terms were popularized through the work of the Independent Commission on International Development Issues, under the chairpersonship of former German Chancellor Willie Brandt (hence it is also known as the Brandt Commission). Its main report, in 1980, was entitled *North-South*. This distinction is based on an understanding of the main developmental division between countries being that of the highly developed countries of North America and Europe, plus Australian and New Zealand and the developing or transitional countries that are almost all located to the south. Other models of understanding regions or groups of countries do not so adequately grasp this primary distinction (such as East-West, Third World and so on). Australia and New Zealand are part of the 'global North', although they are physically in the southern hemisphere, because they are socially, politically and economically comparable with other 'advanced' countries. Such an understanding makes this distinction more robust for considering global relations than regional identities such as Oceania (in which Australia and New Zealand are grouped with the Pacific Islands, Timor Leste and so on although they do not share the same levels of development). Thus, this is the primary term used throughout this book to characterize basic economic and political distinctions geographically.

Globalization – The process by which, it is argued by some analysts, the economic, political, social and cultural systems of the world are becoming increasingly integrated into one overarching system.

Imperialism – Referring originally to 'empire', this is both a set of social relations of dominance and/or an attitude in which a particular country or culture exercises power over others. Professional imperialism, in this sense, means that one particular way of understanding a profession dominates other contexts. This is usually expressed in a belief that the dominant perspective is inherently superior because it originates with a powerful group or country and therefore that it ought to be the dominant perspective.

Indigenization – In the context of social work, the process in which a set of theories and practices is taken from one part of the world to another and then adapted to 'fit' the local circumstances (see discussion in Chapter 5). This term has usually been applied to the development of local forms of social work in the Global South (see above), adapted from the 'North'. Some commentators argue that a more genuinely local approach to social work is required, for which the terms 'authentization' and 'contextualiztion' were coined (see above).

International Association of Schools of Social Work (IASSW) – IASSW is the international organization comprised of schools of social work, other providers of social work education and training and individual social work educators. It provides a network for the exchange of ideas, through dialogue, conferences and co-sponsorship of the journal *International Social Work*. It also campaigns on matters of concern to members and the social work profession generally; in this regard, IASSW has 'Special' consultative status to the United Nations through ECOSOC (see above). Founded in 1928, by 2009 it had 536 member schools across all continents; there are also five regional affiliate regional organizations (such as APASWE, see above). At the time of writing, there is increasing collaboration between IASSW and IFSW (see below) regarding statements on professional ethics and standards of education and training. IASSW is discussed in Chapter 6. Its website is at http://www.iassw-aiets.org

International Committee of the Red Cross (ICRC) – Established in 1863, the Red Cross (as it is more commonly known) consists of the International Committee and national bodies. It describes itself as an independent humanitarian organization that has a mission to protect the lives and dignity of those who are affected by war and other violence. It also has the name Red Crescent in Muslim countries

International Council on Social Welfare (ICSW) – ICSW is made up of non-government (third sector) organizations involved in the provision of social welfare and social development. It was founded in 1928 and in 2009 had members in more than 70 countries that include local, national and international NGOs. ICSW provides a network for sharing ideas and is a co-sponsor of the journal *International Social Work*. It also campaigns on matters of concern to members and those who use social welfare services, for example through 'General' consultative status to ECOSOC (see above) at the United Nations. ICSW is discussed in Chapter 6. Its website is at http://www.icsw.org

International Consortium for Social Development (ICSD) – Originally formed as the Inter-University Consortium for Social Development, ICSD is predominantly made up of social work educators, researchers and practitioners. However, it has increasingly opened its membership to members of other professions involved in social development. Its main goal is to facilitate the exchange of ideas and expertise and to bring together those involved in social development across different sectors, including universities, the UN system, INGOs and so on. It has regional branches and links with the other international social work organizations. http://www.iucisd.org

International Federation of Social Workers (IFSW) – In the 1950s the earlier Permanent Secretariat of Social Workers (defunct since the 1930s) was revived and became IFSW. A peak body of national professional associations, IFSW also has regional committees and commissions on human rights and on ethics. As with other international social work organizations, it promotes dialogue, networking and campaigning, through conferences and meetings, co-sponsorship of the journal *International Social Work* and 'Special' reporting status at ECOSOC (see above) at the United Nations. At the time of writing, IFSW has members from 86 countries and affiliates in four others. Individual social workers may support this work by belonging to 'Friends of IFSW'. IFSW is discussed in Chapter 6. Its website is http://www.ifsw.org

International Labour Organization (ILO) – A specialist organization within the UN system, whose formal goal is to bring together workers, employers and governments, in order to achieve decent working conditions and productive employment. In doing so it seeks social justice and human rights in labour relations.

International Monetary Fund (IMF) – A specialized agency of the United Nations, the IMF promotes trade and economic activity through support to countries in order to assist them to engage in trade and the reduction of poverty. Thus the Fund describes itself as facilitating development. It has an autonomous structure, with membership of the 186 countries that comprise the UN. It was established in late 1944 and its initial role was in economic reconstruction after the world conflict of 1939–45. It had the task of securing exchange rate stability. After 1971 it took on more of a role in assisting countries to deal with economic liberalization. As with the World Bank (see below), it has been criticized for promoting policies that benefit the interests of the more wealthy countries in the global 'North' (see above).

Macro, mezzo and micro (theories and practices) – These words are derived from Greek and literally mean 'large', 'middle' and 'small'. In this context, they refer to the degree of generality or specificity of ideas and actions in practice. Thus, macro-approaches are those that take a 'large' view of social issues, focusing on social structures and systems. At the mezzo-level we are concerned with agencies, administration and similar practices; this level is sometimes not recognized as separate (see, e.g., the discussion in Chapter 5 in this book). Micro-level theories and practices address individuals, families and groups within communities. One of the major debates among social workers, addressed throughout this book, is whether social work ought to focus on one or other level or should seek to integrate them.

Metropolitanism – The attitude that favours locations that are perceived to be the 'social centre' (the 'metropolis'). This phenomenon can be seen within countries, where policies and decisions tend towards the interests of the capital city and its environs, or between countries where large economically powerful nations are treated as being at the 'centre' of thinking about issues.

Millennium Development Goals (MDGs) – In 2000 the UN established a set of goals, with associated specific targets, for world development. These goals include education, gender equality, health, economic well-being, infrastructure, the environment and trade relations. Some critics regard the MDGs as too restricted and limited in their scope, while others point to the way in which it is now clear that the aim of achieving the targets by 2015 is already clearly impossible. See extended discussion in Chapter 4 in this book. The MDG website is http://www.un.org/millenniumgoals/

Neo-colonialism – Although the occupation of countries by other countries from other parts of the world (colonialism) has now largely ended, it is argued that direct occupation has been replaced by economic and cultural dominance through which the former colonisers continue to exert power and control. This relationship is called neo-colonialism (i.e., new colonization).

Neo-liberalism – Liberalism is a social philosophy in which individual liberty is regarded as the paramount value. In recent decades a new (neo) form of liberalism has developed in national and international social, political and economic relations. In this form, the primary value is that of liberty for individuals, organizations and nations to engage in trade and business. Within this position, the actions of states that seek to limit the actions of some people or groups in order to protect the interests of those who are seen to be weaker or in need are regarded as undue constraint on liberty. This position therefore is often associated with the reduction of socially funded services, such as education and health.

Organization for Economic Co-operation and Development (OECD) – The membership of the OECD is nation states, with 30 members as in 2009 and a further 40 affiliates. Formed in 1961, it assists member states with economic growth and development policies and strategies, largely through research and information, providing technical assistance and creating a forum for debate and the exchange of ideas. The members are countries of the global 'North' (see above), while affiliates are largely from the 'South'.

Poverty Reduction Strategy Papers (PRSPs) – In 1999 the World Bank (see below) launched a process in which countries seeking to receive development grants, loans or debt relief should produce policy documents that outline the options available to the country and the strategy that it will adopt in order to reduce poverty. These papers are intended to be prepared by a national government in collaboration with the World Bank, the International Monetary Fund (see above) and civil society organizations in the country in question. Subsequently it was determined that the PRSPs should be aligned with the UN Millennium Development Goals. Critics argue that the process is dominated by the Bank and the IMF and that consultation at national level is often with local branches of INGOs rather than with more widely representative civil society organizations.

Privatization – A major impact of neo-liberalism (see above) has been the transfer of state services and assets to NGOs (the private sector), whether not-for-profit or profit-making. This term can also refer to the policy that seeks to make individual members of society responsible for their own welfare needs, that is in shifting such concerns from the public to the private sphere.

Remedial welfare – Some approaches to the provision of social welfare (see below) emphasize the alleviation of problems and resolving deficits. In this sense they focus on 'remedies' for social problems. When applied to social work practice, the term refers to a concentration on dealing with the outcomes of problems rather than looking at the causes. It also implies that remedial practice looks at deficits rather than the resources that people experiencing problems may already possess. Alternatives include the ideas of 'strengths based' practice and 'empowerment'.

Social systems – Many analysts look at a society as system that is made up of many inter-related parts. These in turn are usually characterized as 'institutions', which can include the formal organizations and entities of a society (such as government, businesses, trade unions, religious organizations, educational establishments, health facilities and the like) together with informal entities such as 'the family', 'communities' and so on.

Social welfare – This term has different meanings in North America and other parts of the English-speaking world. In North America it refers to income maintenance, such as government payments to support people who are unemployed. In the United Kingdom, Australia, New Zealand and some other countries, it refers to the system of social provision, whether government or non-government, that meets human needs. In these latter countries it includes pensions and other financial benefits, but also social housing, public health and education services and social work provision. This wider definition is that used in this book.

Structural adjustment – A technical term coined to describe the policy and practice in which developing countries were required to change their national economies and government systems in order to comply with loans and grants from the IMF (see above) and the World Bank (see below). These 'adjustments' included privatization and deregulation of state assets and services, including in many cases health, education and social welfare, as well as changes in taxation systems, tariffs and market regulation. Critics have argued that these requirements served the interests of wealthy nations to have increased opportunities and lower costs for trade.

United Nations – The United Nations was established in 1945 and now comprises 192 member states. Its explicit purpose is to promote peace and security and to advance social development throughout the world. Its main bodies are the General Assembly, the Security Council and the Economic and Social Council (ECOSOC, see above). The UN seeks to achieve its goals through dialogue and debate, through advice and assistance and through the direct work of its Commissions, Organizations, Funds and Programmes.

United Nations Children's Fund (UNICEF) – As a United Nations agency, UNICEF promotes the well-being of children around the world. It undertakes research and policy development, advocates with governments and other parts of the UN system, advises national governments and engages in direct projects. In 2009 its priorities were education (with a particular emphasis on gender equality), the impact of HIV/AIDS on children, child protection and child rights, and child survival and development (which includes attention to nutrition, access to safe water and other environmental issues). UNICEF has in-country offices in those countries where it has projects and also works into other countries from its regional offices.

United Nations Development Program (UNDP) – The UNDP is an agency of the UN that exists to promote economic, social and environmental development through the provision of technical assistance to national governments and advocacy concerning development issues. In 2009 it was working in 166 countries. The UNDP has increasingly incorporated human rights values in its work and also focused on the empowerment of women. Within the UN system the UNDP has coordinative responsibility for the MDGs (see above).

United Nations High Commission for Refugees (UNHCR) – Originally established on a time-limited basis to look after the interests of refugees after the 1939–45 global conflict, UNHCR now has concern with over 30 million people, including refugees, asylum seekers, internally displaced people and those who have recently returned from seeking refuge. It operates through advocacy, the provision of direct assistance and protection, capacity building and policy development. In 2009 UNHCR has offices in over 100 countries and works also in others when required. Its headquarters are in Geneva (Switzerland).

World Bank – The World Bank defines itself as a 'group', which consists of the International Bank for Reconstruction and Development (IBRD) and the International Development Association (IDA). The former focuses on middle-income countries, while the latter is concerned with the poorest countries. (There are also several affiliate organizations.) Both parts of the World Bank system exist to provide funds to countries, in the form of loans and grants, to support a variety of social and economic development goals. The Bank was established in 1944 and initially co-ordinated post-war reconstruction. The Bank now is managed by a board of directors representing 186 countries. Nevertheless, critics have argued that it has often imposed models of development on poor countries of the global South that meet the interests of wealthier Northern nations.

World Health Organization (WHO) – The WHO is an agency of the United Nations system, with the role of promoting health globally. It does this through standards setting, research and monitoring and the provision of advice and technical assistance to different countries.

World Trade Organization (WTO) – Established in 1995 to replace the GATT (see above), the WTO has 153 members in 2009. It promotes trade liberalization through the regulation of trade between members. Recent years have seen disagreement between those countries with high numbers of sub-sistence farmers and other particularly vulnerable workers and the remaining members. The WTO has also become the focus for vociferous protest by a col-lation of groups opposed to various aspects of its goals, including globalized trade and the associated neo-liberal agenda.

Bibliography

Aamaa Milan Kendra/Centre for Development & Population Activities (AMK/CEDPA) (2004) *Adolescent Girls' Literacy Initiative for Reproductive Health (A Gift for RH)* (Kathmandu/Washington, DC: AMK/CEDPA).

Acharya, S. & Koirala, B. N. (2006) *A Comprehensive Review of the Practices of Literacy and Non-Formal Education in Nepal*, Working Paper #11 (Kathmandu: UNESCO).

Addams, J. (2002 [1907]) *Democracy and Social Ethics*, ed. C. H. Siegfried (Urbana and Chicago: University of Illinois Press).

Ahmadi, N. (2003) 'Globalisation of consciousness and new challenges for international social work', *International Journal of Social Welfare*, 12 (1), 14–23.

Akimoto, T. (1997) 'Requestioning international social work/welfare: where are we now? Welfare world and national interest', *Japanese Journal of Social Services*, 1 (1), 27–34.

Al-Krenawi, A. & Graham, J. R. (1999) 'Social work practice and female genital mutilation: the Bedouin-Arab case', *Social Development Issues*, 21 (1), 29–36.

Allotey, P., Manderson, L. & Grover, S. (2001) 'The politics of female genital surgery in displaced communities', *Critical Public Health*, 11 (3), 189–201.

Alston, M. (2007) '"It's really not easy to get help": services to drought affected families', *Australian Social Work*, 60 (4), 421–35.

Andhari, J. (2007) 'Reconceptualizing community organization in India: a transdisciplinary perspective', *Journal of Community Practice*, 15 (1/2), 91–119.

Anucha, U. (2008) 'Exploring a new direction for social work education and training in Nigeria', *Social Work Education*, 27 (3), pp. 229–42.

Asad, T. (2000) 'What do human rights do? An anthropological enquiry', *Theory and Event*, 4 (4) (electronic journal, accessed at http://www.muse.jhu.edu/journals on 25 May 2007).

Askeland, G. A. & Payne, M. (2007) 'Distance education and international social work', *European Journal of Social Work*, 10 (2), 161–74.

Association Canadienne des Travailleuses et Travailleurs Sociaux/Canadian Association of Social Workers (ACTS/CASW) (2005) *Code of Ethics* (Ottawa: ACTS/CASW).

Australian Association of Social Workers (AASW) (2002) *Code of Ethics 1999* (Kingston ACT: AASW).

Ayittey, G. (2005) *Africa Unchained: The Blueprint for Africa's Future* (New York: Palgrave-Macmillan).

Azmi, S. (1997) 'Professionalism and social diversity', in R. Hugman, M. Peelo & K. Soothill (eds) *Concepts of Care: Developments in Health and Social Welfare* (London: Arnold), 102–20.

Badran, H. (1975) 'Egypt's social service system: new ideology, new approaches', in D. Thursz & J. L. Vigilante (eds) *Meeting Human Needs: An Overview of Nine Countries* (Beverley Hills: Sage Publications), 28–68.

Balagopalan, S. (2008) 'Memories of tomorrow: children, labor and the panacea of formal schooling', *Journal of the History of Childhood and Youth*, 1 (2), 267–85.

Baldry, E. & Green, S. (2002) 'Indigenous welfare in Australia', *Journal of Societal and Social Policy*, 11 (1), 1–14.

Ban, P. (2005) 'Aboriginal child placement principle and family group conferences', *Australian Social Work*, 58 (4), 384–94.

Banks, S. (2006) *Ethics and Values in Social Work*, 3rd edn (Basingstoke: Macmillan).

Banks, S., Hugman, R., Healy, L., Bozalek, V. & Orme, J. (2008) 'Global ethics for social work: problems and possibilities', *Ethics and Social Welfare*, 2 (3), 276–90.

Barnes, D. & Hugman, R. (2002) 'Social work: portrait of a profession', *Journal of Interprofessional Care*, 16 (3), 277–88.

Batstone, D. (2007) *Not for Sale: The Return of the Global Slave Trade – and How We Can Fight It* (New York: HarperSanFrancisco).

Bauman, Z. (1993) *Postmodern Ethics* (Oxford: Basil Blackwell).

Bauman, Z. (1998) *Globalization: The Human Consequences* (Cambridge: Polity Press).

Beauchamp, T. & Childress, J. (2001) *Medical Ethics*, 5th edn (Oxford: Oxford University Press).

Berg, K. (1997) 'Female genital mutilation: implications for social work', *The Social Worker*, 65 (3), 16–26.

Bernasek, A. (2003) 'Banking on social change: Grameen Bank lending to women', *International Journal of Politics, Culture and Society*, 16 (3), 369–85.

Blackstock, C., Trocmé, N. & Bennett, M. (2004) 'Child maltreatment investigations among Aboriginal and non-Aboriginal families in Canada', *Violence Against Women*, 10 (8), 901–16.

Billups, J. O. (2002) *Faithful Angels* (Washington DC: NASW Press).

Bowles, W., Collingridge, M., Cohen, S. & Valentine, B. (2006) *Ethical Practice in Social Work: An Applied Approach* (Crow's Nest NSW: Allen & Unwin).

Boyle, E. H. & Carbone-López, K. (2006) 'Movement frames and African women's explanations for opposing female genital cutting', *International Journal of Comparative Sociology*, 47 (6), 435–65.

Briskman, L. (2003) *The Black Grapevine: Aboriginal Activism and the Stolen Generation* (Annandale, NSW: Federation Press).

Briskman, L. (2007) *Social Work with Indigenous Communities* (Annandale, NSW: Federation Press).

Briskman, L., Latham, S. & Goddard, C. (2008) *Human Rights Overboard. Seeking Asylum in Australia* (Carlton North, VIC: Scribe).

British Association of Social Workers (BASW) (2002) *Code of Ethics* (Birmingham: BASW).

Brook, R. M., Hillyer, K. J. & Bhuvaneshwari, G. (2008) 'Microfinance for community development, poverty alleviation and natural resource management in peri-urban Hubli-Dharwad, India', *Environment and Urbanization*, 20 (1), 149–63.

Bullens, R. A. & Van Horn, J. E. (2002) 'Labour of love: female juvenile prostitution in the Netherlands', *Journal of Sexual Aggression*, 8 (3), 43–58.

Butler, I. & Drakeford, M. (2001) 'Which Blair project? Communitarianism, social authoritarianism and social work', *Journal of Social Work*, 1 (1), 7–19.

Burke, J. & Ngonyani, B. (2004) 'A social work vision for Tanzania', *International Social Work*, 47 (1), 39–52.

Burkett, I. & McDonald, C. (2005) 'Working in a different space: linking social work and social development', in I. Ferguson, M. Lavalette & E. Whitmore (eds) *Globalisation, Global Justice and Social Work* (London: Routledge), 173–87.

Cammack, P. (2002) 'Neoliberalism, the World Bank and the new politics of development', in U. Kothari & M. Minogue (eds) *Development Theory and Practice: Critical Perspectives* (Basingstoke: Palgrave-Macmillan), 157–78.

Carten, A. & Goodman, H. (2005) 'An educational model for child welfare practice with English-speaking Caribbean families', *Child Welfare*, 84 (5), 771–89.

Cemlyn, S. & Briskman, L. (2003) 'Asylum, children's rights and social work', *Child and Family Social Work*, 8 (3), 163–78.

Centre for Development and Population Activities (CEDPA) (2005) *Advocacy for Girls' Education* (Washington, DC: CEDPA).

Chama, S. B. (2008) 'The problem of African orphans and street children affected by HIV/AIDS: making choice between community-based and institutional care practices', *International Social Work*, 51 (3), 410–15.

Chazin, R., Hanson, M., Cohen, C. S. & Grishyeva, I. (2002) 'Sharing knowledge and skills: learning from school-based practitioners in the Ukraine', *Journal of Teaching in Social Work*, 22 (3/4), 89–101.

Cheers, B. & Taylor, J. (2007) 'Social work in rural and remote Australia', in M. Alston & J. McKinnon (eds) *Social Work: Fields of Practice*, 2nd edn (Melbourne: Oxford University Press), 237–48.

Chenoweth, L. I. & Stehlik, D. (2002) 'Using technology in rural practice – local area co-ordination in rural Australia', *Rural Social Work*, 7 (1), 14–21.

Choi, J-S. & Choi, S. (2005) 'Social work intervention with migrant workers in South Korea. Micro and macro approaches', *International Social Work*, 48 (5), 655–65.

Chomsky, N. (1999) *Profit Over People: Neo-Liberalism and Global Order* (New York: Seven Stories Press).

Christie, A. (2003) 'Unsettling the "social" in social work: responses to asylum seeking children in Ireland', *Child and Family Social Work*, 8 (3), 223–31.

Claiborne, N. (2004) 'Presence of social workers in nongovernment organizations', *Social Work*, 49 (2), 207–18.

Clark, C. (2000) *Social Work Ethics* (Basingstoke: Palgrave-Macmillan).

Clifford, D. & Burke, B. (2008) *Anti-Oppressive Ethics and Values in Social Work* (Basingstoke: Palgrave Macmillan).

Coates, J., Gray, M. & Hetherington, T. (2006) 'An "ecospiritual" perspective: finally, a place for indigenous approaches', *British Journal of Social Work*, 36 (3), 381–99.

Connell, R. (2007) *Southern Theory: The Global Dynamics of Knowledge in Social Science* (Cambridge: Polity Press).

Correll, D. (2008) 'The politics of poverty and social development', *International Social Work*, 51 (4), 453–66.

Cox, D. & Pawar, M. (2006) *International Social Work: Issues, Strategies and Programs* (Thousand Oaks, CA and London: Sage Publications).

Cox, E. (1995) *A Truly Civil Society* (Sydney: ABC Books).

Dai, H. J. (2008) 'Community in a diverse society. Using three western approaches to understand community organization in post-socialist urban China', *International Social Work*, 51 (1), 55–68.

Darkwa, O. K. (2008) 'Continuing social work education in an electronic age: the opportunities and challenges facing social work education in Ghana', *Professional Development*, 2 (1), 38–43.

Datta, B. (2007) 'Knowing the difference', *New Internationalist*, 404 (September), 14–16.

Deacon, B. (2007) *Global Social Policy and Governance* (London: Sage Publications).

Dean, R. G. (2001) 'The myth of cross-cultural competence', *Families in Society*, 82 (6), 623–30.

Demmer, C. & Burghart, G. (2008) 'Experiences of AIDS related bereavement in the USA and South Africa: a comparative study', *International Social Work*, 51 (3), 360–70.

Department of Urban and Rural Community Development (2004) *Taking Root... Spreading Wings... Alumni Workshop 3–4 September* (Mumbai: Tata Institute of Social Sciences).

Despotovic, M., Medic, M., Shimkus, D. & Staples, L. (2007) 'NGO development in Croatia: de facto interdisciplinary practice', *Journal of Community Practice*, 15 (1/2), 171–92.

Desyllas, M. C. (2007) 'A critique of the global trafficking discourse and U.S. policy', *Journal of Sociology and Social Welfare*, 34 (4), 57–79.

Doel, M. & Penn, J. (2007) 'Technical assistance, neo-colonialism or mutual trade? The experience of an Anglo/Ukrainian/Russian social work practice learning project', *European Journal of Social Work*, 10 (3), 367–81.

Dominelli, L. (2003) 'Internationalising social work', in L. Dominelli & W. T. Bernard (eds) *Broadening Horizons: International Exchanges in Social Work* (Aldershot: Ashgate), 19–30.

Dominelli, L. (ed.) (2007) *Revitalising Communities in a Globalising World* (Aldershot: Ashgate).

Dominelli, L. (2008) *Anti-Racist Social Work*, 3rd edn (Basingstoke: Palgrave Macmillan).

Dominelli, L. & Bernard, W. T. (eds) (2003) *Broadening Horizons: International Exchanges in Social Work* (Aldershot: Ashgate).

Drakeford, M. (2002) 'Social work and politics', in M. Davies (ed.) *The Blackwell Companion to Social Work*, 2nd edn (Oxford: Basil Blackwell).

Drucker, D. (2003) 'Whither international social work? A reflection', *International Social Work*, 46 (1), 53–61.

Drumm, R. D., Pittman, S. W. & Perry, S. (2003) 'Social work interventions in refugee camps: an ecosystems approach', *Journal of Social Service Research*, 30 (2), 67–92.

Durst, D., Nguyen Thi Thai Lan & Le Hong Loan (2006) *An Analysis of Social Work Education and Practice in Vietnam and Canada* (Regina: University of Regina Social Policy Research Unit).

Eilers, K. (2008) 'René Sand (Belgium) President 1946–1953', in F. W. Seibel (ed.) *Global Leaders for Social Work Education: The IASSW Presidents 1928–2008* (Ostrava: Verlag Albert/IASSW), 57–70.

Elliott, D. (1993) 'Social work and social development: towards an integrative model for social work practice', *International Social Work*, 36 (21), 21–36.

Elliott, D., Jordan, C., Ferreire, M. R., Hernández, S. H. & Díaz, H. L. (2003) 'A binational, bilingual doctoral program in social work', in L. Healy, Y. Asamoah & M. C. Hokenstad (eds) *Models of International Collaboration in Social Work Education* (Alexandria VA: Council on Social Work Education), 71–80.

Engebrigsten, A. (2003) 'The child's – or the state's – best interests? An examination of the ways immigration officials work with unaccompanied asylum seeling minors in Norway', *Child and Family Social Work*, 8 (3), 191–200.

Esping-Andersen, G. (1990) *The Three Worlds of Welfare Capitalism* (Princeton, NJ: Princeton University Press).

Farmer, T. W., Clemmer, J. T., Leung, M.-C., Goforth, J. B., Thomson, J. H., Keagy, K. & Boucher, S. (2005) 'Strength-based assessment of rural African American early adolescents: characteristics of students in high and low groups on the behavioral and emotional rating scale', *Journal of Child and Family Studies*, 14 (1), 57–69.

Ferguson, I. & Lavalette, M. (2005) ' "Another world is possible": social work and the struggle for social justice', in I. Ferguson, M. Lavalette & E. Whitmore (eds) *Globalisation, Global Justice and Social Work* (London: Routledge), 207–23.

Ferguson, I., Lavalette, M. & Whitmore, E. (eds) (2005) *Globalisation, Global Justice and Social Work* (London: Routledge).

Fisher, W. (1997) 'Doing good? The politics and antipolitics of NGO practices', *Annual Review of Anthropology*, 26, 439–64.

Fook, J. (1993) *Radical Casework: A Theory of Practice* (St. Leonards NSW: Allen & Unwin).

Fook, J. & Pease, B. (1999) (eds) *Transforming Social Work* (St. Leonards NSW: Allen & Unwin).

Forgery, M. A., Cohen, C. S., Berger, S. & Chazin, R. (2000) 'Outsiders on the inside: reflections on social work teaching in Vietnam', *Reflections*, 6 (4), 5–17.

Forgery, M. A., Cohen, C. S. & Chazin, R. (2003) 'Surviving translation: teaching the essentials of social work practice in Vietnam', *Journal of Teaching in Social Work*, 23 (1/2), 147–66.

Forrest, K. & Rushton, A. (1999) 'Children with relatives abroad: assessment for placement', *Child and Family Social Work*, 4, 153–61.

Forsyth, W. (1995) 'Discrimination in social work – an historical note', *British Journal of Social Work*, 25 (1), 1–16.

Freidson, E. (1994) *Professionalism Reborn* (Chicago: University of Chicago Press).

Freymeyer, R. & Johnson, B. (2007) An exploration of attitudes toward female genital cutting in Nigeria', *Population Research and Policy Review*, 26 (1), 69–83.

Gabriele, A. (2006) 'Social services policies in a developing market economy oriented towards socialism: the case of health system reforms in Vietnam', *Review of International Political Economy*, 13 (2), 258–89.

Galambos, C. M. (2005) 'Natural disasters: health and mental health considerations', *Health and Social Work*, 32 (2), 83–6.

Gallagher, A. (2003) *Nursing and Human Rights* (London: Butterworth-Heinemann).

Gao, L. Z. & Hu, X. C. (2005) 'Overview of and reflections on Chinese practice of microcredit for poverty alleviation', *Social Development Issues*, 27 (3), 35–48.

Gasper, D. (2006) 'Cosmopolitan presumption? On Martha Nussbaum and her commentators', *Development and Change*, 37 (6), 122–1246.

George, S. (1988) *A Fate Worse Than Debt* (Harmondsworth: Penguin).

George, V. & Wilding, P. (2002) *Globalisation and Human Welfare* (Basingstoke: Palgrave-Macmillan).

Giri, A. K. (2006) 'Cosmopolitanism and beyond: towards a multiverse of transformations', *Development and Change*, 37 (6), 1277–92.

Graham, L. (2009) 'LoveLife, Groundbreakers and Mpintshis: young people engaged for change', *The Social Work Practitioner-Researcher*, 21 (1), 131–9.

Graham, M. (2002) *Social Work and African-Centred World Views* (Birmingham: Venture Press).

Gray, M. (2005) 'Dilemmas of international social work: paradoxical processes of indigenisation, universalism and imperialism', *International Journal of Social Welfare*, 14, 231–8.

Gray, M. & Fook, J. (2004) 'The quest for a universal social work: some issues and implications', *Social Work Education*, 23 (5), 625–44.

Gray, M., Coates, J. & Hetherington, T. (2007) 'Hearing indigenous voice in mainstream social work', *Families in Society*, 88 (1), 55–66.

Green, S. & Baldry, E. (2008) 'Building Australian Indigenous social work', *Australian Social Work*, 61 (4), 389–402.

Gunder-Frank, A. (1969) *Capitalism and Underdevelopment in Latin America*, 2nd edn (New York: Monthly Review Press).

Hall, N. & Midgley, J. (2004) *Social Policy for Development* (London: Sage Publications).

Hattori, T. (2003) 'The moral politics of foreign aid', *Review of International Studies*, 29 (92), 229–47.

Hawkins, C. A. & Rao, P. N. (2008) 'CEDER: a social development response to the tsunami recovery in Tamil Nadu, India', *Social Development Issues*, 30 (1), 29–46.

Hazarika, G. & Sarangi, S. (2008) 'Household access to microcredit and child work in rural Malawi', *World Development*, 36 (5), 843–59.

Healy, L. M. (1995) 'Comparative and international overview', in T. D. Watts, D. Elliott & N. S. Mayadas (eds) *International Handbook on Social Work Education* (Westport CT: Greenwood Press), 421–39.

Healy, L. M. (2007) 'Universalism and relativism in social work ethics', *International Social Work*, 50 (1), 11–26.

Healy, L. M. (2008a) *International Social Work: Professional Action in an Interdependent World*, 2nd edn (New York: Oxford University Press).

Healy, L. M. (2008b) 'A brief journey through the 80 year history of the International Association of Schools of Social Work', in F. W. Seibel (ed.) *Global Leaders for Social Work Education: The IASSW Presidents 1928–2008* (Ostrava: Verlag Albert/IASSW), 1–25.

Healy, L. M., Asamoah, Y. & Hokenstad, M. C. (eds) (2003) *Models of International Collaboration in Social Work Education* (Alexandria VA: Council on Social Work Education).

Heimer, C. A. (2007) 'Old inequalities, new disease: HIV/AIDS in sub-Saharan Africa', *Annual Review of Sociology*, 33, 551–77.

Heske, C. (2008) 'Interpreting Aboriginal justice in the Territory', *Alternative Law*, 33 (1), 5–9.

Hinman, L. M. (2003) *Ethics: A Pluralistic Approach to Moral Theory*, 3rd edn (Belmont CA: Wadsworth/Thomson).

Hobbes, T. (1968 [1651]) *Leviathan*, ed. C. B. McPherson (Harmondsworth: Penguin).

Hodge, D. R. (2008) 'Sexual trafficking in the United States: a domestic problem with transnational dimensions', *Social Work*, 53 (2), 143–52.

Hodge, D. R. & Lietz, C. A. (2007) 'The international sexual trafficking of women and children', *Affilia: Journal of Women and Social Work*, 22 (2), 163–74.

Hokenstad, M. C. (2003) 'Global interdependence and international exchange: lessons for the future', in L. M. Healy, Y. Asamoah & M. C. Hokenstad (eds) (2003) *Models of International Collaboration in Social Work Education* (Alexandria VA: Council on Social Work Education), 133–41.

Hokenstad, M. C. & Midgley, J. (2004) 'Lessons from other countries: current benefits and future opportunities', in M. C. Hokenstad & J. Midgley (eds) *Lessons From Abroad: Adapting International Social Welfare Innovations* (Washington, DC: NASW Press), 1–12.

Holkup, P. A., Salois, E. M., Tripp-Reimer, T. & Weinert, C. (2007) 'Drawing on wisdom from the past: an elder abuse intervention with tribal communities', *The Gerontologist*, 4 (2), 248–54.

Hughes, M. & Wearing, M. (2008) *Organisations and Management in Social Work* (London: Sage Publications).

Hugman, R. (1991) *Power in Caring Professions* (Basingstoke: Palgrave-Macmillan).

Hugman, R. (1998) *Social Welfare and Social Value* (Basingstoke: Palgrave-Macmillan).

Hugman, R. (2005) *New Approaches to Ethics in the Caring Professions* (Basingstoke: Palgrave Macmillan).

Hugman, R. (2008) 'Ethics in a world of difference', *Ethics and Social Welfare*, 2 (2), 118–32.

Hugman, R. (2009) 'But is it social work? Some cases of mistaken identity', *British Journal of Social Work*, 39 (6), 1138–53. .

Hugman, R., Nguyen Thi Thai Lan & Nguyen Thuy Hong (2007) 'Developing social work in Vietnam', *International Social Work*, 50 (2), 197–211.

Hugman, R., Durst, D., Le Hong Loan, Nguyen Thi Thai Lan & Nguyen Thuy Hong (2009) 'Developing social work in Vietnam: issues in professional education', *Social Work Education*, 28 (2), 177–89.

Humpage, L. & Marston, G. (2005) 'Cultural justice, community development and onshore refugees in Australia', *Community Development Journal*, 40 (2), 137–46.

Ife, J. (2001) *Human Rights and Social Work: Towards Rights Based Practice* (Oakleigh VIC: Cambridge University Press).

Ife, J. & Tesoriero, F. (2006) *Community Development: Community-Based Alternatives in an Age of Globalisation*, 3rd edn (Frenchs Forest, NSW: Pearson).

International Association of Schools of Social Work/International Federation of Social Workers (IASSW/IFSW) (2004) *Global Standards for Education and Training in Social Work* (electronic document accessed at http://www.ifsw.org/en/p38000222.html on 26 November 2008).

International Center for Research on Women (2003) *The Intergenerational Approach to Development: Bridging the Generation Gap* (Washington, DC: International Center for Research on Women).

International Federation of Social Workers (IFSW) (2008a) *IFSW General Meeting and World Conference 2008* (electronic document accessed at http://www.ifsw.org/en/p38001447.html on 22 October 2008.)

International Federation of Social Workers (IFSW) (2008b) *History of the IFSW* (electronic document accessed at http://www.ifsw.org/en/p38000060.html on 20 October 2008).

International Federation of Social Workers/International Association of Schools of Social Work (IFSW/IASSW) (2000/2001) *The Definition of Social Work* (electronic document accessed at http://www.Ifsw.org/en/p38000208.html on 27 August 2007).

International Federation of Social Workers/International Association of Schools of Social Work (IFSW/IASSW) (2004) *Ethics in Social Work: Statement of Principles* (electronic document accessed at http://www.ifsw.org/en/p38000032.html on 20 October 2008.)

International Social Service (ISS) (no date) 'Children in public care' (electronic document accessed at http://issuk.org.uk/what_we_do/state_care.php on 8 December 2008).

Jaiswal, E. (2005) 'Community development for asylum seekers in Hungary', *Community Development Journal*, 40 (2), 220–3.

Javadian, R. (2007) 'Social work responses to earthquake disasters. A social work intervention in Bam, Iran', *International Social Work*, 50 (3), 334–46.

Jones, C. (1983) *State Social Work and the Working Class* (London: Macmillan – now Palgrave-Macmillan).

Jones, L., Engstrom, D. W., Hilliard, T. & Diaz, M. (2007) 'Globalization and human trafficking', *Journal of Sociology and Social Welfare*, 34 (2), 107–22.

Juliá, M. & Kondrat, M. E. (2005) 'Health care in the social development context', *International Social Work*, 48 (5), 537–52.

Kawawe, S. & Dibie, R. (1999) 'United Nations and the problem of women and children abuse in Third World nations', *Social Justice*, 26 (1), 78–98.

Kekes, J. (1993) *The Morality of Pluralism* (Princeton NJ: Princeton University Press).

Kendall, K. (2008) 'Herman D. Stein (USA) President 1968–1976', in F. W. Seibel (ed.) *Global Leaders for Social Work Education: The IASSW Presidents 1928–2008* (Ostrava: Verlag Albert/IASSW), 105–21.

Koehn, D. (1994) *The Ground of Professional Ethics* (London: Routledge).

Koggel, C. M. (2007) 'Empowerment and the role of advocacy in a globalized world', *Ethics and Social Welfare*, 1 (1), 8–21.

Kreitzer, L. (2002) 'Liberian refugee women: a qualitative study of their participation in planning camp programmes', *International Social Work*, 45 (1), 45–58.

Kreuger, & Stretch (2003) 'Identifying and helping long term child and adolescent disaster victims: model and method', *Journal of Social Services Research*, 30 (2), 93–108.

Ku, H. B., Yeung, S. C. & Sung-Chan, P. (2005) 'Searching for a capacity building model in social work education in China', *Social Work Education*, 24 (2), 213–33.

Kuruvilla, S. (2005) 'Social work and social development in India', in I. Ferguson, M. Lavalette & E. Whitmore (eds) *Globalisation, Global Justice and Social Work* (London: Routledge), 41–54.

Kwon, H.-J. (1998) 'Democracy and the politics of social welfare', in R. Goodman, G. White & H.-J. Kwon (eds) *The East Asian Welfare Model* (London: Routledge), 25–74.

Laird, S. E. (2008) 'Social work practices to support survival strategies in sub-Saharan Africa', *British Journal of Social Work*, 38 (1), 135–51.

Lawrence, R. J. (1965) *Professional Social Work in Australia* (Canberra: Australian National University).

Leve, L. D. & Chamberlain, P. (2007) 'A randomized evaluation of multidimensional treatment foster care: effects on school attendance and homework completion in juvenile justice girls', *Research on Social Work Practice*, 17 (6), 657–63.

Lorenz, W. (1994) *Social Work in a Changing Europe* (London: Routledge).

Lorenz, W. (2008) 'Towards a European model of social work', *Australian Social Work*, 61 (1), 7–24.

Lowe, A. H. (2007) 'Human trafficking: a global problem with solutions that begin at home', *Praxis*, 7 (Fall), 50–7.

Lundy, C. (2004) *Social Work and Social Justice* (Calgary: Broadview Press).

Lundy, C. (2006) 'Social work's commitment to social and economic justice: a challenge to the profession', in N. Hall (ed.) *Social Work: Making a Difference. Social Work Around the World IV* (Berne/Oslo: IFSW/FAFO), 115–28.

Lyngstad, R. (2008) 'The welfare state in the wake of globalization. The case of Norway', *International Social Work*, 51 (1), 69–81.

Lyons, K. (1999) *International Social Work: Themes and Perspectives* (Aldershot: Ashgate).

Lyons, K. (2006) 'Globalization and social work: international and local implications', *British Journal of Social Work*, 36 (3), 365–80.

Lyons, K. (2008) 'Abye Tasse, 2004–2008', in F. W. Siebel (ed.) *Global Leaders for Social Work Education: The IASSW Presidents 1928–2008* (Ostrava: Verlag Albert/IASSW), 189–207.

Lyons, K., Manion, K. & Carlsen, M. (2006) *International Perspectives in Social Work: Global Conditions and Local Practice* (Basingstoke: Palgrave Macmillan).

Mafile'o, T. (2006) 'Matakainga (behaving like family): the social worker-client relationship in Pasifika social work', *Social Work Review/Tu Mau*, 18 (1), 31–36.

Maker, A. (2008) 'Soul Buddyz: community engagement at grassroots level', *The Social Work Practitioner-Researcher*, 20 (2), 270–6.

Mapp, S. C. (2008) *Human Rights and Social Justice in a Global Perspective* (New York: Oxford University Press).

Marais, L. & Marais, L. C. (2007) 'Walking between worlds. An exploration of the interface between indigenous and first-world industrialized culture', *International Social Work*, 50 (6), 809–20.

Mathbor, G. M. (2007) 'Enhancement of community preparedness for disasters', *International Social Work*, 50 (3), 357–69.

Mathbor, G. M. & Ferdinand, P. A. (2008) 'Progress or regress of the MDGs: South Asia perspective', *Journal of Comparative Social Welfare*, 24 (1), 49–64.

Maxwell, J. & Healy, L. M. (2003) 'Mutual assistance through an on-going United States-Caribbean partnership' in L. M. Healy, Y. Asamoah & M. C. Hokenstad (eds) *Models of International Collaboration in Social Work Education* (Alexandria VA: Council on Social Work Education), 51–60.

McAuliffe, D. (2005) 'Who do I tell? Support and consultation in cases of ethical conflict', *Journal of Social Work*, 5 (1), 21–43.

McDonald, C. (2000) 'The third sector in the human services: rethinking its role', in I. O'Connor, P. Smyth and J. Warburton (eds) *Contemporary Perspectives on Social Work and the Human Services: Challenges and Change* (Melbourne: Longman), 84–99.

McDonald, C. (2006) *Challenging Social Work: The Institutional Context of Practice* (Basingstoke: Palgrave Macmillan).

McGrath Morris, P. (2002) 'The capabilities perspective: a framework for social justice', *Families in Society*, 83 (4), pp. 365–73.

Mégret, F. & Hoffman, F. (2003) 'The UN as a human rights violator? Some reflections on the United Nations' changing human rights responsibilities', *Human Rights Quarterly*, 25 (2), 314–42.

Mendes, P. (2007) 'Social workers and social activism in Victoria, Australia', *Journal of Progressive Human Services*, 18 (1), 25–44.

Mendoza Rangel, M. D. C. (2005) 'Social work in Mexico: towards a different practice', in I. Ferguson, M. Lavalette & E. Whitmore (eds) *Globalisation, Global Justice and Social Work* (London: Routledge), 11–22.

Mericourt, B. (2001) 'Unequal but mutually beneficial partnerships in social development: a case example', *Social Development Issues*, 23 (3), 43–9.

Midgley, J. (1981) *Professional Imperialism* (London: Heinemann).

Midgley, J. (1990) 'International social work: learning from the Third World', *Social Work*, 35 (4), 295–301.

Midgley (1992) 'The challenge of international social work', in M. C. Hokenstad, S. K. Khinduka & J. Midgley (eds) *Profiles in International Social Work* (Washington CD: NASW Press), 13–28.

Midgley, J. (1995) *Social Development: The Developmental Perspective in Social Welfare* (Thousand Oaks, CA: Sage Publications).

Midgley, J. (1997) *Social Welfare in Global Context* (Thousand Oaks, CA: Sage Publications).

Midgley, J. (1999) 'Social development in social work: learning from global dialogue', in C. Ramanathan & R. Link (eds) *All Our Futures: Principles and Resources for Social Work Practice in a Global Era* (Belmont, CA: Brooks/Cole), 193–205.

Miller, J. (2007) 'Neither state nor market: NGOs and the international third sector', *Global Media and Communication*, 3 (3), 352–5.

Mishra, R. (1999) *Globalization and the Welfare State* (Cheltenham: Edward Elgar).

Mohan, B. (2008) 'Rethinking international social work', *International Social Work*, 51 (1), 11–24.

Morazes, J. & Pintak, I. (2007) 'Theories of global poverty: comparing developed world and developing world frameworks', *Journal of Human Behavior in the Social Environment*, 16 (1/2), 105–21.

Moyo, O. & Kawewe, S. (2002) 'The dynamics of a racialized, gendered, ethnicized and economically stratified society: understanding the socio-economic status of women in Zimbabwe', *Feminist Economics*, 8 (2), 163–81.

Moyo, O. & Moldovan, V. (2008) 'Lessons for social workers: Hurricane Katrina as a social disaster', *Social Development Issues*, 30 (1), 1–12.

Muleya, W. (2006) 'A comparative study of social work intervention in Zambia and England', *International Social Work*, 49 (4), 445–57.

Mullaly, B. (1997) *Structural Social Work*, 2nd edn (New York: Oxford University Press).

Muno, A. & Keenan, L. D. (2000) 'The after-school girls leadership program: transforming the school environment for adolescent girls', *Social Work in Education*, 22 (2), 116–28.

Mweru, M. (2008) 'Women, migration and HIV/AIDS in Kenya,' *International Social Work*, 51 (3), 337–47.

Nagel, T. (1979) *Mortal Questions* (Cambridge: Cambridge University Press).

Namdaldagva, O. E. (2004) 'Challenges of social work education in Mongolia', unpublished paper presented to the *Global Social Work Congress*, Adelaide.

Napier, L. & George, J. (2001) 'Changing social work education in Australia', *Social Work Education*, 20 (1), 75–87.

Nash, M. & Trlin, A. (2004) *Social Work with Immigrants, Refugees and Asylum Seekers in New Zealand*, New Settler Programme, occasional paper 8 (Palmerston North: Massey University).

Nash, M., Wong, J. & Trlin, A. (2006) 'Civic and social integration. A new field of social work practice with immigrants, refugees and asylum seekers', *International Social Work*, 49 (3), 345–63.

National Association of Social Workers (NASW) (1999) *Code of Ethics* (Washington DC: NASW).

New Internationalist (2007) 'Sex trafficking, the facts', *New Internationalist*, 404 (September), 12–13.

Nguyen Thi Oanh (2002) 'Historical developments and characteristics of social work in today's Vietnam', *International Journal of Social Welfare*, 11, 84–91.

Nimagadda, J. & Cowger, C. D. (1999) 'Cross cultural practice: social worker ingenuity in the indigenization of practice knowledge', *International Social Work*, 42 (3), 261–76.

Noble, C. (2003) 'What am I doing here, really? Students' and teachers' reflections on international placements', in L. Dominelli & T. Bernard (eds) *Broadening Horizons* (Aldershot: Ashgate).

Noble, C. (2004) 'Social work education, training and standards in the Asia-pacific region', *Social Work Education*, 23 (5), 527–36.

Nussbaum, M. (2000) *Women and Human Development* (Cambridge: Cambridge University Press).

Nussbaum, M. (2001) *Upheavals of Thought* (New York: Cambridge University Press).

Nussbaum, M. (2006a) *Frontiers of Justice* (Cambridge, MA: Harvard University Press).

Nussbaum, M. (2006b) 'In defence of global political liberalism', *Development and Change*, 37 (6), 1313–28.

Odulana, J. A. & Olomajeye, J. A. (1999) 'The impact of the government's alleviation of poverty program on the urban poor in Nigeria', *Journal of Black Studies*, 29 (5), 695–705.

Okitikpi, T. & Aymer, C. (2003) 'Social work with African refugee children and their families', *Child and Family Social Work*, 8 (3), 213–22.

Olson, J. (2007) 'Social work's professional and social justice projects: conflicts in discourse', *Journal of Progressive Human Services*, 18 (1), 45–69.

Osei-Hwedie, K. (1993) 'The challenge of social work in Africa: starting the indigenisation process', *Journal of Social Development in Africa*, 8 (1), 19–30.

Osei-Hwedie, K., Ntseane, D. & Jaques, G. (2006) 'Searching for appropriateness in social work education in Botswana', *Social Work Education*, 25 (6), 569–90.

Palmer, S. & Cooke, W. (1996) 'Understanding and countering racism with First Nations children in out-of-home care', *Child Welfare*, 75 (6), 709–25.

Park, Y. & Miller, J. (2006) 'The social ecology of Hurricane Katrina: re-writing the discourse of "natural" disasters', *Smith College Studies in Social Work*, 76 (3), 9–24.

Parry, N. & Parry, J. (1979) 'Social work, professionalism and the state', in M. Rustin, N. Parry & C. Satyamurti (eds) *Social Work, Welfare and the State* (London: Edward Arnold).

Patel, L. (2005) *Social Welfare and Social Development in South Africa* (Cape Town: Oxford University Press).

Payne, M. (2000) *Teamwork in Multiprofessional Care* (Basingstoke: Palgrave Macmillan).

Payne, M. (2005) *The Origins of Social Work: Continuity and Change* (Basingstoke: Palgrave Macmillan).

Payne. M. & Askeland, G. A. (2008) *Globalization and International Social Work: Postmodern Change and Challenge* (Aldershot: Ashgate).

Pine, B. A. & Drachman, D. (2005) 'Effective child welfare practice with immigrant and refugee children and their families', *Child Welfare*, 84 (5), 537–62.

Pittaway, E. & Bartolomei, L. (2005) *Women to Woman: a Gender Sensitive Response to Tsunami Affected Women* (Sydney: Centre for Refugee Research).

Pittaway, E., Bartolomei, L. & Pittaway, E. E. (2003) 'An examination of the role of identity and citizenship in the experiences of women in Kakuma Refugee camp in northern Kenya', *Development*, 46 (3), 87–93.

Pittaway, E. & Pittaway, E. E. (2004) 'Refugee woman: a dangerous label', *The Australian Journal of Human Rights*, June, 119–36.

Pittaway, E., Bartolomei, L. and Rees, S. (2007) 'Gendered dimensions of the 2004 tsunami and a potential social work response in post-disaster situations', *International Social Work*, 50 (3), 307–19.

Puig, M. E. & Glynn, J. B. (2003) 'Disaster responders: a cross-cultural approach to recovery and relief work', *Journal of Social Service Research*, 30 (2), 55–66.

Queiro-Tajalli, I. (1995) 'Argentina', in T. D. Watts, D. Elliott & N. S. Mayadas (eds) *International Handbook on Social Work Education* (Westport, CT: Greenwood Press), 87–102.

Quinn, M. (2003) 'Realizing dreams: community development in Zambia', in W. Weeks, L. Hoatson & J. Dixon (eds) *Community Practices in Australia* (Frenchs Forest, NSW: Pearson Education), 39–44.

Rao, N. B. (1996) 'Demographic correlates of poverty in tribal households', *The Indian Journal of Social Work*, 57 (2), 337–55.

Rawls, J. (1972) *A Theory of Justice* (Oxford: The Clarendon Press).

Razack, N. (2000) 'North/South collaborations', *Journal of Progressive Human Services*, 11 (1), 71–91.

Reamer, F. (1999) *Social Work Ethics and Values*, 2nd edn (New York: Columbia University Press).

Reichert, E. (2003) *Social Work and Human Rights* (New York: Columbia University Press).

Reisch, M. (2002) 'Defining social justice in a socially unjust world', *Families in Society: The Journal of Contemporary Human Services*, 83 (4), 343–54.

Riga, A. (2008) 'Jan Floris de Jongh (The Netherlands) President 1954–1961', in F. W. Seibel (eds) *Global Leaders for Social Work Education: The IASSW Presidents 1928–2008* (Ostrava: Verlag Albert/IASSW), 71–82.

Ritzer, G. (2000) *The McDonaldization of Society*, 3rd edn (Thousand Oaks, CA: Pine Forge).

Rivera, J. D. & Miller, D. S. (2007) 'Continually neglected: situating natural disasters in the African American experience', *Journal of Black Studies*, 37 (4), 502–22.

Roby, J. (2005) 'Women and children in the global sex trade', *International Social Work*, 48 (2), 136–47.

Ross Sherrif, F. (2006) 'Afghan women in exile and repatriation', *Affilia: Journal of Women and Social Work*, 21 (2), 206–19.

Said, E. (1978) *Orientalism* (London: Routledge & Kegan Paul).

Said, E. (1994) 'Identity, authority and freedom: the potentate and the traveller', *Boundary*, 2 (2), 1–18.

Saith, A. (2006) 'From universal values to Millennium Development Goals: lost in translation', *Development and Change*, 37 (6), 1167–99.

Seipel, M. M. O. (1992) 'Promoting maternal health in developing countries', *Health Social Work*, 17(3), 200–6.

Seitz, J. (2008) *Global Issues: An Introduction*, 3rd edn (Carlton, VIC: Blackwell Publishers).

Selinger, E. (2008) 'Does microcredit "empower"? Reflections on the Grameen Bank debate', *Human Studies*, 31, 27–41.

Selipsky, L. (2009) 'Johannesburg Housing Company: innovation through renovation', *The Social Work Practitioner-Researcher*, 21 (2), 259–67.

Sepehri, A., Sarma, S., Simpson, W. & Moshiri, S. (2008) 'How important are individual, household and commune characteristics in explaining utilization of maternal health services in Vietnam?' *Social Science and Medicine*, 67 (6), 1009–17.

Sewpaul, V. (2006) 'The global-local dialectic: challenges for African scholarship and social work in a post-colonial world', *British Journal of Social Work*, 36 (3), 419–34.

Sewpaul, V. & Jones, D. (2004) 'Global standards for social work education and training', *Social Work Education*, 23 (5), 493–513.

Shera, W. (2003) 'Building a social development approach to social work education: the University of Toronto-Sri Lanka School of Social Work project' in L. Healy, Y. Asamoah & M. C. Hokenstad (eds) *Models of International Collaboration in Social Work Education* (Alexandria VA: Council on Social Work Education), 101–10.

Silavwe, G. (1995) 'The need for a new social work perspective in an African setting: the case of social casework in Zambia', *British Journal of Social Work*, 25 (1), 71–84.

Singer, P. (1993) *Practical Ethics*, 2nd edn (Melbourne: Cambridge University Press).

Sklair, L. (1999) 'Competing conceptions of globalization,' *Journal of World Systems Research*, 5 (2), 144–63.

Smith, M. L. (2007) 'Toward a guide to distance education in social work', *The New Social Worker*, 14 (2) (electronic journal accessed at http://www.socialworker.com/home on 9 February 2009).

Snyder, C. S., May, J. D., Zulcic, N. N. & Gabbard, W. J. (2005) 'Social work with Bosnian Muslim refugee children and families: a review of the literature', *Child Welfare*, 84 (5), 607–30.

Spence, P. R., Lachlan, K. A. & Griffin, D. R. (2007) 'Crisis communication, race and natural disasters', *Journal of Black Studies*, 37 (4), 539–54.

Stiglitz, J. (2003) *Globalization and its Discontents* (New York: W. W. Norton).

Stoesz, D. & Saunders, D. (1999) 'Welfare capitalism: a new approach to poverty policy?' *Social Service Review*, 73 (3), 380–400.

Taylor, R., Stevens, I. & Nguyen Thi Thai Lan (2009) 'Introducing vocational qualifications in care to the Socialist Republic of Vietnam', *Social Work Education*, 28 (1), 29–42.

Tesoriero, F. (2006) 'Personal growth towards intercultural competence through an international field education program', *Australian Social Work*, 59 (20), 126–40.

Tesoriero, F. & Rajaratnam, A. (2001) 'Partnership in education: an Australian school of social work and a South Indian primary health care project', *International Social Work*, 44 (1), 31–41.

Thompson, N. (2006) *Anti-Discriminatory Practice*, 4th edn (Basingstoke: Palgrave Macmillan).

Townsend, P. (2006) 'Poverty and human rights: the role of social security and especially child benefit', *The Hong Kong Journal of Social Work*, 40 (1/2), 3–32.

Trocmé, N., Knoke, D. & Blackstock, C. (2004) 'Pathways to the overrepresentation of Aboriginal children in Canada's child welfare system', *Social Service Review*, 78 (4), 577–600.

Truong, T.-D. (2006) 'One humanity, many consciousnesses: unresolved issues in Nussbaum's new frontiers of justice', *Development and Change*, 37 (6), 1259–72.

Tsang, A. K. T., Yan. M. C. & Shera. W. (2000) 'Negotiating multiple agendas in international social work: the case of the China-Canada Collaborative Project', *Canadian Social Work*, 2 (1), 147–61.

Tsang, A. K.-T., Sin, R., Jia, C. & Yan, M.-C. (2008) 'Another snapshot of social work in China: capturing multiple positioning and intersecting discourses in rapid movement', *Australian Social Work*, 61 (1), 72–87.

UNICEF Vietnam/Ministry of Labour, Invalids and Social Affairs (MOLISA) (2005) *A Study of the Human Resource and Training Needs for Professional Social Work in Vietnam* (Hanoi: UNICEF Vietnam/MOLISA).

UNICEF Vietnam/Ministry of Labour, Invalids and Social Affairs (MOLISA) (2007) *Professional Social Work in Vietnam: A Strategic Framework* (Hanoi: UNICEF Vietnam/MOLISA).

United Nations (UN) (1948) *The United Nations' Declaration on Human Rights* (New York: United Nations).

United Nations (UN) (1951) *Convention Relating to the Status of Refugees* (New York: United Nations).

United Nations (UN) (1989) *Convention on the Rights of the Child* (New York: United Nations).

United Nations (UN) (1995) *Report of the World Summit for Social Development* (New York: United Nations).

United Nations (UN) (2000a) *Millennium Development Goals 2015* (electronic document accessed at: http://www.un.org/millenniumgoals on 20 October 2008).

United Nations (UN) (2000b) *Protocol to Prevent, Suppress and Punish Trafficking in Persons, Especially Women and Children, Supplementing the United Nations Convention Against Transnational Organized Crime* (New York: United Nations).

United Nations (UN) (2008a) *Millennium Development Goals Report 2008* (New York: United Nations).

United Nations (UN) (2008b) *United Nations Declaration on the Rights of Indigenous Peoples* (New York: United Nations).

United Nations Development Program (UNDP) (1999) *The Human Development Report 1999* (New York: Oxford University Press).

United Nations Children's Fund (UNICEF) (1999) *After the Fall: The Impact of Ten Years of Transition* (Florence: UNICEF).

United Nations High Commission for Refugees (UNHCR) (2006) *ExCom Conclusion on Women and Girls at Risk. No. 105 (LVII)* (electronic document accessed at http://www.unhcr.org/excom/EXCOM/45339d922.html on 1 December 2008).

United Nations High Commission for Refugees (UNHCR) (2007a) *Convention and Protocol Relating to the Status of Refugees* (Geneva: UNHCR).

United Nations High Commission for Refugees (UNHCR) (2007b) *The 1951 Refugee Convention: Questions and Answers* (Geneva: UNHCR).

Van Hook, M. P., Gjermeni, E. & Haxhiymeri, E. (2006) 'Sexual trafficking of women – tragic proportions and attempted solutions in Albania', *International Social Work*, 49 (1), 29–40.

Viera, B. O. (1976) 'Brazil: systematizing social services', in D. Thursz & J. L. Vigilante (eds) *Meeting Human Needs 2: Additional Perspectives from Thirteen Countries* (Beverley Hills: Sage Publications), 241–63.

Vietnamese Expert Group on Social Work (2006) *General Review of Social Work* (Hanoi: MOLISA).

Walton, R. G. (1975) *Women in Social Work* (London: Routledge & Kegan Paul).

Walton, R. G. & Abo El-Nasr, M. M. (1988) 'The indigenization and authentization of social work in Egypt', *The Community Development Journal*, 23 (3), 148–55.

Weaver, H. N. (1997) 'Which canoe are you in? A view from a First Nations person', *Reflections*, 3 (4), 12–17.

Weaver, H. N. (2002) 'Perspectives on wellness: journeys on the red road', *Journal of Sociology and Social Welfare*, 24 (1), 5–15.

Weber, L. (2006) 'The shifting frontiers of migration control', in S. Pickering & L. Weber (eds) *Borders, Mobility and Technologies of Control* (Dordrecht: Springer).

Wehbi, S. (2009) 'Deconstructing motivations: challenging international social work placements', *International Social Work*, 52 (1), 48–59.

Weiss, I. (2005) 'Is there a global common core to social work? A cross-national comparison of BSW graduate students', *Social Work*, 50 (2), 101–10.

Welbourne, P. & Weiss, I. (2007) 'Cross-national similarities and differences in social work as a profession: a summary and discussion', in I. Weiss & P. Welbourne (eds) *Social Work as a Profession: A Comparative Cross-national Perspective* (Birmingham: Venture Press), 225–51.

Wieler, J. (2006) 'The long path to Irena Sendler – mother of the Holocaust children', in *Social Work and Society*, 4 (1) (electronic journal accessed at http://www.socwork.net/2006/1 on 20 October 2008).

Williamson, J. (1989) 'What Washington means by policy reform', in J. Williamson (ed.) *Latin American Adjustment: How Much Has Happened?* (Washington: Institute for International Economics).

Williamson, L. (1978) 'Infanticide: an anthropological analysis', in M. Kohl (ed.) *Infanticide and the Value of Life* (Buffalo, NY: Prometheus), 61–75.

Wilson, M. (2003) 'South-North development partnership: lessons from a Nicaragua-Canada experience', in L. Healy, Y. Asamoah & M. C. Hokenstad (eds) *Models of International Collaboration in Social Work Education* (Alexandria VA: Council on Social Work Education), 111–24.

Wilson, T. (2008) 'Isibindi: a model for providing community-based child and youth care services', *The Social Work Practitioner-Researcher*, 20 (3), 407–15.

Wise, S. (1995) 'Feminist ethics in social work', in R. Hugman & D. Smith (eds) *Ethical Issues in Social Work* (London: Routledge), 104–19.

Worrall, J. (2006) 'Challenges of grandparent custody of children at risk in New Zealand', Families in Society, 87 (4), 546–54.

Xu, Q. (2006) 'Defining international social work. A social service agency perspective', *International Social Work*, 49 (6), 679–92.

Yan, M.-C. (2005) 'Journey to international social work: a personal and professional reflection', *Reflections*, 11 (1) (Winter), 4–16.

Yan, M.-C. & Cheung, K.-W. (2006) 'The politics of indigenisation: a case study of development of social work in China', *Journal of Sociology and Social Welfare*, 33 (2), 63–84.

Yan, M.-C. & Tsang, A. K. T. (2005) 'A snapshot on the development of social work education in China: a Delphi study', *Social Work Education*, 24 (8), 883–901.

Yan, M.-C. & Tsui, M.-S. (2007) 'The quest for western social work knowledge. Literature in the USA and practice in China', *International Social Work*, 50 (5), 641–53.

Yellow Bird, M. (1999) 'Radical, skewed, benign and calculated: reflections on teaching diversity', *Reflections*, 5 (2), 13–22.

Yip, K.-S. (2004) 'A Chinese cultural critique of the global qualifying standards for social work education', *Social Work Education*, 23 (5), 597–612.

Yuen-Tsang, A. W.-K. & Sung, P. P.-L. (2002) 'Capacity building through networking: integrating professional knowledge with indigenous practice', in N.-T. Tan & I. Dodds (eds) *Social Work Around the World II* (Berne: IFSW Press), 111–22.

Zimmer, Z. (2008) 'Poverty, wealth inequality and health among older adults in rural Cambodia', *Social Science and Medicine*, 66 (1), 57–71.

Index

Aboriginal, *see* Indigenous peoples
Aboriginal Child Placement Principle
(ACPP), 51
action research, 40
Addams, J., 76, 122, 140
Addis Ababa, 153
Adelaide, 135
advocacy, 26, 47, 77, 80
Africa, 4, 11, 40, 61–6, 72, 85, 94, 108,
110, 117, 125, 127, 131, 137, 139,
154
Ahmadi, N., 157–8
aid, 10, 35
see also humanitarian aid
Akimoto, T., 23–4, 32
Al-Krenawi, A., 131
America, *see* North America; South
America; United States of America
Amsterdam School of Social Work, 1
Annan, K., 154
anti-discriminatory practice, 70, 77, 157
Argentina, 2
Asad, T., 9, 132–3
Asia, 4, 11, 33, 40, 44, 49, 72, 85, 94,
108, 117, 125, 137, 139, 154
Asian tsunami (2004), 44
Asia-Pacific Association of Social Work
Education (APASWE), 89, 160
Askeland, G., 17–18, 108, 113, 117,
149–50
assistant/aide roles, 92
'barefoot social worker', 92, 94–5, 112,
142
Association of South-East Asian Nations
(ASEAN), 6, 9, 11, 160
asylum seekers, 11, 24–7, 37–41, 95–6
see also refugees
Australia, 11, 18, 23–4, 38, 42, 44,
49–52, 75–8, 84, 94, 112–14,
116–17, 125, 134–5, 144, 147, 159

Australian Volunteers International, 28–9
'authentization', 4, 16, 23, 78–82,
110–11, 138–43, 147, 160
Ayittey, G., 68

Bangladesh, 47–8
Banks, S., 122–3, 135
Ban, P., 51–2
Bauman, Z., 8, 11
Bedouin, 131
Beijing, 153
Bernasek, A., 48
Berne, 99
Botswana, 79, 110, 113
Bowles, W., 135
Boyle, E. H., 130
Briskman, L., 38
Bulgaria, 123
Burghart, G., 61–2
Burkett, I., 83
Butler, I., 77

California, 34
Canada, 22, 49–52, 75–8, 84, 100,
112–13, 125, 132, 148
Canadian International Development
Agency, 112
capabilities, human, *see* capacities, human
capacities, human, 47, 69, 133, 154–5
'capacity building', 82–4, 110–13
capitalism, 5
Carbone-López, K., 130
CARE International, 91–3
Caribbean, 26, 28, 137
see also West Indies
Carten, A., 26
case management, 26
casework, 74–5, 79, 83–4, 87, 148
radical casework, 77
Centre for Civil Initiatives, 93

188